GEOGRAPHIES
OF WRITING

GEOGRAPHIES OF WRITING

INHABITING PLACES AND
ENCOUNTERING DIFFERENCE

NEDRA REYNOLDS

Southern Illinois University Press
Carbondale

Library of Congress Cataloging-in-Publication Data
Reynolds, Nedra.
    Geographies of writing : inhabiting places and encountering difference / Nedra Reynolds.
        p. cm.
    Includes bibliographical references (p.) and index.
1. English language—Rhetoric—Study and teaching. 2. Human geography—Study
and teaching (Higher) 3. Difference (Philosophy) 4. Place (Philosophy) 5. Space perception.
I. Title.
PE1404 .R47 2004
808'.042'0711—dc21
ISBN 0-8093-2560-8 (alk. paper)
ISBN-13: 978-0-8093-2787-4
ISBN-10: 0-8093-2787-2   2003009917

For Martin Bide

Contents

FIGURES

ACKNOWLEDGMENTS

Three articles are reprinted within this volume in revised form: "Composition's Imagined Geographies: The Politics of Space in the Frontier, City, and Cyberspace" (*College Composition and Communication* 50 [1998]: 12–35). Copyright © 1998 by the National Council of Teachers of English. Reprinted with permission. "Who's Going to Cross This Border? Travel Metaphors, Material Conditions, and Contested Places" (*JAC: A Journal of Composition Theory* 20 [2000]: 541–64). "Activism and Service Learning: Reframing Volunteerism as Acts of Dissent." With Donna M. Bickford. (*Pedagogy: Critical Approaches to Teaching Literature, Language, Composition, and Culture* 2 [2002]: 229–52).

My semester in Leeds was made possible by a sabbatical leave from the University of Rhode Island as well as a grant from the Center for the Study of the Humanities at URI. For my office space and library privileges, I thank Graham Clarke, chair of the Leeds School of Geography in 1999–2000, and Joyce Hill and David Lindley of the School of English. I am indebted to Kate Housiaux and Matt Stroh, who gave so much of their time to me. Most importantly, a number of third-year geography students allowed me to interview them and gave me their permission to share their responses. I've changed their names, but their voices on tape will be in my head for years to come. Others were in the two streetwork groups who allowed me to tape their collaborative sessions, take notes, and ask questions as they worked. It's been all too rare in my life to work with students without having to *grade* them, and the experience was a sheer delight.

This book came into being in other rooms besides those in Leeds: the Bachelor Reading Room at Miami University in 1999, where I was invited by the Department of English to give a talk; room 103 Independence Hall for a graduate seminar on rhetoric and geography in the spring of 2001; conference hotel rooms in Denver and Chicago. Everyone who shared those rooms with me has added to the conversation.

For her friendship and long-standing support of my work, I thank Susan Jarratt—our work on *ethos* certainly haunts this project. At an opportune moment, Lynn Worsham encouraged me to send her something; her generous and timely invitation resulted in the essay that forms the argument here. John Trimbur, often as an anonymous reviewer, has read more of my work-in-progress than anyone else, and his thoughtful responses are all a writer could ask for. I am also indebted to Joe Harris. The suggestions of all of these people have made this a better book. Other colleagues and friends have encouraged me by word and by example: Jack Selzer, Diana George, Gary Olson, Roxanne Mountford, Nancy Cook, Tom Berninghausen, Libby Miles, Bob Schwegler, Kristen Kennedy, Donna Bickford, Champ and Lisa Starr, and as always, Mary Jean Corbett. Many thanks to those at Southern Illinois University Press—Karl Kageff, Carol A. Burns, and Barb Martin—for their assistance. For any flaws that remain in this project, I accept full responsibility.

This book has been written in a loving home and has made me appreciate more than ever the joys of placemaking. Truman and Bentley faithfully follow me up to my study, and Martin keeps all kinds of things growing around here, including me.

GEOGRAPHIES
OF WRITING

INTRODUCTION

In one of the most well-known and influential rhetoric texts in the canon, Phaedrus is on his way out of the city, going for a walk "outside the walls," when he meets Socrates and shares his belief that his walk in the country will be "more refreshing than a stroll in the city squares" (Hamilton 21). Socrates joins Phaedrus, where they soon come to the Ilissus; Phaedrus spots a tall plane tree, and they settle there to hear and discuss the speech that Phaedrus has with him. Socrates seems so enchanted with the place and waxes so poetically about it that Phaedrus comments, "So far from being like a native, you resemble . . . a visitor being shown the sights by a guide. This comes of your never going abroad beyond the frontiers of Attica or even, as far as I can see, outside the actual walls of the city" (26). Socrates replies that he stays in the city because his love of learning, especially about human nature, keeps him among people. As he puts it, "the fields and trees won't teach me anything." In this opening scene, as the translator tells the reader, Socrates is in unfamiliar territory—and such an excursion "is quite contrary to his usual habits" (21).

Habitually, then, Socrates hangs out in the city, and through these opening lines Plato draws attention to the role of *place* in conversations, persuasion, and learning. While critics commonly note that the scene suggests seduction, the dialogue also develops from the myth and storytelling that accompanies this place. In fact, the myth-laden spot by the stream embodies those foundations of an oral culture that Plato is loathe to lose—and which he believes will be lost through a new culture of writing. The act of writing, Plato worried, diminishes the role of memory and makes other parts of the mind fuzzy and sloppy.[1] Perhaps Plato sets the scene in *Phaedrus* so deliberately because he wanted to help readers to *remember* it: in a memorable setting, his ideas about love, the soul, and philosophical rhetoric are more likely to take hold, not just in the pliable mind of Phaedrus but also in readers of this carefully crafted dialogue.[2]

Within the brief introductory space of this dialogue, Socrates and Phaedrus walk, cross boundaries, attend to the history of a place, settle in beside a stream, and begin to compose speeches from a store of half-remembered and half-created lines of argument. Most acts of composing take place in similar ways, drawn from a store of remembered and well-rehearsed spatial practices that come from the everyday and become engrained, habitual, embodied. And because readers and writers don't just "cross over" the margins of discrete discourse communities from alienation to acceptance, we need a sense of place—for texts and classrooms and cultures—defined by contestations and differences that extend well beyond boundary lines. Places, whether textual, material, or imaginary, are constructed and reproduced not simply by boundaries but also by practices, structures of feeling, and sedimented features of *habitus*. Theories of writing, communication, and literacy, this book argues, should reflect this deeper understanding of place.

As Plato knew and as I explore here, memory and place, location and argument, walking and learning, are vitally and dramatically linked in our personal histories and personal geographies. Places evoke powerful human emotions because they become layered, like sediment or a palimpsest, with histories and stories and memories. When places are inhabited in the fullest sense, they become embodied with the kinds of stories, myths, and legends that the spot beside the Ilissus holds; they can stimulate and refresh—or disturb and unnerve—their visitors.

Socrates, displaced from his usual haunt, may be more "open" to new ideas because he is in unfamiliar territory, or more close-minded or harder to convince because he is not occupying his usual hood. Many educators believe that only when people are "moved"—perhaps literally—can they be persuaded to see from a different point of view. However, *moving them* becomes the hard part when most people, like Socrates, live their daily lives within a very small radius.

How do people experience space, and what might that tell us about how they experience other forms of the social world? How do students, writers, or learners experience spaces and places in the everyday, and how might this inform cultural and material theories of discourse? What do "sense of place," pathways, habits, or dwelling have to do learning? These are the questions this book explores through such concepts as mental mapping, streetwork, and thirdspace[3]—all ideas important to cultural geography that I want to claim in working towards geographic rhetorics informed by the material, the visual, and the everyday. My qualitative research conducted with students in the School of Geography at the University of Leeds informs the argument that composition studies needs cultural writing theories and material literacy practices that engage with the metaphorical—ways to imagine space—without ignoring places and spaces—the actual locations where writers write, learners learn, and workers work. I attempt to re-imagine acts of writing through spatial practices of the everyday—walking, mapping, and dwelling—and through different spatial scales: the body, the street, the city.

This book makes three closely related contributions: one theoretical, to re-imagining composing as spatial, material, and visual; one political, to understanding the sociospatial construction of difference; and one pedagogical, to teaching writing as a set of spatial practices not unlike those we use in moving through the world. *Geographies of Writing* sees writing instruction as rooted in time and space and within material conditions that affect students who are often transient residents of learning communities: "students pass through, and only pause briefly within, classrooms; they dwell within and visit various other locations, locations whose politics and discourse conventions both construct and identify them" (Drew 60).

Many of our experiences in life "take place" in a location, and then we draw upon characteristics of those locations to construct memories and to judge or respond to other places. Because homes, neighborhoods, parks, cafes, or classrooms can be so emotionally loaded, it's difficult, methodologically, to study the relationships of people and places, or to understand how some places can feel like home to some while alienating others. But it is urgent for us to consider how spaces impact upon learning, reading, and writing when opportunities for communicating expand through electronic technologies while, at the same time, moving through the world seems more difficult or more dangerous. This study of space and place, geography and mapping, location and materiality, develops from and responds to a rich and diverse literature on postmodern spatiality, cultural geography, and the sociospatial construction of difference.

Understanding the importance of lifeworlds is one place to begin in understanding difference, otherness, and the politics of exclusion—topics that define the causes of critical literacy, social justice, and liberatory education. Understanding difference via geography, therefore, is the widest territory I want to claim for this project. On a smaller spatial scale, if we could discover more about how people learn about boundaries and borders, when they may cross them without penalty; or how they can slip in without being detected; or what the safe times of day are, then we could apply these findings to a richer understanding of how people learn to read, write, and interact with texts. Imagining acts of writing as material—carving text out of time and space, in particular circumstances that differ for each writer—opens up new spaces in which to study and understand literacy and the construction of meaning.

As rhetoric and composition studies enters its fully mature stage, most disciplines in the humanities and social sciences are searching for curricular answers responsive to new technologies and a postmodern age. Many faculty are eager for guidance in helping students with whom we seem to have little in common—how do we reach students with whom we seem to share little? What we *do* have in common with students are the places where we meet them as well as everyday experiences in space: moving through streets or hallways, working in institutional rooms, or commuting to work and school. Moving through the world, similarly but differently, traversing space and connecting with places, give us common ground.

Many of my readers recognize that movement metaphors are increasingly popular in the discourses of postmodernism: traveling theories, border crossing, and moving from the center to the margins. Particularly when revolutionary advances in technology have changed fundamentally the ways we compose as well as how we experience space, it becomes important to attend to the concrete, to the material, and to the geographic. The traveling theories of postmodern cultural theory don't mean much to women afraid to walk a street at night or children who aren't allowed to leave the block. If movement seems essential to learning or persuasion, I will suggest that inhabitance or dwelling are equally important.

In this postmodern culture, we do need theories of movement, those that advocate travel and mobility, in order to give readers and writers both strategies and tactics for negotiating among different discourses.[4] Writers or learners need strategies for entering unfamiliar areas or ways to recognize the politics of space enacted in various places. But they also need to see discourses as places to be inhabited, not just something to pass through or "try on," like the latest fashion or as a hurried stop on the way to somewhere else. Through research informed by cultural geography, I argue for geographic rhetorics that share much with ecocomposition, the belief that studies of writing should inquire into "the relationships between writers, writing and all places, spaces, sites, and locations" (Dobrin, "Writing" 13). Where the work of ecocomposition looks mostly to the natural world, cultural geography focuses on the interaction of the social and the built environment, but the idea of *inhabitance* is crucial to both geographical or ecological theories of writing. If the first rule of writing is to "know your terrain," or to situate writing within an environment (Dobrin, "Writing" 20), then a geographical rhetoric provides both rich metaphors and particular methodologies for the study of writing, writers, and places. First is to claim writing as a set of practices more spatial than temporal: "spatial practices in fact secretly structure the determining conditions of social life" (de Certeau 96). These spatial practices—acts of writing—are enacted not in stable, always-the-same places but within shifting senses of space, in the betweens, in thirdspace.

Over a decade after Lester Faigley, in *Fragments of Rationality: Postmodernity and the Subject of Composition,* identified the ways in which composition remains a modernist discipline, there is more consensus that process writing, discourse communities, and otherwise linear or bounded concepts no longer construct an adequate theoretical model (Clark), especially in a postmodern era defined by electronic technologies and changing populations. Proposed alternatives tend to be spatial or geographical in metaphor or allusion—contact zones, borderlands, or writing as travel—sites where writers must wrangle or be bold. These spatial metaphors don't replace the territorial and linear metaphors that characterize modernist composition theory; they simply add another layer.

Geographic rhetorics begin with a look at metaphors for space and place since metaphors often reflect and construct accepted ways of knowing. Process metaphors, for example, have dominated the discourses of writing instruction for many years. But process usually means temporal, and therefore writing becomes a time-bound concept. In an article examining the metaphors used by scholars in urban studies, Andy Merrifield says that "process" offers much by way of explanation but that when "space is represented processually, . . . theorists inevitably resort to temporality" (418). Furthermore, to "rely strictly upon a vocabulary of process temporalizes space and overwhelms the everyday" (418). Metaphors of "individuation," which have emerged to counteract process metaphors, tend toward description and express the everyday quality of space but do little to contribute to explanations of the richness of space; they tend to become static (418). From within this clash of metaphors (Henri LeFebvre's vs. Jane Jacobs') Merrifield calls for ways to "translate between different metaphors and vocabularies of urban space" (418).

Process theory certainly offered a satisfying and even paradigm-lurching explanation for how writers write. As Merrifield proposes, we do not need to leave process metaphors behind but to find ways to translate between them and metaphors from the everyday. For example, given the realities of today's writing tools, it has become increasingly silly to ask students for "drafts" that demonstrate their writing process when so much of writing takes place on screen in a more fluid, spatial medium that doesn't lend itself very well to "frozen" representations. Electronic writing technologies enfold, embed, or dilute what we have known as the writing process, make it more invisible, harder to see—often hiding the role of invention as well as the differences among writers and their composing habits. Making acts of writing or composing processes *more* visible is the point, rather than trying to eliminate process from our language or theories.

Geography gives us the metaphorical and methodological tools to change our ways of imagining writing through both movement and dwelling—to see writing as a set of spatial practices informed by everyday negotiations of space. In composition studies, it's important to understand the ways in which writers feel alienated from certain discourses or institutional practices, or why new forms of reading and writing are so difficult. In its ideological function to define and enforce social difference, the academy suffers from acute hardening-of-the-boundaries, and this makes it difficult for its members to think outside of the box. How can we imagine spaces where the borders are continually shifting? Margins and borders are comforting, in some ways, to those of us accustomed to knowing our place, in a text or in an institution. From one-inch manuscript margins to the differences between business writing and technical writing, we recognize and abide by dozens of spatial practices in the everyday. The clearer the boundaries, the more confident we are about keeping some out or letting some in. However, this "border mentality" has made boundaries more important than the places themselves. We are so intent on figuring out where the borders lie and who can cross them that we may be neglecting the places *constructed by* those borders.

In addition, a border mentality leads to entrenched forms of exclusion, like racism. As Victor Villanueva has argued, we need more strategies for combating institutionalized racism, rather than for acknowledging or celebrating difference via multiculturalism. In his chair's address to the CCCC, in fact, geographic ignorance was prominent in his examples of racism: "You're from New Mexico? Then get back to your own country." He argues that our intellectual allegiances are too European and that we need to learn about the intellectuals of the Americas—that we need, for example, a change in our intellectual geography. Thus, as we search for a causal understanding of systemic racism in the U.S., addressing geographic ignorance and enlarging our own and students' geographic imaginations may be one answer worth more research. Finally, as teachers are faced with students from whom they feel distant, either by age or experience, race or languages, or different access to power, it's important to find common ground, shared spaces of concern, and topics of interest. We share with students and colleagues the everyday realities of material conditions and physical spaces of campuses and towns, buildings and streets. I won't argue that these spaces are truly public and democratic, and I won't romanticize city streets or rural footpaths, but I will discuss why we should analyze the rhetoric of the street in order to make connections to composing and writing instruction.

My effort in this book, then, is to illustrate how geography contributes, metaphorically and methodologically, to literacy practices, to conceptions of discourse, and to postmodern composition theory attentive to difference, the material, and the visual. The language and practices of cultural geography help me to make the case for a better understanding of paradoxical space and contested places; "realandimagined" space (Soja); geographies of exclusion (Sibley); and material experiences of place—all of which suggest ways to rethink spatial metaphors, to re-imagine acts of writing, and to attend to the politics of space as they intersect with teaching and research practices.

The five chapters that follow start from an analysis of spatial metaphors and move to an argument about learning to dwell within discourses. Interviews and other qualitative data from my experiences at the University of Leeds inform two middle chapters as well as other parts of the manuscript. Chapter 1, "Between Metaphor and Materiality," introduces the idea of spatial practices and shows how they work in tension with spatial metaphors to construct our notions of place and space. This chapter argues that composition has invested heavily in imagined geographies while ignoring material spaces; however, there is also a mutual dependence or an interconnectedness between the material and the metaphorical. While imagined geographies hide or diminish the consequences of space, we also need the productive tension that results from a "trialectics of spatiality" (Soja), where realandimagined places are co-constructed. To demonstrate how conceptions of space are constructed by spatial practices of the everyday, this chapter analyzes time-space compression as idea and effect; specifically, I look at the impact of cell phones and how these technologies contribute to a discourse of loss regarding public space, a nostalgic discourse that ignores the ways in which public spaces are designed to exclude. The changing nature of public and private space as well as the binding nature of container metaphors for both places and acts of writing, make urgent the critique of spatial metaphors that enforce boundaries without encouraging forms of dwelling. Travel metaphors, a result of or response to postmodernism, are similarly exclusionary and result in the continued proliferation of spatial metaphors, like "the real world," that suggest a binary relationship between writers and their readers. Binaries and boxes limit what we can see, and seeing becomes an important part of cultural geography's theories and epistemologies, presented in chapter 2.

The second chapter, "Reading Landscapes and Walking the Streets: Geography and the Visual," offers an overview of geography and concentrates in particular on its visual epistemology as evidenced by its production and study of landscapes, photographs, maps, and charts. Cultural geography offers ideas and strategies for critiquing and expanding composition's theories and practices: for example, in the direction of visual rhetoric, which demands a response from composition scholars but a response that avoids a dominant visual epistemology, where what can be seen constitutes what can be *known*. A better understanding of geography as a discipline and as a teaching/learning subject results in more complex notions of place and space that, in turn, serve to complicate our notions of difference. Cultural geographers work to unhinge the binary relations between, for example, public and private spaces and to analyze the sociospatial construction of identities through such concepts as *habitus*. Strategies drawn from cultural geography, including feminist resistance to some of its approaches, can contribute to reading landscapes—urban or domestic, electronic or material—and to the development of spatial practices that inform a geographical rhetoric. In particular, the figure of the *flaneur* offers one compelling example of moving through the world, dependent on both walking and seeing, and how place and materiality construct identity. Understanding first the construction of identity *in place* works to situate the next two chapters and their emphasis on the spatial practices of walking and mapping.

Chapter 3, titled "Maps of the Everyday: Habitual Pathways and Contested Places," begins by acknowledging the limitations of and problems with maps but goes on to establish mental mapping as a tool not just for understanding people's spatial thinking or spatial remembering but also for tracing the effects of ideology and differences: perceptions of spaces are very much a reflection of race, gender, age, or level of economic security. This chapter records my mapping interviews with geography students about their perceptions of Leeds, its boundaries and dividing lines, and about their experiences in the city, from their homes to modes of transport. Mapping interviews show the ways in which students exist *apart* from the communities in which they live and learn. Students' comments about Hyde Park introduce David Sibley's notion of liminal spaces, which I use to argue that we can't understand cultural difference without understanding contested places and the social conditions produced within and by them. In illustrating the complexities of contested places, like Hyde Park in Leeds, these interviews establish how difficult it can be for people to leave familiar terrain, a point reinforced in the next chapter.

"Streetwork: Seeing Difference Geographically," chapter 4, presents a range of literature on "the street," clearly one of the most compelling and influential spaces of modern culture, and introduces a research project for cultural geography students that asks them to have "an encounter with place." This chapter presents data collected from two student groups and their processes of approaching and analyzing the places they chose to investigate, all of which convey the complex notion of *sense of place*. My findings further illustrate the workings of geographies of exclusion: the ways in which people feel excluded from certain places because of the landscape, the built environment, the inhabitants, or the force of their own preconceptions and expectations. This bodes ill, I argue, for composition's growing enthusiasm for service learning and literacy projects, which have a tendency to become an assigned encounter with difference. Composition's growing commitment to service learning or to literacy programs "outside" of the academy take on a different shape when approached through a geographic lens, sensitive to the sociospatial construction of difference. Walking and mapping are both forms of *flanerie* (chapter 2), drawn from geographical theories and methods to establish the importance of learning to see and the entrenched and difficult-to-dislodge attitudes toward place and space. Dwelling, then, is a third spatial practice, the subject of the final chapter, one that links the importance of first places or homeplaces—and the importance of memory and arrangement—to acts of writing both material and metaphorical.

Chapter 5, "Learning to Dwell: Inhabiting Spaces and Discourses," turns to implications for imagining texts and reading and writing practices through the lens of "inhabiting." Arranged to address different spatial scales—bodies, homes, cities, campuses—this chapter advocates not travel but *staying put* in order to understand the function of boundaries without glorifying them and in order to dwell within and maintain the places that borders surround. We should be attending to actual locations and the geographies of exclusion that characterize everyday life, even in texts and discourses, where such characteristics as "density" illustrate how social space is reproduced. This chapter illustrates the roles of memory and arrangement, in particular, for geographical rhetorics and uses data from the Leeds study to remind writing instructors that environments for writing are constructed from both tools and material conditions as well as from imagined and remembered uses of space.

I chose the Leeds School of Geography for circumstantial reasons—it fit with other parts of my sabbatical leave. While cultural geography is more prominent at other universities (namely Sheffield and University College—London), one of the earliest cultural studies of literacy took place in Leeds—in Hunslet, home of Richard Hoggart and site of his *The Uses of Literacy.* Visiting some of the same haunts where Hoggart grew up, as well as admiring his analysis of working-class reading practices, has in some small way influenced my own approach. Walking the streets, forming my own mental maps, and reflecting upon dwelling became important parts of my research methodology, one that will help us re-imagine acts of writing as spatial, material, and visual. I learned a great deal from the students of Leeds, not necessarily about geography as an academic discipline, but about geography as a lived event—including how spaces and places are inscribed upon us—and about how our experiences in spaces of the everyday impact upon our identities, our confidence, our senses of self.

It's a cliché to describe learning or education as a journey, but the journeys we take to "expand our horizons" cannot happen without other journeys, like the daily ride on the bus to campus. Without ignoring the "higher" journey that such a bus ride makes possible, I want to start with the bus and stay with the bus, seeing what we can learn about the social production of space that repeats itself from the bus route to the lecture hall to the library to the pub and back home again. I rode that bus with students on many days for seven months. I lived in university housing, surrounded by students for neighbors; I ate the same take-away and drank in the same pubs, occasionally with them, and walked the same routes to campus or to the city center. I shopped in the same shops, and I waited with them in queues to use the photocopiers in the library. I went to lectures, sat with them, and took notes. I was never "one of them," but I shared their space and tried to pay attention.

1

Between Metaphor and Materiality

Spatial metaphors are problematic in so far as they presume that
space is not.

—Neil Smith and Cindi Katz,
"Grounding Metaphor: Towards a Spatialized Politics"

What do bodies, city walls, pathways, streams, or plane trees have to do with rhetoric, writing, or an intellectual discussion? Plato opens the *Phaedrus* with attention to place because the context has everything to do with where Socrates and Phaedrus are located, both in a physical place and in relation to each other. While race, class, and gender have long been viewed as the most significant markers of identity, geographic identity is often ignored or taken for granted. However, identities take root from particular sociogeographical intersections, reflecting where a person comes from and, to some extent, directing where she is allowed to go. Geographical locations influence our habits, speech patterns, style, and values—all of which make it a rhetorical concept or important to rhetoric. For writers, location is an act of inhabiting one's words; location is a struggle as well as a place, an act of coming into being and taking responsibility.

This was Adrienne Rich's point in a well-known essay from 1984, "Notes Toward a Politics of Location," one that marks a great deal of interest in positionality and discursive authority, especially among feminist theorists. Rich wants to resist the abstractions of theory and invite "a struggle for accountability" that begins with the body, "the geography closest in" (212). Rich defines her struggle as "locating the grounds from which to speak with authority *as* women. Not to transcend this body, but to reclaim it. . . . Begin, we said, with the material" (213).

To begin with the material means grounding an inquiry into taken-for-granted spatial metaphors and geographical practices that affect reading and writing, living and learning. An inquiry into these metaphors and practices, into place and space broadly speaking and very specifically,[1] can offer insights into the connections between locatedness and moving through the world; between travel and dwelling; between public and private. In such betweens is where this project resides, raising questions about the socio-spatial production of culture and identities, and about the everyday production and uses of space. How do we read the signs about places that tell us to come on in or to keep out? How might theories of territoriality interact with theories of movement to change our notions of place and space? How can cultural and feminist geography contribute to material theories of rhetoric or discourse?

Composition studies—those who read and write its discourses and construct its spaces for learning—has not, typically, begun with the material but instead has been drawn to the metaphorical and the imaginary, particularly evident in language about texts and textual production. In "The Limits of Containment," Darsie Bowden traces and analyzes the container metaphor in discourses about writing and the teaching of writing. I am interested in her analysis for the ways in which it indicates not only a view of "texts" and therefore composing but also a way of being in the world, one that has serious consequences for learning. In the model of containment, words in a text "become privatized . . . and thus they are closed off from a public that is beyond the perimeter" (374). The public-private split, while illusory in several ways, is one of the most dominant paradigms about space in our culture, one that leads to notions of ownership: "my paper" becomes something fenced off, its contents private property. These "implied boundaries," as Bowden names them, explains the effectiveness of a rule-governed system for composing and students' reluctance to revise (375). In addition, "containerization limits the active participation of an audience, and hence, constantly risks being anti-rhetorical" (374). For those whose comfort zone lies within the parameters of titles with a colon and lengthy lists of works cited, the ambiguities of nonacademic discourse—lying outside fixed boundaries—are much more troubling. When a text is viewed as having an inside and an outside—with the audience, in particular, as a factor outside—writers can't think of texts in terms of movement or exchange.[2]

As Bowden recognizes, container metaphors aren't easily hurdled or disposed of; in fact, because of their work *as* spatial metaphors, they can't be "overcome." Spatial metaphors are inseparable from and embedded in our language, especially our language *about* language; as a result, container metaphors for texts imply that there are visible boundaries to all discourse. One hears routinely, for example, the charge that someone's argument has "gone too far" or "doesn't go far enough." How far can discourse go before it goes too far? Where does the notion come from that arguments, analyses, discussions, or questions have spatial limits? Going too far is perceived to be overly analytical, too critical, almost disrespectful. But if no one ever went too far, logically or emotionally, whose minds would ever be changed? "Going too far" as well as the more recently popular "don't go there," stand for the ways in which spatial metaphors dominate our thinking about language and learning. This chapter attempts to analyze some of these spatial metaphors, especially the attraction to movement and the neglect of material space in many contemporary discourses. I argue that we need both movement and dwelling and that we must pay attention not only to borderlands but also to the places that borders surround.

Spatial Metaphors, Spatial Theory, and Thirdspace

Because space is so abstract and intangible, language to describe it tends towards the metaphorical and the narratable. Space is usually described or represented by making comparisons with familiar objects or ideas—like an academic discipline being called a field (giving it the boundaries of absolute space). Meant to familiarize, metaphoric representations "describe the remote in terms of the immediate, the exotic in terms of the domestic, the abstract in terms of the concrete, and the complex in terms of the simple" (J. Smith 12). As rhetorical theorists understand from Nietzsche's lecture "On Truth and Lies in Nonmoral Sense," spatial metaphors, like the language of truths, become familiar through common usage or repetition. After long usage, as Nietzsche says, "the movable host of metaphors, metonymies, and anthropomorphisms" that make up "truth" become "fixed, canonical, and binding" (1174): "Truths are illusions which we have forgotten are illusions; they are metaphors that have become worn out and have been drained on sensuous force, coins which have lost their embossing" (1174). Worn-out coins become mere metal, their worth lost; similarly, well-used spatial metaphors lose their connection to anything "real."

They did have that connection once, however, or the metaphor would not have evolved. Here's one social researcher on the rise of spatial metaphors in sociological theory: "One major feature of spatial metaphors is simply that they do ultimately allude to some concrete, material 'reality,' be it ordinary physical space or commonsensical understandings of social proximity or distance between individuals" (Silber 346). Spatial metaphors come from somewhere, in other words, and they then go on to influence our responses to other places; they are formed through the material world and the ways in which people experience space and place. Because they do come out of the everyday to begin with, it's even more striking that once the spatial metaphors become commonplace or well known (that of sociology or composition studies as "fields"), their connection to the real is elided even though they can shape theory and research (Silber 324). For example, do we really think of plowed earth, fertility, or crop yield when we call composition a field? Once composition could be named a field, a concept reflecting absolute space, then it could wield power (Smith and Katz 75–76).

What spatial metaphors and conceptions of space tend to ignore are the ways in which people move through the world, or the spatial practices that shape lifeworlds. It is not only *places* and their built-in constraints that determine certain practices, which then become habitual or taken for granted, but also the adjustments and compromises, the shifts and turns in the process of accommodating to a place. For example, a composition instructor assigned to a tiered lecture hall with bolted-down seats is upset by the room assignment; she must make contortionist changes to the collaborative group practices of the class. However, at some point in the semester, the configurations become so routine that the room assignment is no longer an issue—everyone adapts. Once constraints become familiar— whether they are the desktop of a computer interface or the furniture arrangement of a classroom—they become encoded and thus rarely noticed or questioned. The daily routine elides the process of adapting, and the ideology of transparent space takes over—the idea that space doesn't matter. Spatial practices, therefore, evolve from movements or placements that we take for granted, or boundaries that seem clear or uncontested, and they develop into the habitual ways we move through the world.

Despite the pull and the promise of the imaginary, the spaces of the everyday demand equal, urgent attention. *Metaphor* and *material* are often divided to make it easier to discuss or distinguish them, but their combination and interaction creates social space, Henri LeFebvre's term, which refers to the ways in which space is "used," produced and reproduced, and how space participates in forms of production.

Published in France in 1974, but not translated into English until 1991, LeFebvre's *The Production of Space* is one of the most important theoretical works on space of the twentieth century.[3] Politically Marxist and stylistically dense, it takes as its project the rejection of notions of space as a container, as abstract, or as independent of agency. Interested in how space affects and is affected by production, and working within the traditions of philosophy and political economy, LeFebvre attempts to develop "a science of space" that unifies a conceptual triad and that theorizes space as a social product, typically concealed by different types of illusions (27–30). The conceptual triad for which LeFebvre's work is best known constitutes three ways in which space is used, produced, reproduced:

- Spatial Practice (perceived)
- Representations of Space (conceived)
- Representational Spaces (lived)

Spatial practice is perceived space, which "embraces . . . the particular locations and spatial sets characteristic of each social formation" (33). Perceived space, in simple terms, is what we see or smell or otherwise register with our senses; it is the material expression of social relations in space. Spatial practice "has a certain cohesiveness, but this does not imply that it is coherent" (38). Spatial practice both produces and appropriates society's space and "embodies a close association" between one's daily routine and the routes or networks set up to link work, leisure, and private life (38). Representations of Space, or conceived space, are tied "to knowledge, to signs, to codes": think of maps or signs or canons. The dominant space in any society, this conceptualized space takes form through verbal signs and codes; think of "the space of scientists, planners, urbanists" (38). Conceived space is made up of conceptual abstractions like geometry that may in fact inform the actual configuration of spatial practices. This second formation makes the rules for spaces; representations of space "are certainly abstract, but they also play a part in social and political practice" (41). Thirdly, Representational Spaces are the lived spaces of inhabitants and users: "This is the dominated—and hence passively experienced—space which the imagination seeks to change and appropriate" (39). Representational spaces are linked to "the underground side of social life" and may or may not be coded. More *connaissance* than *savoir,* representational spaces overlay physical space but need not obey any rules of consistency or cohesiveness (41). Lived space has its source in history and is "alive: it speaks. It has an affective kernel or center: Ego, bed, bedroom, dwelling, house; or: square, church, graveyard" (42).

Particularly important to LeFebvre's theory is the idea that space is active, not a passive surface; in fact, "space is itself actively produced as part of capitalist accumulation strategies" (Merrifield, "Henri LeFebvre," 172). LeFebvre's triad also loses its force, Merrifield claims, "if it gets treated merely in the abstract: it needs to be embodied with actual flesh and blood and culture, with real life relationships and events" ("Henri LeFebvre," 175). LeFebvre makes this point himself—that the perceived-conceived-lived triad "loses all force if it is treated as an abstract 'model'" (40). To counteract this tendency toward abstraction, LeFebvre offers *the body* to help illustrate the three moments of social space. The three realms, like the various parts of a human body, are interconnected so that a subject can move from one to another without confusion—"a logical necessity" (40). LeFebvre's use of the body is an important one for rhetoric and rhetorical theory;[4] it emphasizes the "embodiment" of the production of space, or how space cannot be studied in material ways without accounting for physical bodies, something I take up again in other chapters.

One brief illustration of how these three parts of the triad work in unison can be found in universities and their production of space. The educational mission of universities (*conceived space*) may conceal from us their status as actual workplaces (*perceived space*), and the two together combine in *lived space:* a university is a place where an internationally renowned researcher can't find a parking place. Cultural geography and postmodern spatial theory insist that there are no "pure" spaces and that space functions in indivisible and entangled ways: as perceived, conceived, and lived space. Understanding sociospatiality means attending to this trialectics of spatiality, present in all forms of the social production of place and space, and not just where there is remarkable difference.

Trying to keep the three points of the triad straight is not as important, as least for my argument, as is maintaining a sense of their interlocked relation. The three concepts cannot be separated, a point well illustrated by Edward W. Soja in his book *Thirdspace,* which continues the project of theorizing space as a product of human practice. A tribute to and an engagement with LeFebvre, *Thirdspace* represents "the trialectics of spatiality" in a swirl, not as a chart or graph or map, and outlines not the difference that geography makes but *the geography that difference makes* (see fig. 1.1). While he would insist on the dialectical relationship between space and time, Soja wants a "trialectics," where the spatial and temporal are joined by the social. In a trialectics of spatiality, then, there is one blended, swirling concern with how space is lived, perceived, and conceived.

This trialectics of space leaves binary concepts, like insider-outsider, floating in the middle or bouncing from one spot to another; thirdspace means exploding or transgressing binaries, not simply flipping them to restore the undervalued term. Lived, perceived, and conceived space fold into and spin across one another, working together to accomplish the production of space. Our marketplaces, bedrooms, bus terminals, theaters, or schoolyards are not isolated from this process, do not stand separate from perceptions and conceptions, but are the sites where representations and uses are reproduced. As it is crucial to realize, the functions of spaces keep changing, particu-

Fig. 1.1. Soja's trialectics of spatiality, from *Thirdspace*. Reproduced by permission of Blackwell Publishers.

larly as they are remade to heighten consumption or to increase profits. The more that spaces are "controlled," the more likely that new uses or practices develop as forms of resistance to order and control.

Modernism, according to LeFebvre, promoted a "decorporealization of space"—making spaces less like bodies and more rigid, where border crossings became more difficult. Modernist conceptions of space (what he names abstract space) made nature recede as plazas and commercial centers took over ("the great empty spaces of the state and the military" [50]). Political and institutional, modernist abstract space "*is not* homogeneous; it simply *has* homogeneity as its goal" (287, LeFebvre's emphasis). Accordingly, modernist urban planning led to the postwar construction, en masse, of high-rise or "tower block" units of flats, as in England, purported to solve all social ills. The clean, spare lines of modernist architecture, with structures devoted to a union of form and function, provide a striking contrast with, say, the ornate features of Renaissance buildings or the confusion and disorder of postmodern ones.[5]

Postmodernism, of course, produces space differently, with more of an aesthetic sensibility or at least less determination to make buildings uniform and entirely functional. Postmodernism views the city, for example, as a labyrinth or as theater (Faigley, *Fragments* 5), neither of which are functional modernist images. Since spaces are created, again according to LeFebvre, by ruptures in the semiotic code, postmodernism alters the abstract space of modernity with a semiotic code characterized by fragmentation, disorientation, the simultaneity of fear and exhilaration, the simulations of reality that have replaced reality itself. Some theorists argue that postmodernism and other vestiges of late capitalism have created a remoteness to our spatial experience that has rendered profound changes in how we experience both time and space; below I suggest that cell phones might illustrate this remoteness. Changing conceptions of space, including the production of new social spaces like the Internet, result from technologies that allow the rapid, almost instantaneous, transmission of information and ever-faster modes of transportation. Twenty-first-century technologies have made border crossings *seem,* at least, as easy as punching buttons.

Our world is perceived to be "smaller" than it used to be, a phenomenon known as *time-space compression.* First named by Marx as the annihilation of space through time, time-space compression means more time to work and thus more profit (Massey 146; Harvey 293; Soja, *Postmodern* 126). As spaces seem to shrink, time seems to expand—and the illusion that there is more time would allow capitalists to get more out of workers, like expecting them to check their e-mail or pager evenings and weekends, from home or on the road. "Time-space compression refers to movement and communication across space, to the geographical stretching-out of social relations, and to our experience of all this" (Massey 147). The perception that the earth is shrinking to the size of a "global village"—a perception that benefits the expansion of capitalism—is problematic, however, because it elides differences.

In *The Condition of Postmodernity,* postmodern Marxist geographer David Harvey claims that the history of capitalism has been characterized by this speed-up in the pace of life. Harvey explains that time-space compression forces us "to alter, sometimes in quite radical ways, how we represent the world to ourselves" (240), the consequences of which "have particular bearing on postmodern ways of thinking, feeling, and doing" (285). The effects of time-space compression would not be felt, however, without the accompanying technological devices: fax machines, pagers, cellular phones, personal computers. Time-space compression could not make the world seem smaller without technologies that construct the illusion of closeness and try to bypass the material world or geographic distance. Particularly through the ability of electronic technologies to simulate travel or movement or a "speeding up" of tasks or activities, we think we're "experiencing" a different culture, otherness, or diversity. We get the false sense of going somewhere when we log on and having been somewhere after we log off, but we're not even leaving the comfortable (or crowded) confines of our homes or offices.

Other examples of time-space compression include: (1) satellites beaming events "around the globe"; (2) the weird sense of mobility that comes from "surfing the net" or from exchanging e-mail with someone in Johannesburg or Berlin or Seoul; (3) the "really there" feeling enhanced by big-screen televisions or expensive sound systems in theaters; (4) Microsoft's slogan "Where do you want to go today?" and (5) the IBM slogan "solutions for a small planet." Notably, these examples are from business, the media, and technology—forces that have combined to give us an onslaught of everyday images about how small our world is and how easily traversed. Within a college or university, the general sensations of a shrinking planet—busier, noisier, and more crowded—trigger the temptation to look out over urban classrooms and think "the whole world is here" (Muchiri, et al. 195). As they say, it isn't. In one of the first geography-influenced publications in composition studies, these four authors show just how distinctly *North American* composition is and how the assumptions and research findings are difficult to transplant to places like Kenya, Tanzania, and Zaire, where the cultural reasons for seeking higher education as well as the material conditions differ dramatically from those in the U.S. This article reminds us that it's important to consider pedagogy, discourse conventions, and textbook production as evolving from specific and concrete circumstances—historical, geographical, political, and economic.

Time-space compression works to make the consequences of space harder to read or makes space or spatial divides seem completely natural. According to geographers Neil Smith and Cindi Katz, absolute space refers to space as a container or as discrete, identifiable locations, like acres or plots or battlefields or city blocks. This is a way of profiting from space by making it something measurable, divisible, or taxable. Directly tied to the rise of capitalism, "it is a conception of space appropriate for a project of social domination" (76). We are so familiar with containerized notions of space, or forms of absolute space, that another danger emerges: as technology and capitalism have combined to make time-space compression more common and familiar, one alarming result has been the idea that space is negligible or transparent. As space flattens out, time becomes both harder to notice *and* more important; the masking of *time* through the changing boundaries for space has consequences for workers, students, women, for all of us who live and work in the everyday. For example, even though many composition instructors are attracted to concepts of shifting boundaries and unstable borderlands, this instability makes acts of literacy risky for those who cannot tell where the safe house ends and the contact zone begins.

Time-space compression is a "high theory" concept that feminist geographers have tried to make more practical and more concerned with the everyday. In *Space, Place, and Gender,* Doreen Massey explains that the usual explanation for time-space compression is internationalized capitalism, but that such an explanation is "insufficient" for women:

> The degree to which we can move between countries, or walk about the streets at night, or venture out of hotels in foreign cities, is not just influenced by 'capital'. Survey after survey has shown how women's mobility . . . is restricted—in a thousand different ways, from physical violence to being ogled at or made to feel quite simply 'out of place'—not by 'capital,' but by men. (147–48)

As Elizabeth Wilson notes, feminists are more interested in policy issues related to space—women's safety, street lighting, or the dearth of public transport—than in theoretical or conceptual considerations (148). Massey and other feminist geographers are working towards notions of space as paradoxical, provisional, contradictory, fragmented, insisting that divides are real, that differences are material and concrete, and that space cannot be treated as transparent or "innocent." Transparent space is an assumption that "the world can be seen as it really is and that there can be unmediated access to the truth of objects it sees; it is a space of mimetic representation" (Blunt and Rose 5). However, it is important to challenge the idea of a single and objective sense of time or space against which we attempt to measure the diversity of human conceptions and perceptions. A notion of paradoxical spaces helps feminists to resist transparent space—a particularly dangerous notion for women and other minorities because it denies differences or neglects the politics of space, especially in domestic or everyday environments.

Where Are You? Cell Phones and Changing Notions of Space

The idea that space is transparent or meaningless gains credence with the proliferation of technologies that, in a variety of ways, challenge or confuse previously stable notions of space. Just as concepts of space and place change in response to changes in transportation, architecture, or urban planning, there is abundant evidence that new technologies are also shifting our understandings of space and are ushering in new forms of writing or talking—forms that many users are still adjusting to. For example, near the end of the first e-mail decade, some people persist in their naive belief that e-mail is private discourse, and their behaviors or responses have yet to catch up with the demands of these new spaces for writing. Declarations of love and assassinations of character, written and sent on e-mail to one person or erroneously to hundreds, have been forwarded and reproduced far beyond the "intended audience," causing people to lose their jobs or at least lose face. *New York Times* writer John Schwartz quotes Sherry Turkle of MIT, professor of the sociology of science, as saying that even people who should know better are "lulled" into thinking that e-mail is private. Her theory is that "many Americans equate e-mail with paper mail, which en-joys strong legal, and social, protections against snooping," and thus they tend to confuse the two different forms of communication. Turkle says that "composition occurs in a zone of intimacy," but receiving an e-mail takes place in a very different context, when a user may download hundreds of messages at once. Writing *one* message or receiving dozens comprise two very different experiences. An "intimate" message loses its meaning in a huge pile or causes the recipient to treat it as just another message. Thus, "any-thing" can be forwarded. This article in the *Times* is accompanied by an illustration from what appears to be the 1950s, a young girl holding a book titled "My Diary" and a pencil, posed in thoughtful contemplation. The "old-fashioned" nature of the private diary contrasts starkly with the pub-lic nature of e-mail. Composing, as we know, has changed dramatically through electronic technologies, altering a number of spatial and rhetori-cal practices, but e-mail provides just one example of how our concepts of space (and time) are shifting.

Cellular phones and networks of mobile communications are changing our notions of space as they also offer forms of resistance to concepts of absolute or container space. Cell phones confuse the divisions between public and private space and offer a way for people to, in a sense, write their own personal geographies by reporting on their comings and goings, their progress or halted movements in space.

Anyone who spends any time "out in public" has experienced overhear-ing phone conversations—or one end of them—that used to be considered private. Numbers of cell phone users are huge in Britain, whose geographic compactness makes service and marketing a breeze. Surrounded by cell phones in an airport I hear a man talking to his family members, one after another; in a women's bathroom of a university building, someone is hav-ing a romance crisis on her phone; walking down a sidewalk just behind me, a young man explains his living arrangements and roommates to an unseen listener; in the stacks of a library, a caller makes plans for later. Despite other conversational threads, however, the most commonly over-heard line in public spaces has got to be "Where are you?"

The often overheard "Where are you?" aptly defines this cultural moment and represents an ambivalence about being on the move or being separated from "home," about postmodernity and its consequences. The September 11, 2001, terrorist attacks on the World Trade Center and the Pentagon illustrated in poignant and dramatic ways our culture's growing dependence on cell phones, as those being hijacked called to express their terror or say their good-byes, or those in the buildings called to report on their locations or progress in making their way out. Even before this disaster's scope was traced by cell phone use, the sight of these small dark plastic objects, held to ears, was ubiquitous, a fully accepted part of street and office culture but more resisted in other places. A recent article in the *New York Times* chronicles the efforts of rail companies, Amtrak and others, to control "cell yell," which as Doreen Carvajal writes, "is the stimulating chat of telephone users who assume others are deaf to their stock tips, dining choices, office numbers, and professions of love. . . . But more often, cell-phone blather consists of periodic reports on geographic location."

Why do most cell phone conversations boil down to reports on geographic location? What motivates this need to report on one's own movements or to map the movements of others? Rather than argue that this insertion of the private into the public is "bad," or that cell phone users are simply rude, I want to suggest instead that those terms, public and private, are rapidly losing their traditional meanings—that in fact, public and private were never divided purely and completely. As Richard Sennett puts it, "We talk about public and private as fixed states, because picturing them is easier so. They were in fact complex evolutionary chains" (91).

When used or heard in public, cell phones actually make people *notice* where they are; at the same time, however, they also seem to make the user oblivious to place. Cell phones seem "out of place" because we have such rigid notions of what constitutes public and private—for spaces or conversations. These phones draw attention to place precisely because they violate social codes about where one can speak (loudly and one-sidedly) to a loved one or colleague. It's not the technology that is the culprit but ideas about space that cause the attitude towards cell phone use.

Cell phones constitute a type of tracking, a mapping of the movements of others, a form of friendly (or not) surveillance. Less insidious, perhaps, than surveillance cameras, cell phones constitute, nevertheless, a new panopticon, where knowing the whereabouts (or reported whereabouts) of one's friend or child becomes comforting in our fast-paced culture where danger seems to lurk around every corner—or does. Cell phones reflect how out of touch and disconnected people feel in this culture and how movement is hugely appealing but also risky. If we know "where" someone is at the moment, we gain a false sense of control over our own environment.

"Where are you?" demonstrates changing spatial practices and uses of space. On one hand, perhaps on the most obvious level, people call each other to report that they are six blocks away *because they can.* Almost as obvious, cell phones serve the interests of capitalism in allowing for "multitasking." People can drive and talk; eat and talk; ride on the train and talk; walk to class and talk. With the phone available to explain the late train or the traffic jam or the sudden 5:00 meeting, cell phones contribute to a support structure in place for getting more out of workers; thus, they reflect and contribute to time-space compression in the service of capitalism. Cell phone users can "get things done" from the car, an airport terminal, or while shopping or eating—all spaces or gaps of time that, before the technological age, were for reading, reflection, or other "unproductive" pursuits.

Even though time-space compression ostensibly works to make the world seem smaller, it doesn't make the world seem *safer*. The ordeal of travel, the complexity of movement, the time commitment and patience involved: these add up to a grind involved in moving through the world. The running commentary about place or one's schedule of arrival, departures, and ETA's may represent, on one hand, a badge of honor to be on the move so much in a postmodern culture that values movement (if the movement is economically productive). On the other hand, self-surveillance and frequent reports become a form of resistance to the tyranny of movement in postmodern culture. The proliferation of cell phone use raises doubts about whether people are necessarily comfortable with so much movement or illustrates their ambivalence. The repetition of "Where are you?" indicates a need for closeness in a culture of distance, well illustrated by teens' seeming addiction to cell phones: feeling connected is particularly important for those who are eager to be mobile but still don't have adult freedoms. Like all good tools, cell phones can be adapted to different situations and purposes. They can be turned on or off; locations can be reported accurately or misreported. Cell phones, then, offer a means of resistance for users—even in such dramatic ways as calling from a hijacked plane to report the terrifying events that otherwise would have been contained within the jet.

Cell phones, in short, affect spatial practices in a variety of ways. On one hand, people *seem* less attentive to their surroundings when they are engaged in conversation or trying to dial a number; this is why some states want to ban the use of hand-held cell phones while driving. At the same time, however, by reporting on their geographic location ("we've just landed at O'Hare" or "I'm getting into the cab now on 14th Street"), users are very much aware of *where* they are. By making users believe that they are always "connected" in ways that being surrounded by other people evidently can't manage, cell phone use is becoming a definable spatial practice characterized by a distrust of the material world and a related reluctance about traveling and movement; by a perceived conflation of public and private space that feeds into a discourse of loss; and by a means of resisting traditional uses of space. In short, cell phones draw attention to place at the same time that they try to overcome it—and this paradox is precisely the type of both/ and situation characteristic of the trialectics of spatiality.

Listeners get annoyed when overhearing "private" cell phone conversations because such conversations blur the lines between public and private space—concepts of space that most people would prefer to keep neatly separate even as technologies and other changes in our culture make them increasingly blurry notions. Feelings certainly run high about public space, about who should be in it and what they should be doing. In our romantic notions of community, before "progress" bulldozed through, people gathered in town squares, on front porches, or at the local shop, to exchange news or talk politics; thus, references to public space invoke democracy and nostalgia and civic participation. Before malls, there were shops along the street run by local merchants; before theme parks, people fished on river banks or went on drives through the country. A consequence of time-space compression, the sense of loss of public space, can be traced in part to cell phones and other technologies: "As phone and modem render the street irrelevant, other dimensions become preeminent. Main Street is now the space between airports" (Sorkin xiii). A sense of loss of public space can also be traced to corporate sponsorship, or selling the right to put a company name on a place—for example, Boston Garden is now the Fleet Center; Cincinnati's Riverfront Stadium is now Cinergy Field. The Fleet Center or Cinergy Field could be anywhere, their names having nothing to do with the town or location of the arena. An important public space, then, a place for gathering and the (at least potential) intermixing of cultures and classes, is named for a company and not a place. Many geographers and urban planners argue that these corporate names diminish a city's unique character or alienate people from the history of a city.

There are hundreds of examples of the privatization of public space, whether those spaces are stadiums or malls or libraries (see Lees). Real or imagined or a swirling combination of both, people feel alarmed and regretful about a perceived takeover of public space. Like the discourse of crisis surrounding literacy (see Trimbur "Literacy"), there is similarly a "discourse of crisis" about the loss of public space, in its real or imagined forms.[6] Those lamenting this loss, however, fail to recognize that public spaces are always about, and have always *been* about, control and consumption—trying to get people to spend their money in subscribed ways while following subscribed forms of behavior.

In a volume titled *Variations on a Theme Park: The New American City and the End of Public Space,* Michael Sorkin and his contributors trace the end of public space along several fronts: for one, urban renewal and gen-trification have actually served to drive "authentic" or long-term residents out while creating sterile, artificial environments, meant for marketing but not for living. Some geographers refer to the "malling" of America (most recently, it's the malling of airports, an effort to increase the consumption function of public space) and others to the "Disneyfication" of America to capture this sense of controlled space where image is more important than livability, where four lanes for traffic crowd out all room for pedestrians or cyclists, and where CCTV equipment tries to convey the illusion of safety.

Public space has never truly welcomed everyone. As Mike Davis details, downtown Los Angeles has several features purposely designed to keep out the unwanted, including park benches rounded like barrels to make lying down impossible—thus the homeless must go elsewhere to find sleep. Teen-agers, who occupy a very fuzzy boundary between childhood and adulthood (Sibley 34–35), are not welcome in children's playgrounds and are fiercely regulated in malls (despite their economic potential for some serious con-sumption). Despite the obvious associations of downtowns, benches, parks, and malls as public space, regulation of these spaces is increasing.

Competing notions of public space result, of course, from different ideo-logical positions. In his article "The End of Public Space? People's Park, Definitions of the Public, and Democracy," Don Mitchell identifies two versions of public space under contestation in Berkeley's People's Park during the 1991 riots that erupted over the proposed construction of volleyball courts. The first, a view held by activists and the homeless, is that public space should be "unconstrained," marked by "free interaction and the ab-sence of coercion" (115). City and university officials held a different view of public space, that it should be a "controlled and orderly retreat" and where users must feel comfortable (115). Do public spaces represent the right to organize and speak out or the right to play volleyball without feeling un-nerved by protesters? In his discussion of competing notions of public space and how they clashed in Berkeley, Mitchell distinguishes public space from public sphere (Habermas) by materiality; that is, public sphere is an abstract realm, but public space is material (116–17). Mitchell, in fact, insists on materiality as a necessary element to public space, largely rejecting the prom-ise of electronic environments to accomplish similar ends of social change. Without political activity and the representation of oppositional movements in a material location, according to Mitchell, then it's not public space.

Others concerned with the loss of public space are less likely to make Mitchell's careful and political distinctions. In a popular book listed as so-ciology, James Howard Kunstler's *The Geography of Nowhere* represents a huge tide of sentiment about the horrors of development and growth in the U.S. Kunstler blasts suburban and freeway development and laments that "two generations have grown up and matured in America without experiencing what it is like to live in a human habitat of quality" (245). In the chapter titled "How to Mess Up a Town," Kunstler writes a history of Saratoga Springs, New York, as a case study of how American towns have sacrificed their "essential character" to progress and development, ignoring design, old zoning laws, and pedestrians (134). Kunstler's book is a particularly "loud" protest of the concern that global capitalism is eroding senses of place and creating pseudo-places, but not all geographers or urban planners agree that public spaces have actually declined.

In "Urban Renaissance and the Street," for example, Loretta Lees questions what the "public" in public space actually means. A building may be open to everyone, but that doesn't mean people will be comfortable entering it. Lees uses two examples of gentrification in Vancouver, Canada, to argue that "public space has always been controlled. It has never been truly 'free' and 'open'" (239). The new public library, for example, is "an excellent example of . . . a privately owned and managed public space offered for public use" (242). With a commercial purpose to its outside perimeter (a food court), the library is patrolled by a private security firm that forbids political activity or leafleting (242). Concluding that the Vancouver Public Library is "an ambivalent space," Lees's essay demonstrates that true public spaces are a myth, but that spaces are continually being remade, used in different ways, and that there are possibilities for resisting the control of public space.

Absolute space must become "thoroughly naturalized"—unquestioned— and only then can it express power (Smith and Katz 76). Some public spaces have become naturalized in this way even though, as Lees points out, there are also openings in the production of public space for resistance. Until the powers-that-be tried to assert new forms of control over People's Park, it was a fairly peaceful place, not a scene of activism and protests. In order to understand the conjunction of control and resistance, it's important to study place and space, the spatial practices of the everyday, and the seductive nature of spatial metaphors without losing sight of lived space. The attraction to "movement" must be tempered with material realities about how people move through the world—or how they resist movement and spaces.

Generally, time-space compression (the world is "smaller"); Disneyfied space (space is artificial and constantly surveyed); absolute space (space is contained); and transparent space (space is negligible) all combine to make spatial practices harder to detect, and then the connections between the real and the imagined get lost.

Composition's Imagined Geographies

Social theories of composition, as Patricia Bizzell illustrated in 1982, tend to be "outer-directed," in reaction against "inner-directed" cognitive theories. The problems and challenges of understanding writing and acts of writing have sent social theorists "outward" to find explanations or models. Such travel has certainly enlarged our horizons: borrowing from many theoretical terrains, composition has created or invoked frontiers, cities, contact zones, safe houses, borderlands, community compacts, and various other territories that have influenced, at least metaphorically, concepts of literacy or learning. These territorial metaphors have also, however, made more rigid notions of insider and outsider.

Composition's push toward disciplinarity—towards legitimacy as an academic specialty—motivated a search for places to stake out turf, to colonize, to call home. Borrowing spatial metaphors from postmodern, postcolonial, and other contemporary theories—that is, border crossing and traveling theory and surfing the net—composition's reproduction of spatial metaphors carries certain consequences. In fact, the ways in which we imagine space and place have a direct impact on how we imagine writing and acts of writing as well as the inhabitants of composition studies—and its outsiders, real or imagined. For reasons that are understandable, given the material conditions, as students crowded into worn, urban classrooms during Open Admissions, the tendency for instructors was to look past those material spaces towards imagined geographies, where an ideal pedagogy was possible. Composition, in short, turned to imagined geographies to build its empire, rather than studying the relationship between the worn, urban classroom and the writing produced there.

As the following sections illustrate, at least for the discipline of composition studies, spatial metaphors can begin to dominate to the exclusion of materiality, and the realities of space get ignored or taken for granted. Space, at least as it is represented metaphorically, hides consequences from us, which the following section argues through the example of composition studies and its powerful spatial metaphors: the frontier, city, and cyberspace, as well as borderlands and travel. The first three, I argue, have served to establish composition's disciplinary status; the other two work to shape notions of discourse and difference within composition and literacy studies.

Because writing teachers recognize both the spatial nature of writing and the importance of controlling textual as well as disciplinary space, composition scholars have developed a rich repertoire of memorable spatial images and referents, everything from webs of meaning to turf wars. Spatial metaphors have served to establish what composition should be or to lament what composition has become. For example, claims of composition as a discipline have called on the lofty spatial metaphors of paradigms and "domains" (Phelps) or on the more mundane: inside Stephen North's sprawling, junky house of lore resides a group of sad occupants who live in the basement (Miller). Feminist readings of the field have concentrated on the domestic spaces of composition, where underpaid women are assigned primarily chores and housekeeping tasks (Slagle and Rose; Neel, "Degradation"). In our discussions of economic and political issues about composition, we refer to heavy course-loads as teaching "in the trenches" because composition occupies the "low" position in the academy, akin to a carnival (Miller).

Generally, as composition has encountered postmodernism, metaphors of inside and outside, margin and center, boundaries and zones have become increasingly familiar, appealing, even comfortable. Mike Rose's *Lives on the Boundary;* Carolyn Ericksen Hill's *Writing on the Margins;* and Mary Louise Pratt's "Arts of the Contact Zone" identify popular spatial metaphors for discussing issues of difference and diversity or for asserting where the work of composition studies should concentrate. Perhaps the most appealing spatial metaphor right now is Gloria Anzaldúa's "borderlands" (*La Frontera*), where cultures are mixed and mingled and where geographic borders do not hold. As I'll discuss below, borderlands is one of the geographies difference makes, creating spaces open to a mix of languages, cultures, and identities.

As composition workers struggled with the impact of Open Admissions and the demands of an expanding population, they faced working in crowded, inadequate building space populated by speakers and writers of many languages or dialects, few of them closely resembling traditional academic discourse. The feeling of "foreignness" and claustrophobia led to the construction, in discursive terms, of spaces where their struggles could be enacted. The only space big enough for such a struggle was a *frontier.*

From the first day of Open Admissions at City College, more space was needed for writing instruction. The *New York Times* reported in October 1970 that tutoring was taking place in coat rooms while classes were being held in former ice skating rinks and supermarkets. At John Jay College, the square feet per student shrunk from ninety-three in 1969 to thirty-one the following year. "With lounge space scarce and college cafeterias jammed, many students study, do homework and eat their lunches sitting on corridor floors and stairways," and this crowding was reported in October, before the weather forced all students inside (Buder 59). Nearly everyone associated with the Open Admissions program has commented on the over-crowded conditions; Adrienne Rich's famous essay "Teaching Language in Open Admissions" refers to the "overcrowded campus where in winter there is often no place to sit between classes" (60), and she gives another account to Jane Maher: "the overcrowding was acute. In the fall of 1970 we taught in open plywood cubicles set up in Great Hall [where] you could hear the noise from other cubicles; concentration was difficult for the students" (109).

The crowding and material conditions at City College led to compo-sition's first imagined geography—and perhaps its most enduring spatial metaphor for arguing composition's legitimacy as a discipline. It is no ac-cident that Mina Shaughnessy's *Errors and Expectations* opens with a fron-tier metaphor: "the territory I am calling basic writing . . . is still very much of a frontier, unmapped, except for . . . a few blazed trails" (4). Her purpose is to offer a guide for teachers "heading to this pedagogical West," but admits the flaws of her map: "it is certain to have the shortcomings of other frontier maps, with doubtless a few rivers in the wrong place and some trails that end nowhere" (4). Shaughnessy's invention of this imagined ge-ography illustrates one reaction to some of the pressure of the crowded con-ditions, but more importantly, it inaugurates the use of an enduring fron-tier metaphor.

Shaughnessy's early reviewers eagerly picked up on this frontier imagery because it allowed inexperienced, tentative, even resistant writing teachers to feel like brave, noble conquerors. Harvey Wiener, for example, describes Shaughnessy's book as the map, compass, and guide for those who dare to venture—or who would be sent—into the "jungle of trial and error" where teachers must "hack branches" through students' tortuous prose (715).

One way to read Shaughnessy's construction of the frontier metaphor is to see it romantically as desire for the open space of the frontier, in reac-tion to the crowded, chaotic conditions of City University in an Open Admissions system. Shaughnessy was, undoubtedly, surrounded by over-whelming needs and demands, and all of her biographers or reviewers connect her frontier imagery to her regional identity, formed in the Black Hills of South Dakota. For example, Janet Emig writes in her eulogy for Shaughnessy, "Mina could not be understood without understanding that she came from the West" (37). To read Shaughnessy's work through the lens of the Western motif is tempting not only because of her family roots in the West, but also because of the contrast provided by her move to New York City and her major life's work spent in crowded, urban classrooms. Imagining her homeland and her own identity as a strong prairie-dweller gave her a form of escape from the multiple and oppressive institutional structures of City College. In this version, sustaining her practical, perhaps even vocational, emphasis can be draining and frustrating because of the enormity of the task; thus, Shaughnessy looks to the West for energy and a sense of mission.

Others have interpreted Shaughnessy's frontier metaphor through the realities of her workload and the crowded material spaces of City College. Robert Lyons claims that "her frequent allusions to the pioneer role of basic writing teachers and to the 'frontier' experience of such work had more to do with her sense of taxing work loads than with nostalgia for her Western past" (175). Indeed, Shaughnessy worked herself to exhaustion, suffering a brief physical collapse in 1971 (Lyons 175). For teachers in the trenches, hard work defines their experience more accurately than large expanses of hope and possibility.

Metaphors of the frontier result from dominant ideologies of space, place, and landscape in the U.S.: the more the better; own as much as possible; keep trespassers off; if it looks uninhabited, it must be. Canonical in American studies, F. J. Turner's thesis, "The Significance of the Frontier in American History" (1893), claimed that pushing west into the frontier was the most defining aspect of the American spirit, that the social, political, and intellectual development of the U.S. can be traced along the line of Western expansion. Settling the frontier, according to Turner, reenacted the history of social evolution. Turner's thesis, along with more recent studies from literature and film, can help to explain the power of the frontier metaphor in composition studies. As critics have shown, Western films capture the harshness and supposed "emptiness" of the landscape. One cinematic shot of rock and desert puts into place "an entire code of values," especially the lure of "infinite access": "the openness of the space means that domination can take place. . . . The blankness of the plain implies—without ever stating—that this is a field where a certain kind of mastery is possible" (Tompkins 74–75).

The frontier metaphor appears again and again in the literature of composition studies, often as a way of establishing or confirming composition's disciplinary status. Janice Lauer, for example, in an article that begins by asking "Is this study a genuine discipline?" reinscribes Shaughnessy's frontier imagery. Lauer traces "the field's pioneer efforts" as it "staked out [the] territory [of writing] for investigation" (21). She characterizes composition's early theorists in "their willingness to take risks, to go beyond the boundaries of their traditional training into foreign domains" (21). According to Lauer, composition's "dappled" character as a discipline holds both advantages and risks: composition can be a "rich field of inquiry" or "a terrain of quicksand":

The immensity of unexplored land presents a subtle seduction, drawing newcomers by promising not to relegate them to tiny plots in which to work out the arcane implications of already established scholarship. But once committed, some individuals have difficulty finding entries or end up losing their way because the role of pathfinder is challenging and thus ill-suited to everyone. The field's largely unmapped territory, therefore, has rewarded some handsomely but been fatal to others. (25)

To construct composition as a risky venture, not for the fainthearted, as Lauer does, gives composition studies a tough image: if only the fittest can survive, then it must be worthy of the status of a discipline. Joseph Harris has argued that Shaughnessy mistakenly assumed the frontier of basic writing was unoccupied, and the frontier metaphor has problematic colonialist echoes that are fairly obvious (79). Harris also makes the case that the frontier metaphor is actually quite innocuous; it gave teachers of literature a dose of missionary zeal about teaching writing to underprepared students but also allowed them to imagine that they were not changing but simply extending the reach of the curriculum (80). Naming basic writing a frontier served to mask the politics of space—the real material conditions that crowded students into classrooms with overworked and underpaid teachers.

The frontier metaphor endures because composition's professional development was dependent on sounding "new," bold, untamed and exciting without really changing the politics of space at all. Frontier was an important imaginary space for the early days of Open Admissions because it seemed to invite "vision," hope, and wide expanses of possibility, but the frontier metaphor was also a reaction against the overwhelming work and responsibility that went along with educating larger, more diverse populations of college writers. Composition's development and growth meant changes in its imagined geographies, and after a brief investment in the geography of "community," composition needed a more powerful and diverse space in which to imagine its work, subjects, and practices—the *city*.

As composition grew and developed, different settlements sprang up all across the wide frontier, communities characterized by differences in philosophy, political allegiances, or research methods. Acknowledgment of the diverse communities within composition was one way of demonstrating its legitimacy, but the appeal of the community metaphor soon wore thin, replaced by evocations of the city. Naming composition a city marks a moment of maturity in composition's history, but there are consequences to any imagined geography, and the politics of space can be either illuminated or disguised by images of the modern city.

As a second generation imagined geography, "community" offered tremendous rhetorical power. As Harris explicates, the metaphor of community is "both seductive and powerful" and "makes a claim on us that is hard to resist" (99). However, like the notion of frontier, community too often assumed transparent space—where there are clear insiders or outsiders; where differences may not be so welcomed or encouraged; or where the goal of consensus silences productive dissensus (Trimbur "Consensus").

Composition scholars were quick to recognize that a warm, fuzzy notion of composition—where like-minded peoples cooperate harmoniously— would not serve the diverse populations of composition dwellers. If the frontier metaphor characterized composition as a tough field, community sounded too "wimpy," and composition continued to need authority or legitimacy within the academy. "Community" was also not geographically loaded enough to be appealing and enduring, not in the ways that frontier and city are geographically expansive and symbolically romantic. In other words, community did not last long as an imagined geography in composition because its spaces were just too limited. An imagined geography big enough to hold composition's ambitions was that of the city. Cities offer diversity of peoples and places, models of cooperation, more sites for public gathering, and more feelings of exhilaration, sometimes a keen sense of "survival of the fittest." A city metaphor seems richer and more exciting; the bustle of a city implies that work is getting done.

Seeing composition as a city also invokes the places where rhetoric flourishes—the agora, marketplace, theater, or coffeehouse. The city, therefore, offers at least two ideologies or dominant sets of images and metaphors: (1) city as an embodiment of postmodernism; (2) city as a reflection of democratic ideals. The material conditions of the city are more "in your face" than those of the frontier, which assumes a blank plain; the politics of space, therefore, seem more obvious in the city or less difficult to identify. Still, notions of the city differ ideologically, and too many views of the city glamorize its appeal.

Contemporary geographers often turn to the city to illustrate their claims about postmodernism. Soja reads Los Angeles as the perfect example of "the dynamics of capitalist spatialization"; L.A. is *the* capitalist city (*Postmodern* 191). One view of the city emphasizes simultaneous stimulation and terror, where postmodern subjects feel most keenly a kind of twenty-first-century panic: the fear of being crowded; that all the space is being taken up; that the planet is overpopulated and toxic. Simultaneously, however, caught between contradictory desires, we also want the excitement and exhilaration of a city. The goal of postmodern city life is not to achieve stable orientation, but to accept disorientation as a way of life.

To invoke a city is, on one hand, to identify composition with post-modernism since crowded urban streets, like busy visual images, are more postmodern. On the other hand, unlike postmodern geographers, Harris and Faigley (in *Fragments*) want to claim the democratic, rhetorical, or public images of the city; for example, the idea that cities revolve around a center (Soja, *Postmodern* 234–35). In contrast to the frontier, cities have a central location, a "polis," or a "heart" (as in "in the heart of the city"). Thus, the city seems a more appropriate, more invigorating site for the exchange of ideas: there is a central place to meet, an especially appealing notion for rhetorical scholars interested in the gathering places of ancient cultures and in public spheres for communication.

The city seems a more sophisticated image for composition's maturity than that of the frontier because it invites a more paradoxical notion of space and represents a different kind of work. Composition as a city invites more diversity because many different activities can go on simultaneously and, following the logic of traffic lights, no one will cause accidents or pile-ups; everyone cooperates. To navigate a city requires more experience, skill, or wits than to navigate a small community, and the alienation or anonymity are outweighed by the opportunities or stimulation. The frontier signifies the hard physical labor of sod-busting and planting and harvesting, with a landscape of plains or rolling hills, capped by big skies. The city holds bolder or more complicated signifiers, but corporate work images come to mind: high-rise office buildings, with photocopiers and air conditioning and water coolers, where the politics of space are both enhanced and complicated by modern architecture and technologies.

In representing the city as a place of either postmodern exhilaration or democratic participation, scholars and theorists may be glamorizing the city and overlooking some of the material realities—the same problem that exists with the frontier metaphor. Visitors to cities almost never see the ghettos, for example, and tourists are herded—through promotional materials, transportation routes, and hotel locations—to the most attractive sites. In addition, time-space compression works to make city-dwellers believe that technologies to shrink space have actually resulted in more time. As most commuters will attest, however, "having more time" is not exactly their experience. As cultural geographer Peter Jackson points out, ideologies of city and frontier do not differ all that much: "frontier ideologies are extraordinarily persistent even in the contemporary city, where they reappear as ideologies of 'pioneering' or 'homesteading' in the urban 'wilderness'" (111). Thus, Turner's thesis is once again reinforced—that the pioneering spirit is deeply American, and that American ideologies celebrate pioneering myths.

While the appeal of frontier turns on the American fantasies of space and place (that it is endless; the more the better; that space can be mastered), the appeal of the city turns on busy visual images, heightened adrenaline, movement, and a desire for public space or mutual co-existence with others. As Shaughnessy found out, however, work in the city was just as hard and taxing. Both of these appeals are present in a potent geographic site—*cyberspace.* Cyberspace is an imagined geography where visitors or homesteaders can be simultaneously stimulated and terrified, where order and disorder co-exist, and where the frontier metaphor continues its hold over our collective imagination. Cyberspace and its attendant electronic technologies also offer the most representative example of time-space compression, where space seems to shrink as time seems to expand.

As electronic writing technologies radicalize the work of our field once again, with an impact probably as large as that of Open Admissions, the pattern repeats itself: in the face of some confusion and an overwhelming sense of responsibility, the frontier beckons. It is tempting to call cyberspace "the new frontier" because it offers a sense of excitement and possibility in the face of otherwise frightening changes, and those influences combine to make cyberspace the latest imagined geography.

The frontier metaphor served well during the Kennedy administration to justify the space program; now the frontier extends beyond space, into new imaginary territory called cyberspace. Without NASA-level technology and equipment—with only a p.c. and Internet access—"anyone" can go there, making it far more accessible. It is not difficult to illustrate the dominance of the frontier metaphor in discourses of electronic technologies. The Electronic Frontier Foundation lobbies to stop legislation limiting the freedom of computer users. Howard Rheingold's *The Virtual Community: Homesteading on the Electronic Frontier* addresses the idea of domesticating space—making a home in unfamiliar territory, staking a claim, naming it ours. Even the moral code of the frontier is reproduced: "The Internet has been like the Wild West before law and order was brought to it" (Vitanza 133).

Composition, like Star Trek and NASA, is so completely "American," as the Muchiri essay argues, that the temptation to claim a new final frontier is strong and appealing. Despite the attractiveness of naming cyberspace a new frontier, cyberspace is not transparent space, as several scholars have recognized. Emily Jessup says it quite succinctly: "The land of computing is a frontier country, and, as in the development of most frontier countries, there are many more men than women" (336). Women and other disenfranchised groups will have to follow the maps, tracks, and instructional manuals written by the techies, mostly men who got to the colony first. Concerns of colonialism have been addressed by invoking democracy— claims that cyberspace offers more opportunities for voices to be heard, that "anyone" can participate. This view has its critics, too; for example, Mark Poster claims that promotions of Internet newsgroups and other virtual communities as "nascent public spheres that will renew democracy" are "fundamentally misguided" because they "overlook the profound differences between Internet 'cafes' and the agoras of the past" (135).

Granted, much about cyberspace is hugely inviting: chat rooms and emoticons and a "web" of access to information (and to "community"). The notion of the web, familiar to composition through both Janet Emig and Marilyn Cooper, touches on ecological metaphors that many writing teachers found more inviting than other mechanistic metaphors for the writing process. The World Wide Web has the same inviting ecological tenor, and the implication is that strands seem to connect the whole world, stretching across and enveloping many sites. At odds with these "warm and fuzzy" notions of the Web are some material realities: the whole world is *not* in the Web. Issues of access aside, the metaphor of a web also evokes entrapment. Webs, as any fly knows, can be sticky traps for the negligent or gullible; not all of us are safe in a web. A web has thousands, if not millions, of intersecting strands. A lot of Web users find it hard to leave—not only from confusion but also from a sense that virtual spaces are more inviting or attractive. When they devote themselves to screens and keyboards, on-line participants are removing their actual bodies from physical spaces, and that creates another set of problems for geopolitics. As Stephen Doheny-Farina argues in *The Wired Neighborhood,* participation in on-line communities removes people from their geophysical communities—the streets and schools, sidewalks and shops that make up a neighborhood. People have understandably turned to virtual communities to fulfill some of their needs not being met by physical communities, but Doheny-Farina critiques claims that the Internet's chat rooms are new public spaces. Admitting his own fascination with MediaMOO, in one chapter, Doheny-Farina shows how the supposedly public spaces are more accurately a maze of private rooms, where one's participation ("socialization") is dependent upon one's technical expertise, including one's skill as a typist (61). Settling upon the analogy of virtual communities being like airport bars, Doheny-Farina admits to the compelling nature of these on-line enterprises, but repeatedly notes the seduction, even the danger, of ignoring the politics of space in our daily environments.

Borderlands and Movement

It's hard to ignore the politics of space if you live, for example, along the U.S.–Mexico border, where the clashing drama of history, economics, politics, and cultures plays out daily. Here, the borders are clearly marked, symbolizing both danger and promise, but the real richness is in the movement between the borders, especially among the more subtle boundaries marking cultural differences. From this position Gloria Anzaldúa writes in *Borderlands/La Frontera: The New Mestiza* about her experiences of straddling *los intersticios,* "the spaces between the different worlds [the woman of color] inhabits" (42). As Anzaldúa's book illustrates, margins and borderlands offer women and people of color a place from which to speak, a site from which to resist the center while finding or cultivating an alternative voice. Her writing illustrates this straddling and crossing of boundaries, as she writes in different languages and dialects and genres: poetry, autobiography, philosophy, myth, history. The hybrid writing reflects the hybrid identity and resists binaries. *Borderlands* exemplifies hybridity and refuses "pure difference" (Friedman 93–95).

Anzaldúa's borderlands imagine new places where the silenced might be heard. Rooted in a premise of exclusion—that is, the reality that women, slaves, and foreigners were not welcome to participate in the agora—this theory of communication begins by acknowledging that occupants of borderlands are outsiders to the dominant culture and therefore must develop freedom of movement and the ability to occupy different perspectives. The power of the borderlands metaphor results from its own "straddling" nature, drawing from concepts of territoriality as well as the need for movement; the power comes from the groundedness of the metaphor in a real, actual place. This place, rooted as it is, can only be negotiated through movement. One has to stay on the move in borderlands, weaving between cultures or communities, languages or dialects. Anzaldúa and other writers from the margins recognize that freedom of movement is often necessary for survival. In dangerous areas or difficult situations, it's good to have mobility, to be able to dodge bullets or slip away unnoticed, and movement offers an important resistance to territoriality or containerization. However, theories of movement must develop from spatial practices of the everyday—walking, mapping, or dwelling—and the streetwork or fieldwork practices that cultural geography offers, the subject of the next chapter. Travel gets glorified in postmodern discourses simply because it isn't static and resists (modernist) absolute space. Other ideas about movement, however, are possible, including those that try to connect movement to inhabitance, dwelling, or embodiment.

When space is parceled out, as in absolute space, the result is boundaries, borders, fences, and no-trespassing signs with varying degrees of subtlety. The wide-open frontier, for example, gradually became a set of territories owned by individuals and protected from intruders. One consequence of absolute space, then, is a binary opposition where people are either in or out. Most treatments of discourse communities imply the territorial nature of specialized languages but also convey that while only "insiders" are welcome, outsiders are not completely excluded. Outsiders have to find a way in that imitates insider discourse (in Rorty's terms "normal" discourse) even if they then proceed to introduce an "abnormal" or hybrid discourse. Because most borders are not impenetrable, outsiders develop tactics to subvert or resist the laws of territoriality and learn how to "move" in ways that will allow them inside, if only briefly or if only to effect one small change. In a postmodern trialectics of spatiality, people would be insiders and outsiders simultaneously or in different ways, or they would shift from one to the other almost imperceptibly.

Territorial metaphors for space also serve an important role in constructing a sense of safety, privacy, or comfort. Home, too, is a territory, one defended and protected by its occupants and a monument to private space. When strangers try to enter a private home, the ultimate form of trespassing occurs. In this culture, "home" carries tremendous evocative and persuasive weight, as evidenced by some Web browsers, which begin the journey through the World Wide Web by starting from "home," the icon that of a single-family dwelling. Journeys that start from home are well worth tracking; they count as the extraordinary movement we might call travel or migration; that is, the effort to leave one's home, neighborhood, city, or country in search of knowledge, money, freedom from persecution, or escape from famine or war. Despite ubiquitous representations of middle-class travel—the business culture of airports and planes—the pull to travel is not limited, either, to the middle classes: as one of my readers points out, many young people are advised to leave home to find work, to get an education, to join the military as a way to see the world, and so on. The cultural pressure to move away is significant—and chronicled in dozens of class-based literacy narratives.

Travel Metaphors and the Rhetoric of Mobility

Opposed to the rhetorical construction of territories, Gregory Clark tries to substitute for discourse communities a notion of writing as travel. Clark's effort in "Writing as Travel" is a postmodern one—trying to use movement to transgress boundaries—with a social writing theory in view. Along with many other contemporary scholars, Clark taps into an attraction to travel that has both a long history and much contemporary currency. The tradition of touring the Continent, a requirement for an educated young man, continues today with popular study abroad and exchange programs for students, and many faculty travel to conduct research or to teach in foreign countries. Travel literature is a hot commodity in publishing markets, and forms of armchair travel, like the Travel Channel on cable television, contribute to our culture's romantic notions of travel. Faster and cheaper modes of transport have made travel more available to the lower middle classes while seductive electronic technologies make some of us believe that we can travel via the Internet. In these ways, the idea that we can now travel with ease (if we can afford or have access to the technology) is one of the most pervasive and appealing ideas of the current era.

Clark's proposal, while informed generally by a number of "traveling theories," and while invoking the itinerant sophists so important to our rhetorical history, relies on a bourgeois ideal of travel and does not acknowledge that traveling involves difficulties, economic realities, safety issues and is exclusionary by race, sex, class, and abilities. Even if the traveler is not well-to-do or highly educated—James Clifford reminds us that migrant workers, exiles, and nomads also travel—our western culture generally admires those who travel for pleasure and enlightenment and considers the well-traveled more sophisticated, more experienced, or more able to understand cultural differences. "Tourism" won't quite qualify; in the elite circles of true travelers, tourists are shunned, especially those who go on group bus tours. Travel writer Paul Theroux insists that tourists are not travelers—and further insists that real travelers go it alone. In any case, there are clearly degrees of travel and many different forms—all of them complicated by material factors and the interplay of identity with place. No single notion of travel exists although many of the discourses of cultural criticism would seem to promote one (Wolff).

Imagining writing as travel would also require multiple notions of travel and should not mean silencing or erasing those whose labor makes it possible—like the conditions that make writing possible. Didn't servants accompany bourgeois Victorian travelers, and weren't they traveling, too? (Clifford 33). Furthermore, it's important to acknowledge that not everyone travels or moves around. Those who are burdened by domestic labor or responsibilities, those who are physically disabled, those who can't afford the time off or the expense, those who simply can't leave home, or, most significant for my argument here, *those who see no need to go.* Anthropologist and ethnographer James Clifford broadens the scope of travel to include "an increasingly complex range of experiences: practices of crossing and interaction that troubled the localism of many common assumptions about culture" (3). Clifford acknowledges that feminist theory in particular has complicated the notion of home as safety or immobility—breaking down the binary oppositions between home and abroad. However, even Clifford's effort to broaden the notion of travel and to recognize feminism's contribution reinscribes the fundamental problem with travel metaphors. In her article, "On the Road Again: Metaphors of Travel in Cultural Criticism," Janet Wolff analyzes the gendered nature of these metaphors and ultimately rejects them because some discourses "are too heavily compromised by the history of their usage" (180). Most interested in how the metaphors and ideologies of travel operate, Wolff says, "My argument is that just as the practices and ideologies of *actual* travel operate to exclude or pathologize women, so the use of that vocabulary as metaphor necessarily produces androcentric tendencies in theory" (180, her emphasis). She asserts that travel metaphors are rife with serious implications because "there is something *intrinsically* masculine about travel" (184, her emphasis).

Although she acknowledges the exceptions—that women do travel and that much research has been done, for example, on the Victorian lady travelers—Wolff also believes that the suggestion of "free and equal mobility is itself a deception, since we don't all have the same access to the road" (189). Interestingly, however, among her strong objections to travel metaphors, Wolff finds borderlands, exile, and margins less problematic because all imply dislocation from a given and exclusionary place (189). Geographer Geraldine Pratt agrees with the promise of borderlands "perhaps because the focus is shifted . . . to a socially constructed place in which difference and conflict is constructed and lived" (243). As long as place metaphors do not suggest neutrality, they can certainly provide imaginative inspiration for those seeking sites of resistance.

But Clifford's purpose in *Routes* is to rethink travel entirely, to try to break down the too-easy opposition between traveling and staying put. What if dwelling, home, the local, the neighborhood were not seen simply as the opposite of travel but as concepts that make the notion of travel possible? Clifford's idea of dwelling-in-travel or travel-in-dwelling complicates the relationship between the two. As Clifford outlines the issue he's addressing,

"Travel" denotes more or less voluntary practices of leaving familiar ground of difference, wisdom, power, adventure, an altered perspective. These experiences and desires cannot be limited to privileged male Westerners—although that elite has powerfully defined the terms of travel orienting modern anthropology. Travel needs to be rethought in different traditions and historical predicaments. (90–91)

What we need, Clifford says, is a way of talking about travel that acknowledges and includes a range of experiences with or relationships to travel—and, I would add, to place. Travel metaphors construct our cultural notions about acts of traveling because liberating travel metaphors represent only men's experiences with travel. New concepts of travel, then, will have to account for dwelling. In this vein, Geraldine Pratt, concerned that the rhetoric of movement privileges detachment from place, recommends more attention to the meaning of dwelling, a point she takes from Stuart Hall (243). In particular, how can languages of travel/dwelling acknowledge fundamental differences in people's sociospatial worlds and their unequal access to modes of travel or their range of reluctances to cross borders?

Writing as travel would seem to treat texts as movement or exchange, which would, in Bowden's terms, help us out of the container model that composing is stuck within. However, travel metaphors and the rhetoric of mobility leave the materiality of place unexamined and reinforce the assumption that places, or their boundaries, are stable. Whether the keyword is travel or journey or border crossing or movement, *how* we get there is a crucial part of the equation, often conveniently ignored. Why do we go, with whom, and under what conditions? These are precisely the questions about materiality that travel metaphors neglect. Concepts of border crossing and boundary transgression, forms of movement, ignore evidence that in the "real world" people don't move around that much, a point I'll return to in chapter 3. Those who are enthusiastic about borderlands assume that speakers and writers are willing to cross lines and to take risks in unknown places, and this contradicts geographic evidence about the importance of "home"—as well as the importance of the body. In the words of Christina Haas, "ignoring the materiality of literacy, its basis in bodily movements and habits, is no longer possible" (227).

A number of rhetoricians and composition scholars, like Haas, recognize the materiality of discourse, literacy, and acts of writing; insist on materiality; and would resist a theory of writing based upon some form of disembodied movement. I turn now to some of them, to highlight the need for geographical rhetorical theories that begin with the material—with the artifacts of culture that make possible acts of reading and writing. As Bruce McComiskey explains it, "material rhetoric posits that things do indeed perform rhetorical acts" (700). Unlike social constructionist rhetoric, which posits that "people perform rhetorical acts *with* things" (700, his emphasis), material rhetorics, out of work within cultural studies, semiotics, and feminist media studies, argue that different kinds of bodies, not just human bodies, construct social knowledge and experience (701, 703).

Linda Brodkey first identified acts of writing as spatial and material in "Modernism and the Scene(s) of Writing," where she argues that "the writer in the garret" dominates our images of writing, limiting them to "Authors producing Literature" in solitary rooms. Calling that image of writing "an artifact of literary modernism," Brodkey wants to move conceptions of writing from the garret into Virginia Woolf's room, to place writing "into the very social, historical, and political circumstances from which garrets have been defending us" (79). In "Writing on the Bias," more of a memoir, Brodkey opens the essay with her pencil and her Big Chief tablet, artifacts of literacy for children of the 1950s and 1960s—items that were her passport into the neighborhood, into people's homes, and into conversations with them; this memoir begins the early acts of a child who "leaves her mother's house to travel the neighborhood under the protective mantle of writing" (30).

Writers and texts interact via the tools and objects that make writing possible. In her article, "Accumulating Literacy: Writing and Learning to Write in the Twentieth Century," Deborah Brandt defines literacy as a "piling up" of artifacts—typewriters or piles of sermons—that demonstrate the ubiquity of print and the "residual" nature of literacies (652). New literacies exist alongside and build upon old ones, and families pass along the artifacts to a new generation.

Artifacts make up part of what is emerging as a material rhetoric, characterized by connections between embodiment and tools or things, like public works of art and the stories or histories they signify. Richard Marback has outlined a theory of material rhetoric in his "Detroit and the Closed Fist: Toward a Theory of Material Rhetoric." Interested in negotiating among the concepts of civic life and rhetorical agency, Marback chooses the figure of the closed fist (represented more concretely by a public statue representing Joe Louis) to signify "embodied articulations of civic space and rhetorical agency," which all depends on "a precarious balance" (75). According to Marback, such terms as *contact zone* and *discourse community* fail "to embody rhetorical theory in the material conditions of urban life; such talk has yet to suggest how either contemporary rhetoric physically inhabits cities or postmodern urban space physically inhabits rhetoric" (76). The contact zone is a disembodied ideal because—and this is crucial—it fails to be a concept "thickly informed by geographic manifestations of borders and communities, assimilation and difference in urban space" (76–77).

Material theories of rhetoric must either reject disembodied ideals—those created through spatial metaphors—or learn how to fold them into corporeal, spatial, and textual efforts to locate rhetorical agency in public life.

Haas, in *Writing Technology: Studies on the Materiality of Literacy,* is interested in bodily acts of writing and the relationship between writers and their texts, at least as it can be investigated via empirical methods. Material tools for writing are embedded in the culture that develops them and they, in turn, shape mental processes. Starting from the premise that writing and technology constitute one another, Haas wants to see writing as an "embodied practice" and its tools as cultural artifacts:

> The spatial and temporal metaphors that writers use to describe their text sense problems . . . then, make a great deal of sense because computers transform writing in the realm of time and space—that is, in the realm of the bodily. It is through these worlds of time and space that writers move as they produce written discourse. Hence, the body . . . is the mechanism by which the mediation of the mental and the material occurs. (226)

To make her argument about the materiality of literacy, Haas considers acts of writing as a connection between the body and familiar practices; thus, she refers to Bourdieu, though fleetingly, in her discussion of the materiality of literacy: "Any embodied practice, including writing, is habitual. . . . a habit is a kind of remembering in and by the body" (228). Through this interest in the body, Haas concentrates on individual writers and their relationships to their texts. What Haas doesn't pursue is the ways in which bodies engage in acts of writing under certain physical or material *conditions.* The body, of course, is imprinted with and affected by the spatial and social world in which it moves. While the writer in the garret is not an image of writing supported by social writing theories (Brodkey, "Modernism"), it's nevertheless true that writers need a place to work: a place to sit, a surface, lighting.

Anne Aronson's study of several adult women writers begins with the recognition that when Virginia Woolf called for a room of one's own for women writers, she meant it literally. "Composing in a Material World: Women Writing in Space and Time" identifies the challenges of space and time that make it difficult—for all but the firmly middle-class, middle-aged student with a spacious home, grown children, and a supportive husband— to engage fully in process writing. The results of Aronson's surveys and interviews provide support for Woolf's position and challenge Ursula LeGuin's claim that one needs only paper and pen to write (Aronson 297). Aronson shows that in the ordinary everyday, writing occurs in a corner of the bedroom or at a kitchen table in a full household (289–90). Despite our fundamental theoretical stake in writing as a social act, social circumstances for writing—being surrounded by other people who have needs or desires—can distract from the writing, from getting the work done.

Brodkey, Brandt, Marback, Haas, and Aronson provide different ways of seeing literacy as embodied practice, of seeing rhetoric as enmeshed in the everyday. My own contribution to this effort, as I'll detail more in the following chapter, draws from cultural geography as a rich source for investigating people's relationships to place, and how subjectivity is shaped by ordinary and mundane landscapes, by ubiquitous visual images, and by habitual pathways. Material conceptions of space begin with the assertion so familiar in cultural and postmodern theories that space is socially constructed—and that identities are constructed as bodies move through the sociospatial world. But material rhetorics also insist upon "reality's construction of the social" and not simply "the social construction of reality" (McComiskey 700). Understanding more about this process can lead to a richer conception of sociospatial and cultural difference and can shift our attention to spatial practices and artifacts that reflect both movement and dwelling, that straddle borders, and that work within material places alongside or as informed by imaginary conceptions of space.

The Production of Space in the "Real World"

Since spatial metaphors construct reality and don't simply reflect it, it's impossible to "get away from" spatial metaphors in our language about language. The goal is not to "replace" spatial metaphors with, necessarily, more attention to materiality since cultural and material space are not an antidote to spatial metaphors but a necessary companion. The goal is, therefore, to recognize how metaphor and the material are interrelated, contributing to a complex production of space and spatial practices. Of all the spatial metaphors or ideas of movement that composition has flirted with or embraced, the concept of borderlands comes closest to a geomaterial sense of space; it emerges from both notions of territoriality as well as movement and sees both as integral to the construction of a sense of place. Movement and change are possible, even welcomed, in the borderlands. Empowerment comes not from a stable position but from the ability to navigate and move skillfully, recognizing the risks and costs of boundary crossing. Spatial metaphors, therefore, can be empowering or offer the possibility of political and social change if they are not constructed in a vacuum and if they engage with the material world. Those spatial metaphors that have little grounding in the sociospatial world thus must repress critical differences in order to be effective. Like the frontier or cyberspace, another well-worn spatial metaphor is "the real world"; it refers to a mythological place that composition specialists are being asked to colonize.

It seems particularly important just now to address our own closely held beliefs about "where" the work of writing gets done when a number of scholars—for example, Anne Ruggles Gere in "Kitchen Tables and Rented Rooms: The Extracurriculum of Composition"—call for expanding the study of writing beyond the classroom. Unfortunately, however, moving outside the classroom walls or away from campuses has become moving into "the real world," as if that exists everywhere except on college campuses. Paul Heilker is one writer who buys into a problematic separation between classrooms and the real world, as Bruce Horner has already discussed (67–68). Heilker makes a case for writing "beyond" the curriculum, outside the academic classroom, with civic discourses: "the classroom does not and cannot offer students real rhetorical situations in which to understand writing as social action" and that "composition students have suffered for too long in courses and classrooms that are palpably *unreal* rhetorical situations. Their audiences are not real audiences; their purposes are not real purposes" (71, his emphasis). The lack of content in composition, according to Heilker, makes students desperate for "the real." His argument has its appeal, but it hardly benefits the work of writers and their instructors to cast writing and its work as unreal or less real than writing done in the "real world" (see Horner 67–71). To claim that writing classes are mere rehearsal for the "real world out there" reproduces a binary relationship between the world and the academy that geographers and many postmodern spatial theorists would reject. Attending to the social production of space, to the interplay of conceived, perceived, and lived space, makes claims of the real world hugely problematic since teaching and learning can only occur within the swirl of the trialectics of space, where the sociospatial world becomes imprinted upon readers and writers, and as they leave their mark, too, on the sociospatial world. The growing popularity of service learning and community literacy programs makes even more urgent a need for rhetorics that will interrogate these artificial splits between the classroom and the real world, rhetorics that would insist upon investigating the production of space within composition, or the multiple, conflicting uses of space that fall under the rubric of composition studies.

Composition classes—from the content to the classroom itself—reproduce spatial practices found in many other "places" in the culture; composing practices circulate from, within, and through a variety of discourses and disciplines. Collaborative learning methods, for example, are drawn from the medical profession (Bruffee) and from corporations, particularly Japanese-influenced values of teamwork. The "unreal" rhetorical situations Heilker refers to have developed from a fairly small pool of genres, modes, and topics that continue to be recycled for very specific reasons: as much historical work in composition demonstrates, its development as a set of practices grew out of concrete, material conditions, like the emergence of an overworked female underclass in composition teaching as the result of a decline of traditional, oral rhetoric instruction at American colleges (see Connors 180–202). Once again, the disciplinary motives of composition— in this case, trying to expand the work of composition studies into service learning—privileges spatial metaphors over material realities. Like the constructions of frontiers, cities, cyberspaces, and borderlands in the discourses of composition, the discourse of "the real world out there apart from the university" assumes that the construction of space is somehow "different" for the academy. While some of the spatial practices do differ, of course— the ways texts are read, treated, or exchanged, for example—the production of space still operates, through ideology and across institutional boundaries to make us think, variously, that space doesn't matter, that public space is truly public, or that borders just need to be stepped over.

The way to address and resist these containerized conceptions of space— though we can never "eliminate" them—is to focus on spatial practices of the everyday—those habitual movements through space that are often taken for granted or ignored—and to try to understand how they inscribe differences. Crossing a street or skimming a newspaper are acts contingent upon a multitude of variables that can never be neatly isolated; they result from a combination of habit, opportunity, strategy, visual evidence, past experience, early learning. Our awareness of our own moves and decisions dims over time: when and how exactly do we decide when and where to cross and how quickly or what to read and what to skip? Habitual moves in our daily life are influenced, too, by our cultural mobility—that is, a combination of factors of race, class, gender, age, ability, or sexuality stretched across a range of other overlapping or interrelated differences. Investigating spatial practices, cultural mobility, and the intersections of difference is not easy. But it seems fairly urgent to ask questions about the connections between spatial practices and literacy, or cultural mobility and learning, since movement metaphors figure so prominently in postmodern discourses about subjectivity and pedagogy, and since movement is such a reflection of our experience in twenty-first-century culture.

The theoretical attraction to movement metaphors competes with abundant geographic evidence that most people are reluctant to travel, or even to leave their neighborhoods, without having a very good reason. Firm stay-at-home attitudes, keeping yourself to yourself, contradict many philosophies of learning that value, for example, challenging texts, the learning of foreign languages, experiencing other countries or cultures, or generally cultivating an open mind. But if not from our own neighborhoods and habitual pathways, where do we develop our spatial sense? How can we balance strategic "movement" with forms of dwelling? How do we account for the blending of lived, conceived, and perceived space in theories and practices of literacy? And how can we learn from the places we inhabit to re-imagine acts of writing? These questions are taken up in the remaining chapters, but as one starting point, Philip Eubanks urges writing scholars to give more attention to metaphors for language and writing: "It is not enough that we recognize, in a general way, the substantive ramifications of metaphor, not if we misunderstand the particular metaphors we encounter" (93). In his argument that the conduit metaphor "grows out of a complex of embodied activity, situated experience, and rhetorical human relationships" (99), Eubanks confirms that the point is not to undo, one-up, or improve upon spatial metaphors for writing. We should instead be asking how metaphors result from, rather than simply shape, our experience in the material world. The cause and effect may run the other way, and in this case, we need to understand more about the embodied activity and situated experience that leads to our dependence on and reproduction of spatial metaphors that so often characterize writing and learning.

My goal, then, is to find ways of keeping the material and the metaphorical interconnected, acknowledging that the real and the imagined are dependent upon one another. Neither material conditions nor imaginary places are constructed out of time and place, and objections to territoriality need to acknowledge that places too—and not just identities—are always in flux. Many theorists and researchers are turning to geography to map their forays into space and place and to understand the sociospatial constructions of identity and difference. As the next chapter argues, cultural geography in particular informs an inquiry into spatial practices of the everyday. In order to find ways to inhabit both places and discourses, we start with walking. Mapping and dwelling, the subjects of later chapters, further our exploration of spatial practices, material rhetorics, the relationship between rhetoric and place, and the interrelatedness of movement and dwelling.

2

READING LANDSCAPES AND WALKING THE STREETS: GEOGRAPHY AND THE VISUAL

Locomotion should be slow, the slower the better, and be often interrupted by leisurely halts to sit on vantage points and stop at question marks.
—Carl O. Sauer, "The Education of a Geographer"

Many of us were introduced to geography by maps on classroom walls or copies of *National Geographic* in waiting rooms. Curriculum reform of the 1960s and 1970s replaced history and geography within the broader category "social studies," and in turn, students' knowledge of geography began to plummet, according to some studies. My own educational experience reflects this national trend: the only geography textbook and geography lessons I remember were in the fourth grade, when I chose to study Chile and had to memorize its imports, exports, and annual rainfall. After about 1968, I didn't receive any direct instruction in geography.

In Great Britain, alternatively, geography has never disappeared as a school subject and is, in fact, a popular and important degree for university students. On the University of Leeds campus in Yorkshire, for example, geography has its own large five-story building (see fig. 2.1), not uncommon among the many universities in the U.K. offering degrees in geography. Since the size and stature of buildings indicates much about how the culture values the work that goes on there, it's safe to say that geography is a highly regarded discipline. The Leeds School of Geography is one of the largest geography departments in British Higher Education, with 230 undergraduates recruited each year, and a teaching, research, and support staff of nearly sixty personnel (School of Geography).

One might suggest that Britain is more interested in geography because

Fig. 2.1. School of Geography building at the University of Leeds, U.K. Photo by Randy Blackburn.

of colonialism—Brittania ruled the waves, and its subjects needed to know the scope of such rule. For England and the British isles, national geography is a more manageable subject given the relatively small size of space compared to the U.S. or Australia, the enormous colonies. In the U.S., a national geography curriculum may seem more daunting; thus students are reduced to memorizing the capitals of the fifty states, a curricular experience so well known it is the subject of a television commercial for breakfast cereal. Geography's status in U.S. education is a direct result of the ideologies of space produced and reproduced in the large land mass that makes up the lower forty-eight.

The sheer size and power of the U.S. give its people a very different sense of space than citizens of small countries of Europe, Central America, or Africa, often surrounded by enemies past and present. Ideologies of space in this culture, especially those of the West, reproduce a false sense of protection in large stretches of land. Another layer to our spatial ideologies is Woodrow Wilson's policy of isolationism and the reluctant entry of the U.S. into World War II, a memory that still lingers for many Europeans. The terrorist attacks of September 11, 2001, have made homeland security a top priority in a world where only 11 to 15 percent of Americans have passports—a telling statistic. Finally, U.S. corporations see the world as their profit-making oyster, but most Americans have no good reason to learn about other people, places, and cultures.

Only when the term "global economy" entered the mainstream media did U.S. educators begin to take a hard look at geography education. Approximately a decade after the claims that schoolchildren could not read or write,[1] the media began reporting on survey and test results showing that college students guessed wildly on geography tests and were unable to read a map, identify important countries, or name boundary rivers or mountains. With the collapse of several subjects into "social studies," young Americans had become geographically illiterate. Surveys confirmed that nearly 70 percent of all secondary students had had no formal coursework in geography, and the media were eager to report the most egregious examples of ignorance, for example, the belief that Canada was a state ("Teachers Lament").

In 1985, in response to "deterioration of geographic knowledge," two professional organizations set forth new guidelines for the teaching of geography in elementary and secondary schools (Shabad), and Congress designated a "National Geography Awareness Week" in 1988 "to combat a widespread ignorance of geography" ("Redoubling"). The National Geographic Society pumped over two million dollars into the D.C. public school system alone, for teacher training, a high-tech classroom, atlases, maps, and software (Horwitz A8).

Just ten years after the nationwide concern with geographic ignorance, interest in geography was said to be soaring, with a declared "Renaissance" in geographic education. From inflatable globes to such popular programs and games as "Where in the World Is Carmen Sandiego?" American schoolchildren improved test scores. Geography's fortunes are changing because of a new push towards geographic education—complete with corporate sponsorship—and because of near-revolutionary changes in map-making technology (Hitt).

One sign of geography's changing fortunes and its move into mainstream intellectual life in the U.S. is a recent article in the *New Yorker* (April 2001) about "the new geography." Nicholas Lemann, the author, is quite skeptical of critical geography's claim to make connections between cartography and social justice, but he does concede that geography is a "rich subject" and that it is "back," thanks largely to a group of "mostly British, mostly left-wing scholars—David Harvey, David Woodward, J. B. Harley" (131). Lemann reviews Harley's book, a collection of essays titled *The New Nature of Maps*, largely influenced by Foucault, and admits that the work of the Harley school, "once encountered, makes it impossible to look at maps in a completely straightforward way ever again"—the urge to decode overcomes the habit of taking maps for granted (133). Another book reviewed in this article, Susan Schulten's *The Geographical Imagination in America, 1880–1950,* discusses the different projection maps and the impact projections have on our views of the world. Sales of geographic material, she notes, soared after Pearl Harbor, when President Roosevelt urged people to go out and buy world maps (Lemann 34). (After the terrorist attacks of 2001, it was flag sales that soared.)

World War II marked a peak in geographic interest, which fell off again until the recent renaissance of geography, driven not just by the intellectual interest outlined by Lemann's *New Yorker* article but more importantly by economics: the interest in geography aligns sharply with the expansion of multinational capitalism across the globe. Satellites, cable, NAFTA, the WTO, and the information superhighway—all of these developments have motivated politicians and educators to argue that American students need to be able to navigate these new horizons for commercialism. Functional illiteracy is bad for the goals of capitalism, and educators recognize the urgency of knowing more about other places and cultures in order to be competitive in the world market.

Thus, the U.S. school curriculum and the learning tools market are beginning to reflect the push towards global awareness. Obviously, however, having students memorize the major rivers, leading exports, capital cities, or currencies of different countries is not going to help them learn about cultural differences, or the ways in which difference is constructed via space and place. Geographic "facts" cannot adequately address the problem of racist ignorance, and fairly sophisticated geographic education in the U.K. doesn't mean, of course, that British schoolchildren are less racist or more able to understand the concepts of difference inherent in a multicultural society. But approaches from human geography can teach about the ways in which cultures adapt to spatial limits or constraints, or how people respond differently to places depending on race, class, gender, sexuality, or ability. Human geography can give students and researchers a richer understanding of place and its role in the formation of identity and the production of ideology. Critical attention to maps, what they show and what they leave out, as well as comparisons between maps and "actual" places can help students to understand the difficulties of representation as well as the complexities of fieldwork. Geography as a school subject can also help to sharpen children's spatial sense, which is important to navigating through the world on a daily basis.

This chapter argues that a better understanding of geography as a discipline and as a teaching/learning subject results in more complex notions of place and space that, in turn, serve to complicate our notions of difference. Cultural geographers work to unhinge the binary relations between, for example, public and private spaces and to analyze the sociospatial construction of identities through such concepts as *habitus*. Strategies drawn from cultural geography, including feminist resistance to some of its approaches, can contribute to reading landscapes—urban or domestic, electronic or material—and to the development of spatial practices that inform geographical approaches to rhetoric and writing. Furthermore, geography's visual epistemology can help composition scholars fashion a response to "visual culture," or the perception that images are bombarding us and "taking over" texts and writing. Such a response might come, in part, from the figure of the *flaneur*, which offers one compelling example of moving through the world, dependent on both walking and seeing—a well-known example of how place and materiality construct identity.

Geography's Borders

Geography is no easier to define in a few sentences than contemporary English studies would be. It is a school subject, a specialization at university, a scholarly discipline, and a set of practices. What it is not, of course, is a series of discrete lists to be memorized, or a map on the wall, or a field trip to an urban housing project. It is all these and more, constituting an academic and intellectual area hugely important to the understanding of society and culture. Still considered a "soft" science in contrast to the natural sciences (Lee 27), like every other discipline in the late twentieth century, geography had its own crisis of positivism in the 1960s and 1970s, and its values, research agendas, journals, and curricula have been transformed via the interventions of feminism, cultural studies, and postmodernism as well as huge advances in mapping technologies. There's an old saying about geography being about "maps and chaps," where physical artifacts—maps— and a boys' club mentality rule. The feminist intervention into geography has been particularly earth rumbling because "maps and chaps" ruled for so long (see Rose).

Overall, geography (literally, writing the earth) is a social science—the study of people encountering the earth. Approaches to this broad inquiry can be divided roughly into physical geography, and its different branches, and human geography, although these lines sometimes blur. A typical sequence to school geography, according to Lee, begins with the physical and progresses on to the human. While geography at university becomes far more sophisticated, both physical and human geography are covered by the required curricula; BA Single Honours students at Leeds enroll in the following compulsory courses: Geographical Modeling and Spatial Analysis; Geography of Natural Resources; Landscape Processes; Interpreting Urban Landscapes; World Issues; Statistics for Geography; Study Skills in Geography; and Field Class, Year 1 (*Student Handbook* 29). The required field courses constitute one of the largest expenses for geography degree students (*Student Handbook* 16). Second-year students, for example, fresh off a two-course sequence devoted to research methods, give up their Easter break for a compulsory field trip to France. As the discussion below will illustrate, the value of fieldwork combines with a strong visual element in the making of knowledge in geography.

Physical geography, not quite so affected by social-change movements and theoretical shifts as human geography, is characterized by its positivist inquiry and the concomitant dependence on technologies to measure changes in soil, sediment, rivers, glaciers, or forests. Informed by cartography, geology, economics, and political science, among other areas, physical geography constructs more or less factual accounts of a terrain, region, or country, and physical geographers study how people navigate the earth, via maps and other instruments; or how they might get the most economic production from the landscape; or how people can predict changes in an environment from development or deforestation. Concerns include migration patterns, global warming, or environmental changes.

Human geography, also the study of the interaction of humans with the earth, is influenced by the humanities and has links with sociology, anthropology, history, and architecture among other disciplines. Social geographers study such topics as housing, employment, crime, or transportation, based on statistics and surveys as well as qualitative data, and always attentive to different spatial scales. Combining the methods of qualitative and quantitative research, with as much emphasis on fieldwork as physical geography—just fieldwork done differently—human geographers might investigate people's reactions to a new mall, or how a fictional place affects people's attitudes toward a region, or how the built environment influences spending patterns, crime rates, or feelings of fear. Informed by cultural studies, literature, and art, some of human geography's most recent concerns include race, sexuality, and disability studies, but according to some commentators, human geography's most significant contribution "may well be to insist on *the materiality* of the terms place, space, landscape, location" (Gregory, Martin, and Smith 8, my emphasis).

Insisting on this materiality leads human geographers to investigate how topography and climate affect the way a culture imagines space and time—

that is, how different attitudes develop toward space for groups of people living in areas distinguished by desert, ocean, woods, plains, or mountains. It seems that the more space can be "seen," the less time matters in traversing it. In other words, if you can see the horizon, it doesn't seem like such a long trip to get there. If you can't see beyond the next bend in the road, you'll be a little nervous about what's ahead. An ocean view or scenic vista gives people a different way of imagining space than those who are usually "surrounded" by tall buildings or forest or mountains.

New Englanders, for example, surrounded by woods and stone walls and winding roads, have a very different perception of time and space than do, say, residents of the Great Plains, where trees are found mainly near river beds or planted purposefully on farms to shield the house and outbuildings from winds. A pickup truck, kicking up dust, can be seen from miles away. In the West, distances shrink, conceptually, and people think little of driving several hours to see relatives, shop, or have a meal. By contrast, southern Rhode Islanders, in a well-known joke, don't even travel to Providence without packing provisions for the long trip! If we do indeed write from where we are, then South County, Rhode Island, where I've now lived and worked for twelve years, has a sense of space both from the ocean (Narragansett Bay and Block Island Sound) and from dense second-growth woods. While "everyone knows" where South County is and where its boundaries lie, it will never be found on a map, for South County is not an official name or place—it's just what locals call the area south of East Greenwich; it's the home of Swamp Yankees and where the earliest Yankees slaughtered Wampanaogs and Narragansetts in the Great Swamp Massacre of 1675. As with all places on the planet, its layers of history, place names, or unmapped boundary lines can be learned only locally, on the ground, navigating from visual cues, memory, and learned responses to places.

Officially named State of Rhode Island and the Providence Plantations— an impressive colonial name for the smallest state—the place names here completely captured my imagination: Narragansett, Weekapaug, Matunuck, all of which existed alongside the Kingstowns and the Kingstons and the Charlestowns. The mix of cultures and histories is evident in the place names—many places have two names, some from Native American culture, some from colonial culture, some from the tourist industry, some from old Yankee farms, subdivided for housing plats. Borders or boundaries prove very difficult to recognize or uphold, at least in this area of Washington County, not to be confused with South County. Because of the villages-within-townships-within-counties structure of this region, learning the differences among South Kingstown, North Kingstown, Kingston, and

West Kingston was an experience in the complexity of borders just un-matched in my experience in towns and counties in the Great Plains, south-eastern Kansas, from the Flint Hills to the Neosho River. With many towns nearly twenty miles from the next one, villages don't blend together out west, and fences are everywhere. The farms and ranches in the plains are larger than the eye can see, but in southern New England, heavy foliage hides houses and farms from the road. Human geographers working within land-scape and place studies, such writers as Yi-Fu Tuan, study the subtle atti-tudes and complex emotions that develop from human's interactions with the earth, most of which are difficult to discover or analyze but all of which, this book argues, contribute to understanding the nature of difference.

Difference on a body is marked by articles of clothing, body art, or jew-elry; the size of yard or garden marks differences in homes; the number of schools, shops, or bus stops marks differences in neighborhoods; different colors and codes mark difference on a map. Spatial difference—the pattern of a river, the design of a boulevard, or the sizes of rooms—can give us cru-cial information or guide us, and spatial scales are one measure by which geographers attend to spatial difference. While spatial scale in analytical geography gets very technical, involving geocomputation, most people rec-ognize the importance of scale from maps (e.g., 1 inch = 1 mile). The Mapquest site on the Web allow users to zoom in and out, from the largest scale of the region to the smallest scale of the street. Most nonspecialists also understand spatial scale in the way that Adrienne Rich did as a girl preparing to send a letter to a pen pal:

> Adrienne Rich
> 14 Edgevale Road
> Baltimore, Maryland
> The United States of America
> The Continent of North America
> The Western Hemisphere
> The Earth
> The Solar System
> The Universe

(211–12)

Human geographers also rely upon this nontechnical but powerful form of spatial scale to demonstrate how the social production of space stretches out from individual bodies to the home, neighborhood, city, region, na-tion, and world (see the table of contents for McDowell's *Gender, Identity and Place,* which is organized by increasingly expansive spatial scales). No matter what the spatial scale, however, geographers rely upon a visual nature to difference, on *what can be seen.*

Geography is very much a *seeing* discipline, whose premises and proofs, methodologies and conclusions, stem from visual evidence.[2] The importance of seeing is a fundamental element, of course, of mapping or cartography—that is, the representation of space in two-dimensional or in digital forms, using lines and measurements and colors and textures. The epistemology of the visual, however, extends beyond cartography to become a contentious area within geography studies. As both boon and bane, geography's visual epistemology links very firmly landscapes and "reading," or place and interpretation, but feminist and critical geographers advocate fieldwork methodologies that do not privilege the observer or (only) the visual field.

Geography's dependence on seeing is especially prominent in traditional cultural geography, a subdiscipline of human geography that first evolved from fears that the natural world was being eroded by modernization. Attributed to Carl O. Sauer and the Berkeley School, cultural geography evolved as a strong reaction against environmental determinism, an approach that reduced explanations of human beings or cultures to the physical attributes of the earth (Leighly 3). In his 1925 "The Morphology of Landscape," a methodological piece, Sauer traces the "chorologic interest" of geography to "the establishment of a critical system which embraces the phenomenology of landscape," a landscape that most definitely includes "the works of man as an integral expression of the scene" (320–21). As one of the first cultural geographers, then, Sauer argued against tendencies in human geography that made geography a study of spatial laws. In his argument for "a science that asked how individual landscapes came to take on their shapes" (Crang 15), Sauer was primarily concerned with "areal differentiation," or what makes places unique (Crang 101).

Sauer influenced at least two generations of scholars in his insistence on first-hand field experience and his firm belief in the virtues of fieldwork (Jackson 10–13). During this first wave of cultural geography, the Berkeley School concerned itself with rural landscapes and with physical artifacts, like fences or cabins, and how "man" had marked (and marred) the natural world. According to Sauer, "the natural landscape is of course of fundamental importance, for it supplies the materials out of which the cultural landscape is formed" (343). Culture itself, however, is the shaping force: "Culture is the agent, the natural area is the medium, the cultural landscape the result" (343). Iconographic in this cultural geography tradition is a photograph of

Sauer, seated on a hillside, smoking a pipe and contemplating a scene below. As we shall see below, Sauer's slow locomotion and leisurely halts are reminiscent of Baudelaire's *flaneur,* in a very different environment.

The Berkeley School was dominant for many years, but different theories and more cross-disciplinary research combined to supply ample critiques about its methods and assumptions. Peter Jackson and others object to Sauer's tendency to refer to geology and the earth sciences rather than history and the humanities; in addition, Sauer, Jackson claims, "tended to see history unproblematically in terms of tradition" (15). While his work put landscape on the agenda of cultural geographers, Sauer also saw landscape mostly as a record of human activity without contextualizing that activity within social systems or ideology. Cultural geographers have since critiqued Sauer's theory of place and his tendency to name "culture" as an agent: "By attributing causality to 'culture' rather than to particular individuals or social groups, Sauer implicitly diverted attention away from the social and towards the physical environment" (Jackson 14). Sauer's ideas also seemed to be developed from the premise of premodern, dominantly agricultural, and largely stable societies (Cosgrove 96). What persists from Sauer, however, is the model of reading landscapes as texts.

The "new" cultural geography, post-Sauer, is more likely to treat landscape as a site for the production of culture—as ideologically loaded as a city street or suburban neighborhood. The new cultural geography is also more likely to use qualitative research methods to examine how people and artifacts interact to create a culture, a culture *out of* that place but not overdetermined by it. This approach also asks how identities are constructed "in place," where and how place and identity intersect. Jackson's version of cultural geography focuses "on the way cultures are produced and reproduced through actual social practices that take place in historically contingent and geographically specific contexts" (23).

Influenced heavily by cultural studies, cultural geographers no longer limit themselves to the landscape studies of the Berkeley School but explore both theoretical and practical concerns with the social production of space, and how differences of gender, race, class, age, or ranges of access or abilities impact those spaces.[3] Cultural geographers study the ways in which cultures are contested spatially and how identity and power are reproduced in the everyday, in mundane, ordinary landscapes. How do particular sites acquire meanings, and how do different subcultures use places and sites (Crang 5)? According to Linda McDowell, cultural geographers examine

> how the increasingly global scale of cultural production and consumption affects relationships between identity, meaning, and place. Attention is fo-

cused on the ways in which symbols, rituals, behaviors and everyday social practices result in a shared set or sets of meaning that are to greater or lesser degrees, place-specific. Thus a geographic perspective has become central to the cultural studies project more widely. ("Transformation" 147)

Generally, cultural geographers want the construction of identity understood as a *spatial* process, but a process that resists a "one-to-one correspondence between the image and consumption of a place and its *reality*" (Keith and Pile, 7, their emphasis). Indeed, cultural geographers influenced by Sauer have long resisted a one-to-one correspondence between the land and the culture—like that living on the Great Plains means being a farmer, or that living by the sea makes one a fisherman. Just because someone spends her whole life in one place, a neighborhood or house, doesn't mean that she has a resultant stable identity, or adopts the same habits as all of her neighbors, or uses all the same pathways. Being raised in Brooklyn or L.A. or Crabapple Cove doesn't mean having a stable identity, either, as recognizable as a sitcom rerun. Therefore, in their attempt to understand how identities are constructed in space, through experiences with place, cultural geographers insist on explicitly material notions of culture, not abstract ones.[4]

Like cultural studies, then, cultural geography asks how material artifacts are appropriated and their meanings transformed through oppositional social practices (McDowell, "Transformation" 158). The new cultural geography, which can only be defined in relief against the old, concerns itself with spaces "contemporary as well as historical . . . ; social as well as spatial . . . ; urban as well as rural; [it is] interested in the contingent nature of culture, in dominant ideologies and in forms of resistance to them" (Cosgrove 95). Cultural and feminist geographers recognize the ways in which the body and movement are intertwined, that actions and habits are constructed by the spaces in which they are enacted. Material geographies focus on the everyday, on the politics of space, and on both emotional and physiological attachments to place and space. Such concepts as habitus and structures of feeling emphasize sense of place and sociospatial practices and offer a way to interpret people's ordinary journeys in the everyday.

Cultural geography resists explanations of culture divorced from materiality and derives, in part, from cultural materialism, via Raymond Williams (Jackson). For Williams, culture cannot be reduced to ideology, "narrowly conceived, because it is part of a social and political order that is *materially produced*" (47, his emphasis). According to Jackson, Williams's concept of structures of feeling is particularly important for cultural geographers because it connects to the important geographical idea of "sense of place" (39).

In *Marxism and Literature,* Williams identifies structures of feeling as "meanings and values as they are actually lived and felt" and "specifically affective elements of consciousness and relationships" (132). Intended as a cultural hypothesis, structures of feeling can be used to understand, in particular, art and literature, a way of recognizing "their specific kinds of sociality" (132–33). Williams asserts that social forms become social consciousness "only when they are lived, actively, in real relationships" (130). Cultural geographers like Jackson are attracted to Williams's structures of feeling because experiences within landscapes or the built environment are often very much like responses to art and literature, and these responses are materially produced, not simply aesthetic. Cultural geographers want to claim, from Williams, that geography is lived, actively, in real relationships.

Jackson also sees structures of feeling as related to Bourdieu's concept of habitus. Habitus attempts to represent how social behaviors, habits, become so naturalized as to be inscribed onto the body, a result of "the sedimented history of particular practices" (Jackson 39): for example, an English professor who can't read without a pen in hand, or a seven-year-old ballet student whose legs and posture already show the signs of dance training, or someone abused as a child who often cowers at a raised hand or sudden movement. Practices and habits become inscribed upon the body, and many of these habits evolve from places, from where we hang out or from our usual haunts.

Habitus brings together social class and learned behaviors, the body and the material, and habits and practices. Like Williams's structures of feeling, habitus is an attempt to theorize the social as a process, as actively present. The two theories also have in common the analysis of class differences; Williams acknowledges the historical variability of structures of feeling, as well as "the complex relation of differentiated structures of feeling to differentiated classes" (134). Bourdieu, in his overall study of "taste," proposes the habitus as a structure through which to read differences of social identity: "an agent's whole set of practices . . . are both systematic . . . and systematically distinct from the practices constituting another life-style" (170).

Habitus has become a useful concept for scholars interested in the study of social practices. Clifford cites Bourdieu's use of habitus, in a "generally recognized social-scientific sense," as

> the social inscribed in the body: a repertoire of practices rather than rules, a disposition to play the social game. It makes conceptions of social and cultural structure more processual: embodied and practiced. . . . The older sense of "habitus" sees subjectivity as a matter of concrete, meaningful gestures, appearances, physical dispositions, and apparel without reference to

these determining structures, which became hegemonic only in the late nineteenth century. (354)

Bourdieu's habitus, as these various references to it illustrate, doesn't neglect the body or material circumstances; both together form practices. In addition, Williams's structures of feeling, especially when combined with Bourdieu's concept of habitus, gives cultural geographers a more complex notion of sense of place, one that attempts to account for difference (Jackson 39). This is important because sense of place cannot be treated as singular or stable; neither can the identities that are shaped within them. Places (or territories) are contested, with competing and shifting interpretations of their meanings, and these meanings are tied to signs and symbols that carry cultural weight.

As a set of embodied practices, habitus keeps us in our place, so to speak, or defines the tactics and strategies we rely upon for moving through the world. Modes of transport or preferred pathways are part of one's habitus, as are clothing and style, gestures and movement, accent and expressions. A person's sense of place, while a result of many layered effects, is quite directly related to her body in space.

Feminist Geography and Visual Epistemologies

Feminist geographers have been particularly attentive to the relationship between bodies and spaces and the ways in which some spaces get figured as female. Nature, historically, has been feminized, and the persistence of the Nature-as-Woman metaphor can be traced throughout the literature on feminist geography. Whether the landscape is rural, urban, or domestic, seeing landscapes as texts, in the tradition of cultural geography, is problematic for women since "the conception of landscape as female [has] facilitated a masculinist relationship to place" (Nash 237). In *Feminism and Geography: The Limits of Geographical Knowledge,* Gillian Rose argues that geography's fixation on landscape—on reading landscapes—is "a version of the discipline's aesthetic masculinity" (101). She uses landscape painting and feminist art history to show how most (male) geographers are reluctant to engage critically with "the gaze," or to acknowledge the pleasure of gazing upon the land, usually configured as female Nature (89–99). Rose believes that the "metaphor of landscape as text works to establish an authoritative reading, and to maintain that authority whenever emotion threatens to erupt and mark the author as a feeling subject" (100–101). If the landscape is constructed as feminine, then the gaze is masculine, and Rose reviews the work of Annette Kolodny and others who address the implications of Nature as woman, which also has implications for "seeing the land" (110). As one way of confronting this dominant image of nature, then, feminists have turned to other sites to demonstrate the social production of gender—namely, urban and domestic environments. Learning to read these "landscapes" means attending to the politics of space by focusing on issues of sexism, colonialism, and complicity with the military-industrial complex.

Feminist geography, in particular, can help us to understand the construction and reproduction of difference since the fundamental concern of feminist geographers is the ways gender is implicated in the social construction of space and place. To this end, feminist geographies tend to rely on qualitative research methods that put them into interactions with real women and everyday situations. Feminist geographers have brought geographic analysis into the home and other domestic sites, seeing them as important to cultural analysis as workplaces or centers for consumption. In recent years, these geographers have been hugely influenced by the work of bell hooks, whose essay, "Homeplace: A Site of Resistance," both celebrates the home for black women and names "that terrifying whiteness" of the world outside the home. In hooks's memory, the journey across the (white) town was filled with fear and bitterness, contrasted by the sweet arrival at her grandmother's house (41). In this piece, hooks argues that *home* operates for African American culture not just as a place to do (more) domestic work but as a site of resistance: "This task of making homeplace was not simply a matter of black women providing service" (42). Instead, making homeplace was about creating a safe port in the sea of white supremacy—a place where one could rest and restore her dignity. Traditionally, homeplace has not been valued because of sexist thinking about domestic labor. The dedication to home was consciously exercised in practices of the everyday, which supported "the philosophical core of dedication to community and home" (45). Thus, hooks calls for contemporary black women to reconceptualize ideas of homeplace as a site for subversion and resistance—and to resist above all white bourgeois norms that frame the home as a politically neutral space (47).

Feminist cultural geographers try to promote a similar understanding of homeplace, not as the private sphere or as a place for "'merely' domestic" activities, but as a site for complex social relations (McDowell *Gender* 73). In order to deflect attention from the backbreaking labor that women have performed in homes for centuries, industrialization brought a new emphasis on the "spiritual" qualities of dedication to the home (McDowell, *Gender* 75). McDowell traces the various ways in which the association between women and domestic work became institutionalized, supported by the capitalist system that provided goods for consumption that women needed in order to fulfill their role. Issues of domestic labor have been much discussed and theorized especially by socialist feminists, but McDowell also admits that only recently have "more nuanced arguments" been put forth that avoid the binary between home as haven or home as prison, site of domestic violence and patriarchal oppression (88–89). The contradictory nature of the home, according to McDowell, "has been more widely recognized in recent feminist work" (89). In moving in the direction of third-space, then, homes are being re-imagined as neither public nor private, neither heaven nor hell, but somewhere in between.

Homeplaces reproduce both traditional subjectivities and sites for resistance. In studying the complex issues of domestic labor and family life, feminist theorists move cultural geography away from romanticized landscape studies of fields and farmlands. Urban, domestic, institutional, or imaginary landscapes are just as important to understand for their roles in creating identities through place and for analyzing the connections between the built environment and identity formation. But whatever "landscape" is in view, feminists have been reluctant to interpret it through a dependence only or solely on visual evidence, and critical geographers have also expressed concern about geography's dependence on the visual particularly when the visual images produced by geographers can be used for any number of purposes.

For contemporary research in geography, a reliance on visual evidence is particularly difficult to avoid or resist. Maps and photographs provide the most obvious cases of geography's investment in the visual, but new technologies are also expanding the visual terrain and putting pressure on geographers to be vigilant about the social and political consequences of, in particular, cartography and imaging systems. Geographic information systems (GIS) and global positioning systems (GPS) are a major growth industry. GIS is a "toolbox" of spatial processing functions, widely used in research projects where geographic information from a number of different sources must be integrated; for example, when evaluating the suitability of a site for building a new industrial complex or a baseball stadium (Martin 213–15). Not intended to simply display geographic information, GIS manages the input, storage, manipulation, and output of such information: local street maps, maps of sewage systems, census data, wetlands, demographics of many types. Both GIS and GPS rely on digital map data that can be stored and manipulated on-screen. Digital map data is then brought to life on-screen through a computerized geographical information system (GIS). GPS is most familiar as the navigational systems in rental cars and luxury cars that guide drivers to their destination with satellite imagery, although these technologies are also increasingly affordable as hand-held models. With commercial names such as Onstar or Magellan, drivers or hikers are able to program their desired destination and then follow the on-screen directions, never having to consult a compass or the angle of the sun—since different, more technological, literacies are required.

In processing cartographic and spatial data, GIS can also manage data from remote sensing, or the visual representation of a portion of the earth's surface. Remote sensing satellites "orbit the earth . . . collecting data through electromagnetic radiation . . . . [This] enables data to be collected and then digitally re-presented visually as an image that looks like a photograph or even a map, but in origins is neither" (Roberts and Schein 187). The military was the first to develop these technologies, and the oil industry, in particular, has made profitable use of them.

The connection between cartography and the military-industrial complex has not gone unnoticed by critical geographers. As Derek Gregory and his coauthors put it:

> human geography, by virtue of its involvements in cartography, remote sensing, spatial science and geographic information systems, and its sometimes tense association with physical geography, probably still provides one of the most technically sophisticated arenas within contemporary social sciences and humanities. This plainly imposes an obligation to reflect carefully on the cultural politics of the technologies in which it is implicated. (7)

The maps, charts, and databases developed by geographers inside and outside of the academy have, in fact, been used towards colonialist and military domination. Critical or politically left geographers were concerned during the Vietnam war about the uses to which maps were put; for example, strategic bombing to cause the maximum damage (Cloke et al. 38–39). Some geographers have long been aware of their responsibility and the "commodity"— the buying and selling of images, for example—of maps and databases.

However, the growth of GIS and other geographic technologies relies upon the commodification of spatial images and, more broadly, on a visual epistemology.[5] Susan M. Roberts and Richard H. Schein, in analyzing advertisements for new geographic technologies, begin from the geographic given that "vision is privileged as a way of knowing. That which is seen is real" (183). New geographic technologies and global imagery represent the world from above, which is a particularly striking—and disturbing—god's eye view (185). Nonetheless, visual data is crucial to our understandings of place and space in part because images, like public spaces, can be commodified, a process that intensified with the expanse of modern cities and the "images" with which they became associated: Paris = Eiffel Tower; a pyramid = Cairo; New York = Statue of Liberty. As geographers know, certain images, reproduced and consumed, create our conceptions of particular places, to the point that we assume we "know" Paris if we recognize a picture of the Eiffel Tower. Visual images are often tangible, physical, and reproducible; they can be bought and sold, copied and distributed, enlarged or reduced or sharpened. While this is mostly true for photographic or digital images, it's also important to consider the power of memory in archiving and reproducing visual images: while pictures from memory cannot usually be reproduced or shared, they do have a huge influence on people's experiences with or responses to place. The ease with which images can be produced and consumed is one of the reasons theorists react against the dominance of the visual—because a reproduced image can come to stand in for reality, erasing the consequences of space and time.

Some cultural theorists and feminist researchers have taken a strong theoretical and political stance against a privileging of the visual, against the "god's eye view." De Certeau begins his chapter "Walking in the City" (1984) by looking down on Manhattan from the 110th floor of the World Trade Center, but he calls the view an "optical artifact," a simulcram, a picture, a Concept-city; it is *not,* in other words "real"—not produced by actual spatial practices, like walking (91–95). Doreen Massey claims that, in modernism, "vision was systematically and symptomatically prioritized over other senses. . . . the sense which allows mastery"—a mastery that comes from "the very detachment which it allows and requires" (224). And while Gillian Rose acknowledges that fieldwork, first and foremost, "is all about looking," the result is often that seeing becomes conflated with *knowing* (86). Then, Elizabeth Wilson points out, "the feminist critique of visualism thus becomes part of a new problem, rather than the solution of an old one" (103n). A relentlessly negative stance against "ocular imagery" (Wilson's term) ignores the growing importance of the visual in popular culture and electronic technologies. Feminist geographers are not the only ones to find a dependence on the visual unnerving. In a different form, anxiety about the visual persists in mass culture and in some academic disciplines like composition.

Composition's Visual Interests—and Ambivalence

Many people working in composition, literacy, and cultural studies recognize that new technologies are generating more attention to visual culture, a broadly inclusive term that sometimes refers to a perceived onslaught of

visual images, or a tendency for images to "replace" language. The terms
visual literacy or visual rhetoric are becoming more common as well; that
is, the ability to "read" images critically, analyze the way they work, and
choose or design images that communicate effectively (see George). There's
a direct correlation, of course, between the rise of (visual-based) electronic
technologies—screen culture—and the scholarly or pedagogical interest in
visual literacies. But the attention might also grow out of an anxiety that
reading and writing, in an electronic era, will become less essential; this is
a fear that began with television, or television criticism, and still persists.[6]
Composition, like many other disciplines, is engaged in fashioning a response to visual culture but with a great deal of ambivalence.

Composition's loss of its fourth C—communication—as Diana George
and John Trimbur argue, "plays out a deep-seated ambivalence on the part
of writing teachers toward the means of mass communication that predates
the establishment of CCCC" (686). George and Trimbur review the history of the communication movement (and the battles), in part to show
how composition and rhetorical training were to serve as "'inoculation, a
means of resisting mass culture'" (694–95). From this standpoint, then, the
ever-popular "analyze an advertisement" assignment in first-year composition courses throughout the country rest on a pedagogical imperative that
says, "Don't be a sucker for these images." George and Trimbur show,
through the work of Charles Paine, that these attitudes are a legacy of A. S.
Hill and the first-year course "as a means of providing students with a defense against mass communication and the mass media" (694). They conclude with their relief that communication is still our fourth C because of
the work that it does to keep composition grounded in the material:

> [Communication] is a persistent reminder that to write is to operate a tech-
> nology that makes visual signs—that encodes messages by inscribing marks
> on a page or screen. "Communication" pulls us toward the worldly, the
> actual, the material. It makes writing, like other types of composition (mu-
> sical, graphic, handicraft, engineering design), into an act of labor that quite
> literally fashions the world. (697)

Many of us are willing to harness the rhetorical clout of images for our
teaching, but without really believing that visuals can do the same work as
text—and they don't, in fact, perform the same rhetorical or intellectual
work. Best to leave the terms in tension, George concludes, and I agree:
"some tug of war between words and images or between writing and design can be productive as it brings into relief the multiple dimensions of
all forms of communication" (14). Many composition specialists, in fact,
are coming to a conclusion shared by Faigley, that the exclusion of visual

thinking from the mainstream literacy curriculum has serious implications, and that the persistent myth of the transparent text and the grand narrative of alphabetic literacy have combined to make people believe that the World Wide Web and other technologies are going to destroy academic literacy as we know it ("Material" 188, 175). If images (have) become appropriated by advertising media, this argument goes, then how can we reclaim the power of images to sell critical, political, or intellectual ideas? The rapid-fire delivery of images on television or the Internet seems to make us immune to seeing; the more we are hit with, the less discrimination we can exercise, or the more difficult it becomes to pause and analyze an image or its placement. The piling up and easy reproduction of images contributes to the uneasy sense that the intellectual thought and sustained activity required by composing are becoming irrelevant for navigating the Internet or watching a film.

Of course, in the analyze-an-advertisement assignment, students are also asked to *write* about them, so here the reading and writing link is secure; however, George asks students to write *visual* arguments.[7] As she displayed her students' work at a recent conference, she engaged with the almost inevitable question, "are these truly arguments?" While we have learned much about literacy in recent years, and most composition instructors no longer believe that reading and writing mean "marks on a page," giving too much classroom time to visual images or a variety of media signals to some a diminishment of the work of writing instruction. Not especially interested in easing our ambivalence about visual culture, I do want to understand these anxieties and their sources. Increasingly, different strands of composition research explore visuality or identify new literacy practices that result from screen culture and may translate into acts of composing. Habitual uses of so many technologies—videogames, personal computers and organizers, interactive software, DVDs, and so on—may in fact result in a confident spatial sense, one guided by colorful images and icons and plenty of "movement."

In a chapter titled "Living on the Surface," Johndan Johnson-Eilola analyzes the modernist world of history (i.e., depth) and the postmodern world of surface in order to argue that we do the new generation a disservice if we insist that learning can only be represented through a depth model and if we devalue the epistemology of surface dwelling. He uses the term "surface dwellers" to identify a new generation and defines living in space as living on the surface, where things happen "in a state of continuous stimulation" (185). Those who dwell in cyberspace adopt its habitus; their movements and identity emerge from the places they visit and from the mental maps they develop.

Johnson-Eilola's research, some of it informal observations of children working with computer learning programs, indicates that a new generation is developing, on the whole, keen spatial senses and sharp spatial memories.

Children with home computers, electronic games, and other interactive toys or learning tools navigate electronic sites by remembering where they were before, which link they clicked or which site had a vivid image. They develop rich mental maps of computer interfaces and the best pathways through a program's options or features. For example, his eight-year-old daughter masters a computer game called "Per.Oxyd" that requires her to "hit blocks"—to make rapid decisions about which ones to hit in order to "get to the next level." When asked how she knows what to do, her reply was "you just play." She had figured out how to maneuver and navigate the space of a game screen without a manual or instructions—without, that is, modernist devices. Johnson-Eilola argues that her confidence and experience with the computer game illustrate a postmodern ability to accept chance and work with it actively, to experiment, "to deal tactically with contingency, multiplicity, and uncertainty" (195).

His anecdote fits with my own experience watching my twelve-year-old niece play a videogame, "Banjo Kazooie," a 3-D Nintendo game in the familiar pattern of "different levels" that increase in difficulty; players move up as they gain the dexterity and the memory to get the two characters in the game to work together. When the bear and bird cooperate to solve problems, and when the backpack opens to the right tools, *success.* Here's how the promoters describe it: "Banjo and Kazooie can learn more than 20 different moves, and they'll need them all to make it through the nine nightmarish worlds inside Gruntilda's Lair" (Nintendo).

Rachel also discussed her moves as trying to get to the next level or trying to get somewhere she'd never been before. Her confidence in getting around was a result of her comfort level with disorientation; she didn't mind not knowing where she was—and there wasn't necessarily a (modernist) center or starting point that she needed to find her way back to. At the same time, however, she was also comfortable because she remembered so well where she "had been" and where particular spots would take her, as in "I've got to stay away from that or I'll end up in a deep well." The imagery of the places she encountered, then, helped her to remember the best pathways through the levels or the trouble spots she should avoid. As with a well-illustrated story, she liked the characters and wanted to see what would happen to them, but the action also took place in space, in different environments, in the colorful 3-D environment on the screen. The program was complex enough, with enough richness and hidden places that she kept going back, playing the same game for weeks but never exactly the same game, motivated by both the continuous stimulation and the visual representations of space.

Modernist notions of space are linear and hierarchical, apparent in the ordered list of information that still characterizes many Websites. However, Johnson-Eilola points out that more "information-rich screens" are being developed that model computer games: that ask users to understand things in multiple, contingent spatial structures rather than in serial and chronological orders. In addition, more and more information is available "on the surface," rather than in locations of depth, like archives:

> In the face of surface-oriented information spaces such as Per.Oxyd . . . , history-oriented people attempt to understand these communicative spaces under the old paradigm: they attempt to focus on one element to the exclusion of all others. . . . [However,] these spaces can be navigated and negotiated from a simultaneous, surface perspective that does not attempt to find single facts or linear structures but has learned to process information along parallel lines without relying on a single focal point or goal. . . . In learning to understand communication in terms of simultaneous, contingent streams and structures, users also lose the ability to anchor themselves anywhere with certainty. (205)

College students in the early twenty-first century, it's fairly safe to say, have played videogames—some of them many games and some of them for many hours; many also spend hours surfing the Web. Do those experiences in the spatial world tell us anything about the way writers or composers learn to negotiate electronic/spatial environments? Examples of kids and computer games encourage us to rethink writing from a spatial and visual perspective. Habitual movements developed from these games develop from the interaction of memory and spatial sense. At work in these games, Gunther Kress would say, is the "spatial-simultaneous logic of the visual" (68). Kress argues that written language "is being displaced from its hitherto unchallenged central position in the semiotic landscape, and that the visual is taking over many of the functions of written language" (68). There's evidence everywhere of the multisemiotic landscape of communication in the 1990s, but Kress uses a contrast of two textbooks to make his point about the fundamental shift in the role of writing. Both are science textbooks aimed at ninth graders, one published in 1936 and the other in 1988. As he demonstrates through a comparison of the two textbooks, "writing is not the vehicle for conveying all the information which is judged to be relevant" (74). Through a linguistic analysis of two passages, Kress demonstrates that images are taking on certain functions formerly carried by language (82).

The visual, according to Kress, is a spatially and simultaneously organized mode, using the medium of light and the materiality of certain kinds of substances. The logic of writing draws upon both the logic of the visual and the logic of speech (81), but where writing depends more on narrative, the visual depends more on display (82). Display and arrangement are the fundamental features of the logic of the visual (versus speech which is sequential and temporally organized), demanding more attention to the product. As images do the work formerly performed by language, the logic of sequence is diminished. Written passages, then, become blocks of text, visual elements in a visual unit (81).

Perhaps the logic of sequence is highlighted by the more physical or tactile act of writing with pen and paper. Christina Haas's research with ten experienced writers shows that pen-and-paper composers spent more time planning and could recall their texts better than on-line composers; she posits that on-line writing makes the text more "distant" somehow and harder to manipulate spatially. If writing instructors don't find much in the way of prewriting or planning in students' folders when they rely on the two-dimensional space of electronic writing (versus the three-dimensional space of pen-and-paper), Haas might say that the tools are to blame.

According to Haas, the more writers can "touch" their texts, the more time they will spend planning them and the better they will remember them; in this way, literacy has a distinct materiality. Faigley argues that literacy "has *always* been a material, multimedia construct" ("Material" 175, his emphasis). At the end of his historical overview of writing as material, Faigley analyzes the ways in which images on the Web have material consequences, demonstrated by the Zapatistas' successful understanding of the material effects of visual literacy (194–98). Understanding the power of visual rhetoric means choosing images for persuasive ends or adding visuals to the available means of persuasion.

This brief review of research by Johnson-Eilola, Kress, Haas, and Faigley demonstrates that those who study writing can no longer afford to ignore visual and material elements to communication. As we know from Deborah Brandt's work, literacy practices pile up, accumulate, and are passed on, residual traces evident in the next generation, where tools or practices are recirculated. On-screen practices, like street practices, are worth more study and may help loosen the hold of ambivalence about visual culture.

Material and geographic rhetorics can help us understand the implications of visual culture and its relationships to or effects on literacy practices. As we try to prepare our students for work and life that are saturated by both

images and technology, and as we consume and are consumed by the proliferation of technologies, we need to look both to the screen and to the
street for an understanding of how space matters. Although geographers do
not have a monopoly on "seeing" as a research practice, they might suggest
that understanding spatial and cultural difference begins on the ground,
for example, by walking through neighborhoods.

Learning to see takes place at street level, through walking. While other
ways of moving through the world might also teach us to see, only walking embraces so many senses and has the "hands on" (or feet first) materiality of place. "Walking in the City" is Michel de Certeau's attempt to claim
walking as a rhetorical practice. In searching for a theory of everyday practices, of lived space, de Certeau turns to "the disquieting familiarity of the
city," (96) not the view from a skyscraper, but from the "ground level, with
footsteps" (97). De Certeau goes on to claim that "the act of walking is to
the urban system what the speech act is to language" (98). In a spatial act-
ing-out of place, walking becomes "a space of enunciation" (98), but one
that must work within the constraints of the spatial order. The spatial or-
ganization of the city, after all, structures the possibilities for movement: a
wall, for example, prevents one from going further, but one can crawl over
it or go around it. Walking is a continual improvisation, a type of perfor-
mance that continually privileges, transforms, or abandons the spatial elements in the constructed order. Spatial practices like walking, then, are a
form of resistance to faster and more mechanical means of transportation
but also are a way of exercising agency: walkers can pause, cross, turn, linger, double-back, and otherwise have control of their actions. Walking is
more than a cheap means of transportation; it's an art, practiced with a great
deal of style in some cases, as the figure of the *flaneur* illustrates.

The *Flaneur,* Walking, and Ways of Seeing

With the rise of the modern city, new ways of seeing became possible; rather
than sitting on a hillside gazing at the valley below, urban observers walk the
streets, mixing with people from "all walks of life." Characterized by paradoxical spaces, confusion between public and private, and resulting identities in flux, the modern city becomes a text made up of both material and
metaphorical elements, the *flaneur* its composer. In the histories and literatures of modernism, one of the most compelling street figures is that of
the *flaneur,* urban rambler, or street prowler, known best through Charles
Baudelaire and Walter Benjamin and more recently through Edmund White.
I explore this figure as a way of representing both actual physical movement
through the streets and ways of seeing in built environments.

69

Strolling through the literature of modernity, geography, urban studies, and critical theory, the *flaneur* embodies the spatial practices of walking as writing, writing as walking; his main focus is to absorb and render the city through writing. A writer, artist, and journalist who collects as he saunters, sketches as he watches, the *flaneur* organizes and juxtaposes material in various ways.[8] Forms of *flanerie,* this section argues, are important to claim for material and geographic rhetorics, for ordinary journeys of the everyday, those defined by images of the built environment and determined by pathways through the built environment. The rambler is a figure worth habilitating for material rhetorics and geographies of writing not because he *solves* something in our dilemmas about visual culture but because he embodies method.[9] Forms of *flanerie* stand for an approach to street life, a way of moving through the world, collecting, arranging, and remembering, dependent on seeing.

The growth of the modern city provoked much commentary about urban life and accompanying social changes:

> the menace of the cities was not only disease and poverty; even more threatening were the spectres of sensuality, democracy and revolution. One particular cause for alarm was the way in which urban life undermined patriarchal authority. Young, unattached men and women flocked to the towns to find more remunerative work. There, freed from the bonds of social control, they were in danger of succumbing to temptations of every kind; immorality, illegitimacy, the breakdown of family life and bestial excess seemed to threaten from all sides. Perhaps worse was that, in the rough and tumble of the city street and urban crowd, distinctions of rank of every kind were blurred. (Wilson 91)

This blurring created betweens, or possibilities for new identities, a result of architectural and related changes. In eighteenth-century London, specific building acts made possible new forms of movement, those that shaped the city "as a series of spaces or flows of movement rather than discrete architectural elements" (Rendell 76). The Building Act of 1774 gave the West End a uniform design, with wider and regular streets, in contrast to the east end, where haphazard growth led to narrow, irregular streets (Rendell 77). In addition, Lighting and Paving Acts of 1761 provided drainage, curbs, and improved street lighting, all of which contributed to a walker's mobility. As more consumer culture industries began to develop—for example, advertising, industrial design, window display and fashion—they contributed to the process of "the exoticisation of the urban landscape" (Featherstone 914). There was, quite simply, more to see and more to buy.

The French poet and commentator Baudelaire identified the *flaneur* in 1859–60 as a new kind of public person (Wilson 93). A wandering spectator, an observer watching but not participating in the scenes of modern urban life, the *flaneur* was mobile and detached. Dressed to be seen, both spectacle and spectator, the *flaneur* has become an emblem of the public sphere, a product of changes in the physical landscape and forms of movement those changes made possible. As Rendell chronicles, new architectural forms such as the arcade—"a privately owned street of commodity consumption"—helped to provide a new kind of public space, where, protected from the weather and from the hustle of the streets, wealthy patrons could feel safe in a semipublic environment (87).

The arcade is where one could find Benjamin, who walked the streets, wedded the crowd, and wrote a huge volume, over a thirteen-year period, of notes and reflections. *Passagen-Werk,* published by Harvard as the Arcades Project, became over a thousand pages of fragments, organized chronologically in key-word files (Buck-Morss 5). Benjamin gave the *flaneur* another layer of meaning, in this version more of a scientist of human nature who "as Benjamin put it 'goes botanising on the asphalt'" (Featherstone 913). Mike Featherstone tries to capture the many contradictory qualities of the *flaneur,* which of course reflect the many contradictory qualities of modern cities: "On the one hand, the *flaneur* is the idler or waster; on the other hand, he is the observer or detective, the suspicious person who is always looking, noting and classifying" (913). *Flaneurs* wrote occasional pieces for magazines and newspapers, the city their subject. In *The Flaneur: A Stroll Through the Paradoxes of Paris* (2001), Edmund White draws from writers, artists, and photographers (Mercier, Baudelaire, Atget, Breton, Benjamin) to define the *flaneur* as a modern artist "who immerses himself in the bath of the crowd, gathers impressions and jots them down only when he returns to his studio" (36). Interested in experience rather than in knowledge, a *flaneur* observes the habits of everyone, across classes and occupations.[10]

Drawn to bohemia, the *flaneur* was a type of middle-class artist, without perhaps a natural gift or inherited skill, but a commitment to a craft of seeing. Misunderstood as an idler, the *flaneur* is a writer, a chronicler, a collector, who uses the fragments of consumer culture to make meaning. The *flaneur's* craft entails what Featherstone calls a hermeneutic of seeing and what to Susan Buck-Morss is Benjamin's "dialectics of seeing":

> Benjamin's goal was to take materialism so seriously that the historical phenomena themselves were brought into speech. . . . Corsets, feather dusters, red and green-colored combs, old photographs, souvenir replicas of the Venus di Milo, collar buttons to shirts long since discarded—these battered

historical survivors from the dawn of industrial culture . . . *were* the philo-sophical ideas. (4)

Benjamin had a "topographical consciousness" and a compulsion to "map" everything he had experienced, giving spatial order to his imagination (Demetz xvii). His ideas develop directly from the cities he visited or lived in: Berlin, Moscow, Marseilles, Paris, Naples (see Demetz). Benjamin was not interested in describing modern urban experience, or in the *flaneur* as an actual social type, Mike Savage argues, "but as a theoretical, critical, counter to the idea of the mass, as an attempt to indicate the sorts of po-tential for critique which continued to exist" (38). Benjamin's interest was in the city as a "'labyrinth'" and related to his "'critique of narrativity'" (39–40).

The streets of cities are the haunt of the *flaneur;* the Paris arcades, in particular, were the site of the emergence of *flanerie:* Approximately thirty arcades were constructed between 1800 and 1850, providing enclosed spaces for people to stroll and look, to idle and dawdle. "Paris was the home of bohemia and the dandy: the artists of life, who sought to cultivate a lifestyle, a stylish demeanour and appearance" (Featherstone 913). The work of the *flaneur* took shape, then, from the city's form. The city, in this view, is the organizing principle for the material: the shops, houses, signs, posters, and so on that one finds in a street become not only the organizing principle to the writing but the launching point for the reflections, aphorisms, tales, memoirs. Benjamin's "One-Way Street," for example, proceeds by sections titled, variously, Filling Station, Breakfast Room, No. 113, Gloves, Mexi-can Embassy, Construction Site, Caution: Steps, Post No Bills, This Space for Rent, in what represents a modernist aesthetic, "like so many pieces in a photomontage or a Cubist collage" (Buck-Morss 18).

Just as building acts and new architectural forms made rambling a popu-lar pastime, subsequent changes led to the reported decline of the *flaneur,* or at least its hybridization. Featherstone attributes the perceived decline of the *flaneur* "to the reconstruction of Paris in the 1850s and 1860s under the guidance of Haussmann's plan to cut boulevards through the old city" (914). The growth of department stores, in particular, had a huge impact: "The rise of the department store, mundane a subject as it may seem, is in fact in capsule form the very paradigm of how the public realm as a active interchange gave way in people's lives to an experience of publicness more intense and less sociable" (Sennett 141). Restaurants, museums, and the resulting increase in traffic meant that the *flaneur* of the early nineteenth century, male and middle-class, "declined" while forms of *flanerie* lived on in, some argue, shopping.

The new modern city made new identities possible—but only for men? Perhaps needless to say, feminist theorists have interrogated the concept of the *flaneur* for its gender bias, and left to be acknowledged in this discussion is the gendered identity of the *flaneur* and the debate about whether the *flaneur* can be a female figure. Janet Wolff argues that the *flaneur* or the modernist urban identity can only be male, but Elizabeth Wilson wants to claim the possibility of a female *flaneur*—a *flaneuse.* (Their debate is discussed in McDowell, *Gender* 155.) Because of the blurring that the new street life caused in previously firm notions of public/private, Wilson believes, there were actually more opportunities and freedoms for women. With the development of department stores, arcades, tea rooms, restaurants, museums, galleries, and exhibitions, middle-class women had vastly increased opportunities for being visible in public, for walking the streets, even in lower-class areas where they may have been involved in charity work (Featherstone). In "The Invisible Flaneur," Wilson argues that it proved impossible to banish women from public places—though the male ruling class certainly tried, and women "continued to crowd into the city centers and the factory districts" (93). In rejecting Janet Wolff's position that women were wholly excluded from the public sphere, Wilson wants to reclaim the street for women.

Jane Rendell's attention to historical, *material* changes in London streets serves to make her argument about a "dialectical relation between gendered identities and urban space," one far more complex than that allowed by separate spheres ideology (89). To reduce space to the binary opposition of public and private ignores the multitude of actual places in cities that are both/and or neither/nor. A geography limited to public/private distinctions is mostly relevant to white, middle-class feminism and ignores the importance of multiple locations as well as provisional, fragmented, or contradictory spaces (Blunt and Rose 4). Rendell's discussion demonstrates that changes in urban design fashioned new forms of movement for men *and* women: "The rambler's activities . . . took him all over the city. But if men had important roles as consumers, the development of commodity capitalism also encouraged an increasing movement of women outside the family home as workers and consumers" (85). The modern city changed many aspects of everyday life for women as well: middle-class women had more opportunities to go out shopping or dine in respectable restaurants while non–middle-class women became "streetwalkers" in the broadest sense, living by their wits and causing the status of women to become open to interpretation (McDowell *Gender* 154). Too many women moving about led, however, to the Vagrancy Act of 1822, which attempted to control the movement of women through the new urban spaces. As Rendell notes, "the figure of the public woman . . . represents the blurring of public and private boundaries, and the uncontrollable movement of women and female sexuality" (88). Others believe that despite the elitism of the earliest *flaneur* figures, the concept has been "democratized" and "now often stands as a metaphor for the contemporary urban dweller, moving through the flux and transience of the city" (Edensor 217). In this reading of the *flaneur,* it now stands for "a mode of being in the world" (Edensor 217).

Feminist theorists have, understandably, been divided on their responses to the *flaneur,* but the *flaneur* nevertheless provides a striking example of how identities are formed through place and how places can be embodied: in the planning and architecture of the modern city, the figure of the *flaneur* emerged. Because the advantage of the *flaneur* was simply leisure time, time to linger and dwell, he is also very much a middle-class figure, a beneficiary of the leisure time available to the rising middle class. As Sally Munt points out, the features of the *flaneur* also "tend to be articulated within a heterosexual paradigm, reliant upon heterosexual discourses of the city" (116). But like Munt, I am also "interested in this observer as a metaphor" because "within the labyrinth, the process of *making up meaning in movement* becomes the point" (116, my emphasis). Making up meaning in movement, however, cannot be neatly separated from the identity, sexuality, or abilities of the one walking. In the narrow, labyrinthine, dirtier streets of the east end, a different subjectivity would emerge from Victorian London: the prostitute, pick-pocket, street urchin, whose behaviors and means of moving through the world were far more clandestine, tactical, and based upon survival rather than entertainment or aesthetics. To completely disentangle the *flaneur* from its origins as a modernist, male, middle-class dandy is probably not worth the effort, but claiming forms of *flanerie* for material and geographical rhetorics provides a starting point, a way in, and emphasizes the connection between place, movement, and identity, between visual and spatial practices.

The modern city used store windows for display, capturing the attention of *flaneurs* who wandered the streets, observing, collecting, and arranging. A contemporary *flaneur* has far more "windows" to observe, framed by screens that aren't store windows but CRTs. Just as the modern city, streets, and shops made possible forms of *flanerie,* contemporary environments—screen culture—make possible other moves and new identities. A contemporary *flaneur* would be as much "at home" in screen culture as on familiar streets, practicing many of the same moves of a confident and curious street dweller, with keen attentiveness to the environment and an eye out for anything "new." Making up meaning in movement happens in composing, too, not just on the streets but also in a number of spatial environments.

Because it is such a visual discipline, geography can contribute in compelling ways to composition's response to both screen and street culture and our notions of what constitutes reading or composing. In Kress's analysis, writing depends more on narrative, the visual on display (82). Both, however, involve acts of composing:[11] decisions about design or where things go. Composing draws in part from memories of other narratives, from mental maps of well-known visuals. The *flaneur* embodies a confident spatial sense that all composers and navigators need; it's a figure that offers one model for forms of movement in certain environments, illustrates the connection between place and identity, and emphasizes the importance of learning to see through walking and mapping. The *flaneur,* with its emphasis on the visual, is a way of taking materialism seriously.

Learning to see at street level might help us understand how it is that images are taking on certain functions formerly carried by language (Kress 82). "Sequence," for example, becomes less important, but remembering where one is, in relation to other places, becomes more important. In geographical rhetorics, then, memory and arrangement become critical. Where do things go, and how can we keep track of them in different types of texts, not all of them organized by text running from left to right? How do memories of other texts or images influence arrangement? What visual representations of texts are lodged in readers' and writers' memories that affect their arrangements or "moves"—their pauses, clicks, page downs, or bouts of re-reading? I'll come back to this point in the final chapter, but imagining rhetorical theories as nonsequential and nontemporal invites us to develop writing and teaching practices centered on the logic of the visual, on display, arrangement, or design. At the same time, our conceptions of "the visual" need to expand as well, becoming less bounded by 8.5 X 11 dimensions. A photo taken with a digital camera, then printed out, centered on a page, and photocopied, is not, of course, much of a contribution to visual rhetorics or visual arguments. Geographic and material rhetorics are more likely to invite the study of banners for a street festival in a neighborhood in, say, Chicago (Cintron, "Just Places").

Material rhetorics invite a type of seeing and forms of movement that help writers or other composers pay more attention to how they navigate space, inhabit places, or encounter difference. "Learning to see," as some urban planners argue, can result in collaborative projects to restore neighborhoods, to reclaim buildings, and embrace community life. For example, published by the Design Center for American Urban Landscape, *Planning to Stay: Learning to See the Physical Features of Your Neighborhood* offers a framework for neighborhood preservation and planning, a step-by-step process that groups can follow. The book opens with the explanation that what began as a book about neighborhood planning became a book about *seeing*. The authors argue that we "must learn the 'visual rhythm' of open spaces, houses, churches, public buildings" in order to transform neighborhoods (Morrish and Brown 7).

With color photographs on every page, *Planning to Stay* illustrates the "Neighborhood Made Visible," with chapters on homes and gardens, community streets, neighborhood niches, anchoring institutions, and public gardens; and five organizing themes dependent on geographic concepts: location, scale, mix, time, and movement (27–29, 55–65). These organizing themes are offered as a friendly methodology for evaluating a neighborhood's qualities. Armed with these five tools or approaches, residents and merchants and those interested in neighborhood planning head out into an area looking for visual evidence of, for example, ease of movement or uses of lighting.

While not all of us in composition studies or literacy studies are interested in transforming neighborhoods or urban planning, reform and change begin with learning to see. Location, scale, mix, time, and movement, as a set of *topoi,* help to expand the work of maps and provide a way of encountering new and unfamiliar places, encounters that are often intimidating or uncomfortable.

The next chapter turns to the concept of mapping in order to further illustrate geographies of writing and rhetoric and the importance of spatial practices in movements of the everyday. I learned a great deal about cultural geography, mapping, and streetwork from a small group of undergraduates in England as they took ordinary journeys of the everyday, often into contested places, and as they attempted to understand an unfamiliar place from the perspective of cultural researchers. Their experiences with encountering difference demonstrate the extreme limitations of traditional maps, which cannot include "the breeze [that] carries the smell of the lake, or the Swedish bakery, or grilling kielbasa" (Morrish and Brown 23). Maps can never capture the operations of walking or the well-trodden paths: "Surveys of routes miss what was: the act of passing by" (de Certeau 97). The activities of passers-by—walking, wandering, or window shopping— are transformed, de Certeau says, into points on a map, and then "the trace left behind is substituted for the practice" (97). The geographical system of mapping, therefore, can transform action into legibility, "but in doing so it causes *a way of being in the world* to be forgotten" (de Certeau 97, my emphasis). Other forms of mapping might make experiences in space more legible or transferable, forms that come not only from cartography but also from stories and legends about places. One spatial practice, walking, over-laps with another—that of mapping. As the next chapter shows, mental maps and not just textual maps affect deeply our sense of place; mental maps are "written" through our identities and means of moving through the world.

3

MAPS OF THE EVERYDAY: HABITUAL PATHWAYS AND CONTESTED PLACES

Mapping is too important to be left to cartographers . . .
—J. B. Harley,
"Deconstructing the Map"

What the map cuts up, the story cuts across . . .
—Michel de Certeau,
The Practice of Everyday Life

Who is felt to belong and not to belong contributes in an important way to the shaping of social space . . .
—David Sibley,
Geographies of Exclusion: Society and Difference in the West

In one episode of the popular television drama *The West Wing*, White House officials meet with groups that wouldn't normally have the ear of the White House.[1] The character C. J. is assigned the group "Cartographers for Social Equality" and meets with them reluctantly. The Cartographers for Social Equality had come to the White House asking for a mere million dollars or so to replace the thousands of Mercator projection maps still hanging in classrooms across the country with Peters projection maps that depict continents with more accuracy. In a scene where three (geeky) geographers demonstrate the different views of the world as evidenced by the Mercator projection map and the Peters projection map (Peters), C. J. is mesmerized, her "world view" decidedly shaken up, especially by an image where the map is flip-flopped so that the northern hemisphere occupies the "bottom" of the map, and the southern takes over the top (see fig. 3.1).

While some may be skeptical that different maps, created through different projection systems, could alter world politics or influence social justice

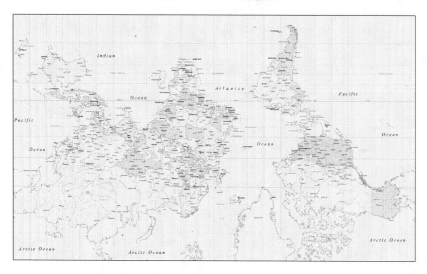

Fig. 3.1. Upside-down Mercator map. Reprinted from Map Resources, <www.mapresources.com>.

(Lemann), critical geographers insist on the connection. J. B. Harley, in "Deconstructing the Map," asserts the rhetoricality of maps:

> rhetoric is part of the way all texts work and . . . all maps are rhetorical texts. . . . All maps strive to frame their message in the context of an audience. All maps state an argument about the world, and they are propositional in nature. All maps employ the common devices of rhetoric such as invocations of authority. This is *especially* so in topographical maps. . . . Rhetoric may be concealed but it is always present. . . . (242, his emphasis)

Many areas of geographic study have changed dramatically in response to both poststructuralist claims about knowledge-making and new technologies, but perhaps none more than the science of maps and attitudes toward mapping. Our ideas about maps need to change in order to reflect how technology is revolutionizing map-making as well as map-reading, document design, and technological reproduction.

For decades if not centuries, the dignified authority of library atlas cabinets, flat drawers with neat stacks of two-dimensional maps, as well as the generally reliable accuracy of glove-compartment maps, led to dominant notions about maps not as "texts" to be interpreted but as documents to be trusted. Following Harley's lead, critical geographers address the politics of mapping and admit that map-making is a political and interpretive act, and scholars in human geography and cartography have acknowledged in recent years the rhetoricality of map-making. The collection *Writing*

Worlds: Discourse, Text, and Metaphor in the Representation of Landscape (Barnes and Duncan), for example, engages with the cross-disciplinary emphasis on intertextuality, signification, and deconstruction to argue that *discourse* creates maps and dominant images of regions, not measurements, surveys, or instruments. In *The Power of Maps,* Denis Wood asserts that maps work by serving interests, and this "interested selectivity," embodied in the map as both presences and absences, allows the map to work, to have meaning, and in turn, to reproduce the culture that creates them in the first place (1). In nearly every field or discipline, scholars use the language of mapping to show how the field is configured, where the borders lie, and who works where. (In rhetoric and composition studies, for example, see Phelps; Lauer; Sullivan and Porter; Glenn.)

As academics and the writers of *The West Wing* recognize, mapping is an important spatial practice that illustrates the link between geography and culture, between images of the world and world power, between the concept of space and actual places. Maps and their significance loom large in both traditional assumptions about the discipline of geography and in people's habitual ways of navigating the world. This chapter concentrates on mapping as another spatial practice that informs geographies of rhetoric and writing and that illustrates the complexity of thirdspace, where maps can be informative and useless, accurate and empty, image and text, exemplary of logic and measurement but also unreadable to a first-time user.[2] The maps we spread out onto a dashboard or view on a screen have very little to do with our mental maps, the images and associations of places that we carry around in our heads.

This disparity means that we must change our notions of mapping, just as we must re-imagine acts of writing, to account for paradoxical and contested places and for places that are laden with risk or the perception of risk for trespassers, the unwelcome, or "intruders" marked by difference. People move through space, in large part, very cautiously, particularly if their (visible) identity puts them at risk in certain areas or neighborhoods. Movement through the spatial world is determined largely by contested places and geographies of exclusion, by (invisible) markers of boundaries. In addition, even the finest maps—created via satellite and updated every twenty-four hours—cannot capture the contested places that are difficult even for insiders to characterize or predict.

Computer technologies and Geographic Information Systems have made maps more public and democratic, easy to reproduce, available in more than one dimension, and, via satellite technology, precisely "accurate." Like most advances, this presents a double-edged sword, and the dual nature of these advances encapsulates the changing nature of geography and the complications of place and space. Maps achieved much of their cultural capital in colonialist and imperialist enterprises; obviously much rarer in ink on parchment, maps and mapping services are consumed today by many professional groups as well as by farmers or fishermen and all those whose income and livelihood depends on the weather. The group of consumers gets larger, too, when you add in the avid gardeners, boaters, golfers, and other middle-class outdoor enthusiasts who now want maps that move, as on weather sites, where radar images of rain march from west to east, illustrating a "speeding up" of weather patterns and the projected paths of fronts or storms. Maps are colorful, often portable, collectible, or valuable, but their value comes, of course, from the culture's demand for positivist, precise, measurable, and reproducible forms of "reality" and representations of regions that are meaningful to people.

Familiar to some readers, a poststructuralist critique of mapping is offered here alongside a practical fondness for maps, an admiration for their logic, and a confidence in their usefulness. Despite the wealth of persuasive arguments that maps are everything from inaccurate to instruments of oppression, I don't want to dismiss something that we depend on so much in the everyday. The image of travelers and tourists poring over maps is a common one, but walkers and residents also depend on different types of maps, memories, or landmarks to find their way around, even for such mundane activities as errands or appointments: street names, subway maps, big trees, crosswalks, billboards, hills or rivers, bus stops or benches, shops or stores, signs of all types. Habitual pathways, of course, are characterized by signs that have faded with familiarity; the routine byways of a pedestrian, for example, may have originally been marked by signs of the built environment, but they are no longer needed when the routine becomes naturalized.

The dignified authority of maps dies hard, but it has by now been challenged rigorously by a number of geographers and cartographers—and also by revolutionary technologies of map-making. Affordable software, increasing access to GIS databases, and a growing reliance on satellite imagery might be making possible the "democratization" of cartography, but technological advances, while they may be useful in settling disputes over boundaries and borders, do not alone make new maps "more" accurate or true. Harley worries, in addition, that the

> effect of accelerated technological change—as manifest in digital cartography and geographical information systems—has been to strengthen its posi-

tivist assumptions and it has bred a new arrogance in geography about its supposed value as a mode of access to reality. (231)

In other words, there is a danger of investing in technologically sophisticated maps as the new source of truth without also acknowledging the shifting, fragmentary nature of all forms of knowledge and information.

If we assume that people who never leave their neighborhoods don't really need maps, that assumption ignores the power of a globe or atlas for armchair travel, for dreaming about traveling or imagining other places. Those who do explore unfamiliar places, by choice or by circumstance, often depend on a map and often have the experience of "Hey, here it is! Just like on the map, just like the map says." Something about maps is hugely satisfying, and there's nothing quite like "a good map" to a hiker, tourist, new resident, or real estate agent. However, as this chapter will argue, mapping takes many different forms, and we need to look beyond published and copyrighted two-dimensional maps to understand mapping as a spatial practice. Rhetorical mapping addresses questions of "How do you get there from here?" that have more to do with practices of the everyday than with expeditions of the Royal Geographical Society or van trips on blue highways. "Which bus will take me to Stop and Shop?" "Don't go that way during rush hour." "How far to a good flea market?" "Turn right where the old post office used to be." Since maps have been the subject of intense debate within human geography for several years now, it's important to contextualize that debate and to come to terms with the kinds of information that maps can and cannot give us.

Mental Mapping, Maps That Move

While print and electronic maps are the most familiar forms, "mapping" is increasingly used as a metaphor for charting, understanding, exploring, or organizing. Mental mapping and cognitive mapping are both terms used by educators and researchers to refer to a person's cognitive capacity to understand where things are in relationship to one another, sense of direction, or sense of distance. It's the ability to carry around in our heads organized information or images of cities, especially images that are "soaked in memories and meanings" (Lynch 1).[3] A form of imagined geography, mental maps hold the cognitive images in our minds about a place, a route, or an area. We have mental maps of our hometowns or the most familiar places of our childhoods; we have mental maps of our current neighborhoods or campuses. Based on these mental maps, many of us could give directions to a stranger or could sketch the way from A to B. In *The Image of the City*, Kevin Lynch introduced the concept of cognitive mapping to city planning by testing the idea of "imageability" through interviews with inhabitants. Principles for urban design, Lynch believed, would develop from a comparison between group images of their city and visual reality. Residents were asked to describe places, sketch locations, or take an imaginary trip through the area.

The techniques of mental mapping are not only useful to city planners. Educators, like the fictional cartographers portrayed on *The West Wing*, know the importance of teaching children spatial sense: children should be able to make a short trip alone to the school library; or tell a driver how to get to their house; or know how far it is to other neighborhoods reported to have better playgrounds. The point of teaching "spatial sense" is not to turn schoolchildren into cartographers, but to make them safe in their lifeworlds and to expand those lifeworlds gradually without endangering or intimidating them. In geographic education, mental mapping usually begins with freehand drawings of a place, proceeds to fieldwork or other types of investigation, and then returns to revising or redrawing the original map, based on new knowledge and understanding (see Mental Mapping and Mental Mapping Project).

Geography educators argue, rightly, that it is an important form of visual and global literacy to be able to read maps. Children should understand something about the relative size of countries, the differences among continents, the way that the sun, for example, affects cultures in dramatically different ways. It matters, for purposes of employment or to increase one's opportunities, to have good map literacy or a strong spatial sense. For example, the navigational skills required for reading a map are similar to those found on a computer interface, but also in very practical terms, how can someone get to a job interview without finding their way there? Here's the case that geography educator Patrick Wiegand makes for children's spatial literacy:

> Children's need to understand the spatial relationships of the Earth's land masses will become more important. For example, increasing school use of the Internet and the opportunities offered by videoconferencing will enable children to undertake interactive investigations around the world. They will need a sharper awareness of where places are in relation to each other and how time zones operate. Having a reasonably accurate image of the way the continents are arranged around the globe and the limitations of world maps not only allows us to make better sense of travel and world events, it is [also] one of the building block of international understanding. (6)

Using mental maps, researchers have learned about people's ability to navigate space and to remember places based on mental maps. Wiegand

and Bernadette Stiell, in "Mapping the Place Knowledge of Teachers in Training," asked geography student-teachers to draw a freehand sketch map of the British isles—a "mental map" or "free recall" map as an admittedly partial test of place knowledge. The results, while varied in theme and significance, showed that "all students in the sample drew England 38 percent larger than its actual relative size. The Republic of Ireland and Scotland were shown 45 percent and 20 percent smaller respectively" (195). Similarly, in a large-scale study of mental mapping, researchers collected 3,568 maps of the continents drawn by students in seventy-five universities in fifty-two countries (Monastersky 222). A predictable "home-turf exaggeration" emerged, but even more striking was the consistent pattern by which Europe was enlarged in scale while Africa's dimensions shrank. No matter where students lived, they exaggerated the size of Europe, and a full 80 percent of the maps featured Europe in the middle (Monastersky 222). The point is not, then, that students need to be taught the right scale, but that mental mapping can tell us a great deal about how people perceive the world, and how ideology (i.e., Eurocentrism) is reproduced in images and school exercises.

The legitimate criticisms of mental maps are that most exercises or experiments using them require people to draw, and then drawing ability comes into the picture. Some research subjects may have very accurate and even unique mental maps but not feel comfortable with the activity of drawing or putting those images on paper. This has always been a disadvantage in using mental maps for research, and, of course, as composition readers know very well, cognitive research is often problematic when divorced from the social production of knowledge.

Mental maps, however cognitively housed, are socially constructed. They are a particular form of "imagined geography" that illustrate the complex relationships between the social and the spatial. Most importantly, maps and spatial memory have been shown to relate to gender and class. This means they are not "cognitive" topics but social ones. The research of Peter Orleans from 1967 in Los Angeles provides the most striking example of this: asking residents of L.A. to share their mental maps of urban space, Orleans questioned a wide range of groups and then created composite maps from their responses (Gould and White). Unsurprisingly, the higher the income and the whiter the neighborhood, the richer and more wide-ranging were residents' knowledge of L.A. White respondents from Westwood represented tourist areas and the coast, for example, while black residents in Avalon identified main streets leading to downtown, but other districts were vague entities. Finally, Spanish-speaking residents in Boyle Heights constructed the smallest mental maps of all, representing only the immediate area, the City Hall, and the bus depot (Gould and White 17). In other words, leisure time, access to affordable transportation, and above all, feelings of empowerment and safety allow people to explore little-known regions and to broaden and deepen their own "mental maps" of a place or region.

Soja pins a fondness for mental mapping on secondspace epistemologies,

> immediately distinguishable by their explanatory concentration on conceived rather than perceived space and their implicit assumption that spatial knowledge is primarily produced through discursively devised representations of space, through the spatial workings of the mind. (*Thirdspace* 78–79).

Artists and architects, urbanists and designers can be found in secondspace, according to Soja, where "the imagined geography tends to become the 'real' geography, with the image or representation coming to define and order the reality" (79). Despite his criticisms, others believe that mental maps and a variety of forms of mapping can become vital tools in exploring people's understanding of space, or the cultural and social spaces that mark inclusions or exclusions: "Just as individuals need cognitive maps of their cities to negotiate their spatial environment, so we need maps of society to intelligently analyse, discuss and intervene in social processes" (Gregory, Martin, and Smith 10).

One form of mapping can be found in William Least Heat-Moon's *PrairyErth*. Subtitled "A Deep Map," his book captures the character, history, and richness of Chase County, Kansas, in the Flint Hills, "the last remaining grand expanse of tallgrass prairie in America" (12). Using the image of a grid to organize Chase County into twelve quadrangles, and hoping that coordinates would lead to connections (15), Least Heat-Moon's chapters—his in-depth visits to each quadrangle—all begin with sections "From the Commonplace Book" and "In the Quadrangle." His deep map is mostly textual rather than visual; the rare visual maps he includes are two-dimensional and not even in color. But to make this map, for thirty months Least Heat-Moon walks across approximately 780 square miles of landscape and explores a dozen small towns; he searches county records, talks to residents, and collects Native American legends. Partly geographic and partly anthropologic, the deep map merges botany, geology, history, and anthropology; Least Heat-Moon is explorer and recorder and narrator. Least Heat-Moon's deep map is a story written geographically, and illustrates vividly how much we need stories for our maps as well as maps for our stories.

Within rhetoric and composition studies, Ralph Cintron uses mapping to situate his ethnographic study of *Angels' Town: Chero Ways, Gang Life, and Rhetorics of the Everyday.* His second chapter, titled "Mapping/Texting," uses a map of Angelstown (the size of a double bed) as an example of the discourses of measurement, particularly reduction (17); distinctions between grids and circuity; and the rhetoric of place names (20). A map is "one kind of optical knowledge that comes into being after real space overwhelms the eye" (29); it is a material representation of space, one that furthers "the desire to conquer and colonize," desires made possible by the processes of mapping and texting (35).

Influenced by Lynch, Least Heat-Moon, Cintron, and others, I rely in this chapter on overlapping versions of mapping to argue that mapping as a concept helps us understand the social production of space and people's experiences in space, but our concept of mapping must include the realandimagined and needs to be drawn from the actual experiences of sociospatial beings. Mental maps are drawn by people's experience in space and with specific places or locations—experiences that have everything to do with class, race, gender, age, mobility, and sexuality. Identity is constructed in place, via place, and I hope to build on that assertion both by qualitative research methodologies and through the rich literatures of cultural geography.

A Study: Mental Maps and Living in Leeds

I often rode the bus in Leeds from St. Michael's to the Headrow, observing the politics of space even on a double-decker bus: young adults in groups, probably students, always go upstairs. Young men riding alone go up, too. Young women alone, though, stay down. Do the students and younger riders consciously leave the lower level seats for pensioners or mothers with children—those who cannot navigate the stairwell—or do they want to "claim" the upper deck, where the view is better and the driver's gave removed?

In order to explore the relationship between the spatial and the social in a concrete and practical way, I interviewed eight students in a cultural geographies class at Leeds University about their experiences in Leeds, with getting around the city, with living and working there as students.[4] My purpose was to explore the everyday material existence of university students in the "mundane landscape" of the campus, the surrounding area, their housing, and the other places of their social and spatial lifeworlds. What places did these students see as contested, desirable, or dangerous? Which places did they avoid or feel excluded from? How are their experiences in space shaped by their identities as students, who are typically transient members of learning communities? In what ways do students—straddling the borders of a number of communities—describe geographically-constructed difference? My analysis of the interview transcripts suggests that an awareness of the workings of geographic exclusion helps us come to terms with the "invisible" types of difference that are the hardest to identify and understand. Geographies of exclusion (Sibley) are worth far more of our attention as we attempt to understand the various ways in which difference is encoded.

I asked for volunteers and conducted managed conversations with eight students from the third-year cultural geographies module in which I was a participant observer in the spring term of 2000. While participants were certainly not randomly selected, they were all third-years, all seeking BA degrees in geography, and all white. With the social advantages of race and excellent educational backgrounds (only about the top 10 percent of all eligible college-age students are accepted into university), the students with whom I worked were very representative of "the student body" at Leeds.

Here's how the interview project began: during a workshop early in the term, the lecturer asked students to do a version of a mental mapping exercise as a sort of pre-writing activity to their research project on a place new to their experience. "Tom" (all names are pseudonyms) gave students, in pairs, a photocopy of an Ordnance Survey map of Leeds (see fig. 3.2) and asked them to identify four types of areas: no-go, ethnic, conflict, and normal. Using colored markers, students were to shade in or outline these types of areas and then get together to compare and discuss their shadings.

I was immediately struck—and troubled—by Tom's terms for these categories. "Normal to whom?" I wanted to ask. "No-go for whom?" "Doesn't it depend on gender, race, class, modes of transport, and abilities?" I didn't raise these questions that day, but the classroom activity—observing students and listening in on their decisions about what to mark—sparked my interest in one-on-one interviews with students about their mental maps of Leeds. I combined, then, a form of mental mapping with one-to-one semistructured interviews.[5] The interviews, like the activity in class, asked students to sit with a map of Leeds and colored markers and to talk about their *personal* definitions of and experiences with the following categories (changed slightly from those in class): "no-go," "ethnic," and "desirable."

The interview transcripts (a total of approximately seventy-eight pages) touch on a range of issues well beyond the three categories. The eight students (four males and four females) talked about their main modes of transport and their habitual routes in getting around the city; they described types of housing that worked as signifiers for them; they shared anecdotes of feeling fearful or excluded; they discussed how they had "come to know"

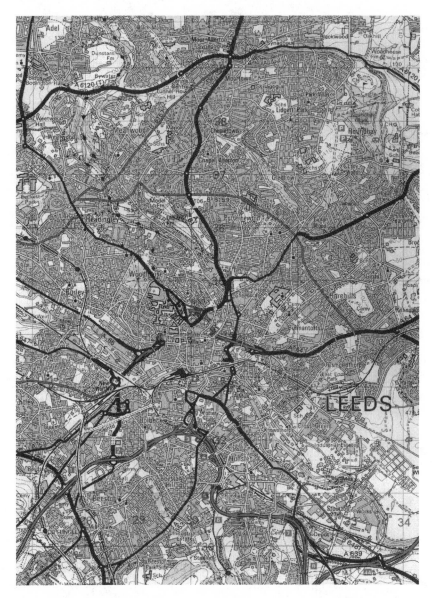

Fig. 3.2. Ordnance Survey map of Leeds proper. Used with the permission of Her Majesty's Stationery Office, © Crown Copyright, NC/01/577.

about certain places; and they made comparisons between Leeds and their own hometowns. One of the striking findings of this data is that these students, despite their training as human geographers, stuck to a very limited area within Leeds and were either reluctant or totally uninterested in exploring other parts of the city. They also held strong opinions—some of those uninformed—about particular neighborhoods. The interview data I share below supports the argument of feminist geographers Geraldine Pratt and Susan Hanson, "that most people are fixed in and by space. Understanding these processes provides one way of seeing differences as socially constructed" (12).

The (Confined) Spatiality of Social Lives

In "Geography and the Construction of Difference," Geraldine Pratt and Susan Hanson point out the tension between postmodern views of experiencing space and more everyday and down-to-earth realities:

> Much has been made of the shrinking world, of the increasing ease of travel and communication, and of the resulting homogenisation of space around the globe. Although the world is indeed increasingly well connected, we must hold this in balance with the observation that *most people live intensely local lives;* their homes, work places, recreation, shopping, friends, and often family are all located within a relatively small orbit. The simple and obvious fact that overcoming distance requires time and money means that the everyday events of daily life are well grounded within a circumscribed arena. (10–11, my emphasis)

A passage from my interview with "Elaine," which highlights students' reluctance to stray from well-defined student areas, offers considerable support for Pratt and Hanson's assertion. Here's the passage in full.[6]

I: Anything else you want to say about your map of Leeds?

E: Not many details is there? [laughs]

I: Well, why do you say that or why do you suppose that is?

E: It's just a general knowledge that I don't really have of the area; I think I know Leeds well, but all I know is like Headingley to the city center—I know the city center quite well, but there's a general lack of details thing.

I: Well, do you think that's because . . you're a student?

E: Uh-huh.

I: And your particular place and time in life?

E: I think so but not necessarily 'cause when I was working in Comet [a retail store] back in the summer, there were people there that didn't have a clue about north of Leeds or where I live.

I: Any part?

E: Yeah, and most of them had lived there all their lives.

I: So it's not necessarily about being a student; it's about . . .

E: It's like your neighborhood is your whole life, isn't it? . . . People identify with their neighborhood, and if you've got everything there, then you didn't need to go out of it, and you're safe in this area where you live 'cause that's where the home is.

I: So you haven't really felt compelled to explore . . . the areas of Leeds that you don't know.

E: No, not really, no. I suppose it bring questions of home into it, doesn't it? 'cause Headingley is my home at the minute, so therefore that's where I'm going to spend the majority of my time.

All eight of the participants commented on their own neighborhoods and their limited knowledge of the city of Leeds. Mitchell says, "I don't really know too many areas of Leeds because when you're a student you're only really going between the university, your house, and into the city center," and he repeats the point about his ignorance of Leeds twice more. Anna puts the issue rather succinctly: "because I have no need to go very far out, I mean my knowledge of Leeds is pretty much concentrated into that student area or where students live." Zoe compared her limited sense of place in Leeds with her similar experience in London:

> I don't really feel like I know Leeds at all really 'cause I only know a narrow corridor; . . . a bit strange really [. . .] but I suppose like if you're living in London, I mean I only knew my borough, I only knew that really well; I didn't know that much of the rest of London at all.

Julian believes that most people's familiar territory occurs within a limited radius:

> I only know sort of a limited, I think you'll find this with everybody else, they've got a sort of chunk of Leeds that they know quite well [. . .] You've got a sort of radius—if you live in that, like I live in that so I've got a radius of about five miles either side of that which I know quite well, which is everywhere within walking distance basically.

Some were quite matter-of-fact about their ignorance of the city while others seemed a bit regretful that they had not done more to explore a wider range of places. Sheila, in particular, seemed to feel that she had failed somehow as a geographer in her tendency to stick to student areas, but she explains her behavior in terms of security and convenience.

> *S:* I'm totally ashamed of myself for the fact that I've just basically been on this road here which is just basically where students live—the town center and—

I: Between the city center and—

S: And I'd say even as far as Headingley—

I: Just up the A660, right?

S: That's it. That's the area where students all live; that's where all the pubs are, the clubs are in town and basically I mean, I've been, the area that I've functioned in is so restricted I'm almost ashamed of myself, but—

I: It's not because you're afraid, it's because—

S: No, it's because I can't, it's because . . . everything I want is here [taps finger on map] which is really bad. I've got friends who've gone out into the countryside and explored all around, but I'm bored with that because that's what it's like when I'm at home [in Wales]. Everything I want is, has been along this road, and students do feel like quite secure there I suppose as well.

I: Well it's their, their culture.

S: Yeah, put it this way: [. . .] I wouldn't *not* go to Bramley for the day 'cause I'm a student, but I wouldn't want to live there amongst . . . I'd want to live—

I: With students?

S: Yeah! Definitely and that's probably some sort of security issue there and also because you know it's just that there's four cinemas, . . . there's all my friends, there's loads of pubs, and it's just—

I: Convenient?

S: It's convenient, yeah, which I'm quite, I am ashamed of it, I should've been around a bit more but—

I: Well, it's about who you are right now, I guess.

Students were able to name the reasons for their restricted knowledge of Leeds, namely the convenience and a desire to share in "student life," defined in part by being surrounded by other students. If "everything they need is there" in the student neighborhoods, why should (white, middle-class) college students venture into unknown territory? They relied very much on what friends and acquaintances had told them about certain places, and "things they'd heard" as well as their own impressions of places formed through their regular routes through Leeds. Except for Sheila, they accepted their confined spatiality as a fact of life, a reality connected either to their position as students or to the geographic given that "for many people in the world, everyday life continues to take place within a restricted locale" and that "the 'localization' of most of everyday life is indisputable" (McDowell, *Gender* 2–3).

Students' identities as students—their embodied practices—kept them from venturing into certain areas where they had strong feelings that they weren't welcome or would feel "out of place." At my suggestion, students used the term "no-go" to name and discuss places where they personally would not feel safe.[7] Anna talks about one no-go area, determined for her by one (accidental) drive through the area and information from others:

> I wouldn't feel comfortable walking down Chapletown at any time just because I'm obviously not [a resident]; I don't think I would fit in there, I mean the kids that hang about on the streets there [. . .] the people who are sort of my age tend to be hanging around in, we call 'em pikeys which is like Adidas pants and all the girls have their hair scraped up onto their heads and spiral perms with blonde hair and I'd be, just by standing there it'd be obvious that I wasn't one of them, so I just wouldn't stop.

Students were well aware of the features that marked them as students and used these differences to explain their isolation from many areas of the city. Elaine can't really name the areas but says "some of the ones down here [in south Leeds] because, just because of my position in Leeds at the moment as a student they wouldn't appreciate us going there." When I asked her to elaborate, she admits that she is stereotyping the areas or basing her notions on hearsay but also is clear that her reluctance to enter these areas comes from her identity: "just because I'm, mind, a student with student feelings putting myself into one of these like council estates it wouldn't be a wise thing to do; you just don't go there, just for your own safety."

These students have good reasons to worry about their own safety, as most of the participants mention incidents where they had abuse directed at them or felt vulnerable because of crimes against students. Elaine clarifies that things can happen even in daylight, even in residential areas: "I've had little groups of kids throw stones at you and stuff." Liam talks about being spat upon as he walked by "kids who sit on walls," but he emphasized that he didn't take it personally. In naming no-go areas, Liam describes an area near his house: "There's footpaths down at the bottom of that—I wouldn't actually go up there for fear of being, well, I get abuse shouted at me, every now and again, all students do I suppose, but then there's bricks in there, and I wouldn't walk down that way at night." While he seems quite casual about the verbal abuse, Liam avoids an area where greater physical harm could be done. In addition, both Sheila and Anna narrate the details of a crime scheme in this area of Leeds where (male) students are grabbed off the streets at night and taken to cash points, where they are forced to withdraw money to give to their attackers. This pattern had been repeated three or four times over a few months, and most students were well aware of it.

In less threatening ways, however, students were also made aware that they were unwelcome in certain areas, that they were trespassers in areas that "belonged" to other social groups. Half of the students interviewed talked about their tentative status, even in neighborhoods—in this case,

Hyde Park—full of student dwellers. Hyde Park, a neighborhood near the university occupied by both students and Asians,[8] is the epitome of a contested place, where the local businesses' economic dependence on students bred an attendant feeling of resentment of them. In this space, students realize their economic clout but are equally aware of their temporary status as residents. In the next section, I try to illustrate further the complexities of Hyde Park as both realandimagined space, where the construction of difference can be illustrated by conflicts related to liminal spaces and residential segregation.

Contested Spaces

On a gray afternoon in February, taking my usual route from campus to Headingley, I overheard one side of a mobile phone conversation, where a male student said to his caller, "I'm walking through Hyde Park. . . . No, the dodgy one. In *Leeds*."

Hyde Park is most often associated with London, but that confusion is only one of many layers of complicated meaning affixed to this place. I begin with Hyde Park, the dodgy one in Leeds, because it emerged in these interviews as a place marked by contestation and controversy, while it was also obviously a gathering place and a playground. It served the functions that city parks fulfill—it was a pleasantly green respite from the otherwise brick and stone environment—and it was also perceived to be a dangerous place. As one geographer has noted, "Parks are typical of those spaces that make the edge of the street ambiguous, that extend the space the street signifies" (Crouch 165). It was often filled with people using the space in various ways; on a nice day, you could see dogs being walked, children on the playground, older teens on the skateboard ramp or basketball court, pick-up football matches, and many people just passing through on their way to and from the university or towards the Hyde Park bus stop on one edge of the park. However, at dusk or after dark, it took on a different identity, and for women, at least, even the streets surrounding the park take on a sinister quality.

For residents of Leeds, "Hyde Park" refers to both a park, with clear borders, and a neighborhood, with boundaries less obvious. Hyde Park is both a clearly bound green space, with playground areas and trees lining the sidewalks, and also a residential area characterized by red-brick terraced housing, a shopping area, and at least one major traffic artery (the Otley road). I often had to ask students to clarify whether they meant Hyde Park as *park* or as neighborhood, and this distinction is just one layer of the contestations surrounding this space. On the city of Leeds ward map, Hyde

Park is part of the Headingley ward. One would have to "know the area," in experiential ways, to distinguish the boundaries between Hyde Park and other parts of the Headingley ward (including Headingley the residential and commercial district within the voting ward of Headingley) (Leeds City Council). Rates for rentals, higher in Headingley, and the number of "ethnic" shops, higher in Hyde Park, can serve to distinguish between the two areas.[9] On the northwestern edge of the university, the park serves as *a space in between* the campus and some of the most student-populated neighborhoods in Leeds—streets that are also more permanently occupied by a very diverse group of residents.

Hundreds of pedestrians and cyclists, making their way to or from the university, walk through Hyde Park, both as a shortcut to certain parts of campus and to avoid or take a break from the busy and noisy main road. My first reaction to it was a very pleasant one—after a mile of walking on an exhaust-fumed main road, I welcomed a calmer green space. However, I was to learn later that Hyde Park is considered by most students to be unsafe at certain times or in certain situations. In addition, students consider Hyde Park the neighborhood to be, simultaneously, terrible, rundown, and full of character. Even though those I interviewed called it "student land," it is also presented in social geography lectures as one of the most ethnic areas in Leeds, occupied mostly by South Asians, many of whom run businesses: shops, taxi stands, takeaway restaurants. I want to write about Hyde Park here to illustrate how contested places can be. Hyde Park operates as a complicated signifier for the students I interviewed and supports the argument that even the most precise, sophisticated map cannot represent much about a place except where it exists in (geometric) relationship to other places.

My own understanding of Hyde Park, and all its contestations, comes from walking through the area a few days a week and from living in Headingley, adjacent to Hyde Park the neighborhood. But none of my experiences as a transient resident prepared me for the strong reactions most of the students I interviewed had towards Hyde Park or the strong associations or a particularly resonant sense of place.

When asked how she knew that Hyde Park was an ethnic area, Elaine replied, "I know about Hyde Park because we live round there, so we have to walk through that." She doesn't pause to clarify what *"that"* is, but given her wording and tone, it is clearly distasteful (why didn't she say "we have to walk through *there*"?). Elaine also says: "I've been in Hyde Park in the middle of the night, and it's like oh my gosh I'm so scared." When I asked her whether she meant the park itself or the neighborhood, she said "both

94

really," but she emphasized that "when it goes dark, you don't walk through the park, you walk around it."

Elaine lives nearby, in Headingley, but she doesn't hesitate to draw firm boundaries between the two (despite the fact that firm boundaries are not drawn by the city). Headingley is, in fact, considered by Elaine to be a desirable area: "I suppose at the minute, I'd say Headingley is desirable to me because it is a student area and it's very accessible to the center of town. Hopefully when I finish next year I want to stay in Headingley; I don't want to move out; everything is just there for you." She clarifies that it's not so much physical attractiveness that makes the area desirable but "it's just everything's there in a community; there's young people and lots of services, like good bus routes into town and takeaways, the cinema, everything." Elaine ignores the fact that Hyde Park is also accessible to the city center; also has a cinema (see fig. 3.3) as well as a number of shops. What Hyde Park does not have, unlike Headingley, is a number of pubs; what it *does* have are a number of nonwhite and nonstudent residents.

Anna's boyfriend lives in Hyde Park, but she attributes her avoidance of the area to her upbringing in a small village, a small-town experience that cultivated in her a sharp awareness of her surroundings for city life: "Because I'm from a little country village I'm more aware of that than a lot of other people; I never walk through Hyde Park even though a lot of my friends don't believe it's violent."

Her geographic upbringing and gender make Anna notice many of the details that then contribute to her judgment about Hyde Park:

> Even walking through Hyde Park, you can see that it's not a desirable place to live. It's the sort of place that people go and live when they're students, and they're fine 'cause they can treat it as student land, but then when they leave, you know, as soon as they stop being students they want to go somewhere nice. The reason it's not nice is because there's bars over all the windows, there's robberies and people driving around in cars with darkened windows a lot with the music coming out—. . . so I'm going to ring that in ethnic as well. I don't know if that's because it's ethnic or not, or if it's just because it's so run down . . . there's rubbish in the streets; there's stray cats everywhere; there's gangs and gangs of Asian kids playing behind the terraced houses on the back streets.

According to Anna and others, Brudenell Road (see fig. 3.4) is the clearest signifier of an "Asian street," but Anna says, "To be honest, the students and the Asians live side-by-side."[10] Brudenell Road is characterized by, says Liam, "a lot of ethnic shops and food places—there's a big concentration of them. When I walk round there—I've got a couple of friends who live

Fig. 3.3. Hyde Park cinema. Photo by Randy Blackburn.

down there—there's always more ethnic minorities walking around than you see white people." Mitchell, who calls Hyde Park "definitely one of the ethnic areas," also specifically mentions "a lot of Asian shops like grocery shops and meat shops' Halal signs."

Sheila was the only student of the eight interviewed who lived in Hyde Park by choice: "I live in this area here—it's Hyde Park and it's definitely ethnic 'cause there's a lot of like Asian families that live in and around here; I've been there so I know." Since all of her friends live there too, Sheila is careful to distinguish between Hyde Park the neighborhood and Hyde Park the park.

Fig. 3.4. A small section of Brudenell Road, Hyde Park. Photo by Randy Blackburn.

I: Would you walk in Hyde Park, at night?

S: Hyde, the actual park? No, you never walk through Hyde Park, that's definitely a no-go area; I'll mark that one actually. . . . The actual park is not lit; it's really dark; actually the council should probably spend a bit of money on lighting. Of course I'd walk through at night but in a massive gang, I'm talking four plus. Walk through coming back home from the university union Old Bar and go home; I'd walk through there if there's more than four of us usually—usually if there's a lad as well but *never* just me and my friends walking in from the union, always round the side of the park, never through the park.

I: Even in the daytime you go around?

S: The worst time apparently for like student muggings or other incidents is around five or six o'clock at night when it's dark, so going home from uni, that's the time I usually go, between half five and seven at night I'm usually on my way home so then I would always go around the side.

I: And that's better lit?

S: It's better lit and there's just traffic and houses.

I: More people?

S: Yeah, there's loads of students walk down there; I mean 'cause it's terrifying when you're walking through the park and it's dark and someone comes from the opposite direction and you're oh no, and you realize that there's students so it's okay, and you think oh it's just students so they're legitimate, which is a bad thing to think anyway. [laughter]

Sheila's relief at seeing other students, which she admits is problematic, may illustrate the high ethnic population of Hyde Park. Even Sheila, who enjoys living in Hyde Park for its diversity, expresses her sense of relief at encountering other students at night—rather than, one assumes, other locals who may not be white.

Mitchell and Anna both talk about the contested claims to residency status or the about the contestation over who belongs in this neighborhood and who doesn't. Mitchell says,

> I know people who live in the Hyde Park area, and their next door neighbors who're Asian come round and knock on their door and say, "Why are you living here, this is an Asian area." So I think as well as white people saying it's is an ethnic or Asian area, Asians see it as an ethnic area themselves.

Anna relates her own experience as a visitor and nonresident:

> *A:* Basically I went to a friend's house there [in the Hyde Park area], and we're all sitting in the lounge having a cup of tea or something, and these kids were climbing on the bars in front of the windows climbing across the bars [imitates them], "Oy mister, mister, give us this, give us that," and they [my friends] can't put any, any of their washing out, and there are literally—there are sort of bars over the windows to stop the kids coming in, and they're inside the house and that's their territory—soon as you step outside the house then it's almost like it's Asian people's territory, really, . . . so
>
> *I:* They'll ask you things like—
>
> *A:* What are you doing here, what are you doing here. If you're in the way, or if you're wanting to get past them, it's fine if . . . you, you know, keep yourself to yourself and you've been quite separate about it, but if you— if there's any attempt to mix in any sense then, that, you know, I'd be nervous about it, definitely, so you tend to sort of keep yourself to yourself and walk with your head high and hopefully no one will bother you.

Anna identifies in this passage what David Sibley, in *Geographies of Exclusion,* calls a liminal zone, spaces of ambiguity where the categories of inside/outside, public/private, or home/street become blurred or uncertain. Sibley asserts "for the individual or group socialized into believing that the separation of categories is necessary or desirable, the liminal zone is a source of anxiety" (33). If students are in their homes, they are "safe," but Anna's anxiety begins when she has to cross the threshold, enter the streets, and move through the neighborhood.

In these mixed residential areas, where races and classes share limited space, inevitable conflicts arise, not just from racial or economic differences but from a whole set of issues that are deeply embedded in English culture and the experience of immigrants. Elaine tells a story that illustrates these layers of tensions:

> On our street, there's an Asian lady that lives opposite us, and we've always said "Oh look, she's got a lot of plants." Everything in her garden looks really nice. We had a friend come and stay with us and she gave us a window box, so we put it out on the back of our kitchen window which doesn't face her house—we put it inside. Well, one day in the summer came a knock on our back door, and we never use our back door, so it's like, oh, who's that? So we open the door, and there's this lady, and she accused us of stealing her window box, and we were just like [laughs], "Come on now this is ridiculous." And then she started going on about how we were students and we come from middle-class families, which isn't necessarily true, and how just that we think we're better than everybody else and tra la la.

Several things about Elaine's brief narrative give us some insight into the sociospatial construction of difference and everyday conflicts related to coexisting in shared neighborhoods. The permanent resident takes great pride in her garden and works hard at maintaining the flowers and plants, which the students do notice and appreciate; however, one assumes that the student residents have never shared their appreciation with their neighbor in a conversation that may have preceded this encounter. When a single window box appears on the students' otherwise unadorned flat, the gardener notices, even though it doesn't face her house. The gardening neighbor comes to the back door, a door that the students never use, giving an immediate sign that this visitor does not belong—and doesn't want to. (Does she walk around to the back because she wants this conversation to take place "off the street"? Because she feels unworthy to come in the front? Or because she wants to make her case next to the window box in question?) For whatever reason, the neighbor woman resists the students' habitual spatial practice of always using the front door. Her decision to knock at the back door forces students to encounter her in different territory, somewhat unfamiliar to them. As this woman's confrontation of her student neighbors suggests, Asians' own exclusions from so many neighborhoods and from "middle England" in general leads them to want to claim Hyde Park as their own. They see students as trespassers in the streets where they, in fact, feel somewhat protected, by virtue of residential segregation, from confrontations with non-Asians. They want to keep students out to increase their own sense of belonging.

The students I interviewed did not openly challenge others' claims that they didn't belong; they recognized that other residents were far more permanent, with more of a stake in the area. Some students were willing to admit that they didn't always make "good neighbors"; Mitchell talks about how students don't care for their houses (because they'll lose their security deposit anyway). Elaine, however, describes an "antistudent sentiment" that she claims is held by most locals: "The locals think that we come in and make loads of noise and create rubbish and get drunk and we're hooligans; and they've just got quite a lot of negative feelings against us."

Sheila thinks the antistudent attitudes result from a very limited form of contact between the two groups: the Asian businesses provide services to students, and students are interested in or dependent on the Asians only as "service providers." The students are consumers, and the businesses need them to survive.

> Yeah, the only thing I do dislike about [Hyde Park] a lot is the fact the community's so divided, students and you know, the Asian families and businesses. The only thing you ever come into contact with people for unfortunately is buying burgers from the takeaway or taxis; that's the only contact.[. . .] I think that students, well I know that students are really resented by the locals—cause we can really misbehave.

For the residents, students' economic clout often overrides residents' resentment of their noise and "hooligan" behaviors. Sheila remarks about how "welcomed" the students feel when they return to Leeds in September: "We come back and the taxi drivers always say 'Oh I'm so glad to have you back.' You know, students do bring most of the money into the area and businesses, especially all the takeaways."

As Sibley says, "In the interaction of people and the built environment, it is a truism that space is contested but relatively trivial conflicts can provide clues about power relations and the role of space in social control" (xiii). It's impossible to tell how serious or how trivial some of these encounters were between students and the Hyde Park residents; however, it's clear that the mix of social differences, beyond "race" or "class," causes boundaries or borders to shift and slide; those unsure of their place use tactics, like Anna's, of "keeping herself to herself" in order to get through territory that belongs to others.

These students' accounts of their experiences in and reactions to contested places like Hyde Park can tell us a great deal about the construction and reproduction of cultural difference. Places can only be contested, however, if there is some conflict, a mix and diversity that some students will find unnerving while others will find it refreshing. With one exception, these students were willing, theoretically, to live in Hyde Park, or they knew plenty of students who did; it was convenient and relatively inexpensive. Other places in Leeds, however, were no-go, a category that Tom introduced in the initial mapping activity in the class workshop and that I also used to question students about areas of Leeds into which they would not venture.

No-Go Areas

As I walked to and from campus that spring, geography lectures in my head, I tried to pay attention to my habitual pathways and variations from it. In one spot along the Otley Road, in front of several billboards, pedestrians had worn a path between the billboards and the backs of several buildings. Shadowed and often damp, it was a mathematical shortcut but too intimidating for me, too narrow and deserted looking. I couldn't make myself walk through it alone.

In the mid-1980s, following violent clashes between the police and the black community in London, the press and political discourse used repeatedly the term "no-go area," as Michael Keith explains, a phrase with roots in Northern Ireland, "a phrase that implied that there were parts of British cities which the police were unwilling or unable to patrol" (39). Calling it term a surrounded with mystification, Keith acknowledges the pejorative use of the term but presents two fallacies of its use: "one that this phenomenon is new to mainland Britain, the other that it is causally related to the number of crimes committed by black people" (40). These students did report one such area in Leeds, an area that the police entered only reluctantly and therefore a distinct no-go area, in keeping with the evolution of the term. For this mental mapping exercise, however, I encouraged students to define no-go areas (and the others as well) with whatever terms they chose; Liam, for example, defines no-go areas as those where "I wouldn't feel safe at night, but I suppose in the daytime as well." Elaine says for her, no-go areas are all about fear, "whether or not I've got myself in a position of vulnerability."

Liam identifies Chapletown as "notorious," something he knows by reputation rather than experience. Chapletown was, in fact, the most often named no-go area for these students. Elaine says that there's a special police force unit there, and Mitchell refers to information they received in the halls of residence during first year:

> There was quite a big thing about not going to Chapletown during the day, and don't even think about going at night, because it's unsafe and you'll get mugged. Also in lectures on social geography, we were told that it's an area where if you do get mugged the police won't do anything because they'll say, "Well, what are you doing here in the first place?"

Sheila confirms this, that first-years are advised to stay out of there, and that social geography lectures identified Chapletown as a site of deviance and crime, that it is a no-go area for the police.

Liam and Sheila and most of the group agree about what constitutes a no-go area in terms of the physical characteristics. Sheila lists "some of the characteristics of urban deprivation like more graffiti, more litter, vandalism; . . . and the shops tend to have physical barriers like grilling on the windows." Liam mentions twice the feature of terraced housing as well as vandalism: "housing is terraced, . . . litter everywhere, kids running around screaming." Note the similarity to Julian's description of a no-go area: "Everything's boarded up, and there's nobody about. . . . You see burned out cars and broken windows; you see high security fences everywhere and rubbish strewn everywhere and a few kids perhaps running around the place looking wild." Zoe mentions litter repeatedly to describe no-go areas, as well as "back-to-back houses, really run down."

Although there was considerable agreement about one no-go place (Chapletown) and about the physical signs of urban deprivation, no-go, like all neat and tidy categories for capturing a sense of place, didn't quite apply to some more nuanced or complex places. Mitchell: "So I suppose although Hyde Park's quite a green area, it's seen as an undesirable park with undesirable houses around it." Liam makes it very clear that he considers Burley "quite a scrubby area," but he's not exactly frightened to be there: "I mean if I walked through Burley, I wouldn't think someone's gonna come at me. I just don't like the feel of the place; I just don't like it."

Anna explains that for her, Hyde Park is not exactly no-go but that she approaches it with some trepidation or what she calls "provisos"—her own improvised rules for navigating the area:

> So yeah, I walk a lot, I walk from university home to Headingley, but I always walk along the Otley Road; I don't walk through Hyde Park, unless someone's walking through Hyde Park with me and they prefer to go that way. Once I'm out of Hyde Park, I walk up Cardigan Road without a problem; Cardigan Road's fine, it's just . . it's just Hyde Park that I don't like, and walking down Victoria Road's fine as well 'cause it's on the edge, isn't it?

"On the edge" is safer, then, than being in the thick of it. Liam is one of the few students who acknowledges that people actually *live* in no-go areas:

> Having said that [about Burley], I live in Woodhouse, and a lot of people think of Woodhouse as being a not very nice area because it's inner city and it's not aesthetically pleasing to look at, but in fact, living there I know it's really only kids that cause trouble. I feel quite safe walking around Wood-

house, but I suppose that's only because it's my home. . . . I think of Burley as being quite a scrubby area, for want of a better word, but people who live there might not think so.

Mitchell also mentions Burley, but as a no-go area based on "what people told me about it, because of the riots that happened there." According to newspaper accounts, however, the riots were in Hyde Park.

Riots in Leeds erupted in both July 1995 and May 1997. According to newspaper accounts, the 1995 conflicts, in Hyde Park, left a pub in smoking ruins and on successive nights, attracted between fifty and a hundred youths to the area, where they attacked police with stones (Wilkinson). Those who set the pub alight were reacting to police raids on The Jolly Brewer and claimed that it was "the center of a police surveillance operation" for drug dealing and robbery, which the reporter confirmed. Although there were no arrests and only one person slightly injured, these are the "riots" that Zoe, for example, referred to in trying to name her aversion to Hyde Park.

The 1997 riot was more complicated. Centered in Harehills, where the minarets of a new mosque are visible on the skyline, an Indian shop owner made a "'tactless' decision to stock a video about the Indo-Pakistan conflict which features a Koran being flung to the ground" (Wainwright). A crowd of three hundred Muslim youths gathered, throwing stones and threatening arson. The police response, a "high-profile response" (i.e., with riot police) was blamed for making the situation worse, and officials called it the worst violence among British Muslims since *The Satanic Verses* was publicly burned in Bradford. None of the students I interviewed lived in Harehills, but one group did explore part of it for their streetwork projects, the subject of the next chapter.

Liam also assumes that there have been riots in Chapletown, though he's quick to point out that he hasn't actually been there himself. From his knowledge of Manchester, Liam draws parallels between the worst-by-reputation areas of Manchester (Northside and Hume) with Leeds's Chapletown and assumes that the area is defined by drugs and prostitution. But the main marker for no-go areas for Liam, is that of housing: "See, I'd actually go around Burley rather than walking through the center, you know there's quite a lot of terraced housing near the bottom of the hill from the university; . . . there's a lot of housing around there that I wouldn't walk through at all."

In describing where she lives and how she gets around Leeds, Zoe mentions an area that, while surrounded by places she considers safe, is nevertheless an island of no-go. Near her home in Meanwood, this area represents a complicated set of boundaries.

Z: This is Meanwood Road, and I live just off the ridge just up here, but as you walk into the center of town like here, it's not nice—actually I shouldn't have put that bit as desirable 'cause that's Little London there, in here [see fig. 3.5.].

I: Is Little London good or not?

Z: No, it's horrible. [laughs]

I: Why?

Z: Little London is . . . , well it's in Woodhouse I suppose . . Little London is like here.

I: Okay.

Z: I live just before Little London; it's not nice at all.

I: So what characterizes Little London, I mean how do you *know* that that's Little London?

Z: Because all the houses are the same—it's all council houses; there's a lot of tower blocks as well; I mean there's about five tower blocks; they're all—all the roads are called after London stations, and there's a Little London community center, but basically all the houses look the same, and then it suddenly changes when you get out of that. But it's not nice at all because I suppose a very poor area and what people have said about it as well; I think there's quite a lot of crime that goes on round there.

I: Okay, so, in getting from your house to the city center, do you avoid Little London?

Z: Oh, yeah, definitely. Where I live it would be quicker for me to just walk down the main road to get on to the interchange here, and then there's this sort of pedestrian park that goes through the tower blocks of Little London towards the city center, but there's no way I'd walk there because, I just wouldn't want to.

Desire and Place

Despite students' claims not to know much about Leeds, they could be quite precise, like Zoe is above, about the places they feel comfortable in and those they are determined to avoid, even if it means going the long way round. Students were also quite clear about the desirable areas of the city, characterized by the amount of green space, the type of housing, feelings of familiarity, and a sense of community. Open space, green space, and unoccupied land hold a very high value in England, of course, and students' comments certainly reflected this ideology as well as their middle-class upbringings and general inexperience in strange cities. With a couple of exceptions, none of the students was living in a place they identified as desirable, and while their definitions of desirable varied depending on students' background or future plans, students unfailingly pointed out the same areas as being "very nice, very posh."

Fig. 3.5. A part of Little London. Photo by Randy Blackburn.

Elaine identifies a specific area of Leeds, Adel, "'cause it's rich with big houses; that's the majority of the north really," and when asked to identify what she meant by desirable, Elaine answered, "Mine's materialistic I suppose, big house, nice car, everything that you can visually see in the neighborhood . . . big houses, nice cars and a kind of suburban life, middle England [laughs]." Anna names Beckett Park as an area where she feels "quite happy walking around; it's quite green and tidy and everyone's got their green wheelie-bins out, and people wash their cars on Saturday mornings [laughs]."

The type of housing is one of the most obvious indicators of desirability. Students most often mentioned detached or large semidetached houses with walls and cul-de-sacs. And as Mitchell explains it, houses need gardens to be desirable:

> I think the houses in this area are still back-to-back houses, but they've made real front gardens and are set back off the road, so they appear to be more desirable . . . whereas if you're living in the back-to-backs in Hyde Park or Burley, your front door is right on the pavement.

Without a driveway as well, according to Mitchell, your car (your stuff) belongs to "the actual street."

These definitions of desirable hinge on green space, so Woodhouse, where Mitchell is living now, doesn't qualify: "I think the area of Meanwood and

Weetwood's quite desirable. . . . [There are] sports pitches up there, the university sports pitches so when you're traveling by bus to that area you can see the big houses and posh cars and lots of grounds." But perhaps the biggest "hinge" is that of ethnic identification. In talking about an area near where he does his weekly shopping, Mitchell says: "If you go a bit past [the Sainsbury's in Moor Allerton], you can see slightly posh houses, and that's the Jewish cluster so I suppose that's an ethnic area as well." This part of the transcript with Mitchell is worth quoting at some length.

I: How do you know that [that it's a Jewish cluster]?

M: 'Cause I'm Jewish so.

I: Okay.

M: I've been there; it's quite well publicized that that's a Jewish area of Leeds and northwest Leeds, . . . and obviously they perceive Jewish people as having a bit more, a bit more wealth.

I: Have you learned in your social geography classes that people tend to congregate, in particular areas?

M: Yeah, we learned about clusters, positive and negative segregation. We learned about people clustering because they felt they have to live together because of discrimination they'd get if they lived in separate areas. Also people want to live together because, if they have to go to mosque five times a day . . . then they can walk to the mosque and they can walk together. That's the problems and the sort of themes you get in a social geography class.

I: I'm just now noticing that there are synagogues marked on the map.

M: Yeah, I think there are two synagogues in the vicinity of the Ring Road, and there's also a lot of golf courses around here, so you can just look on a map and see that that's quite a posh area.

Liam wants to mark the whole of "outside Leeds" as desirable because of the "masses" of green space. Outside of the Ring Road is "the beginning of the great green expanses," he says. Anna also notes that the area around Bodington Hall is desirable because "there's lots of country side, the playing fields were wide open green spaces, and to get into university . . ."[11] it was a simple direct route, there and back, very safe, very familiar." Anna particularly liked living there because you could "choose the city, but it wasn't in your face," and she mentions the comforting presence of a police station nearby. For Anna, "the further out you get the better it gets. . . . Out towards Adel behind Bodington Hall all of these houses—they're all old-fashioned, high-walled houses but not threateningly so, very sort of private residences that you feel quite safe walking around."

Along with the desirable suburbs, however, several students noted how happy they would be living downtown, in the new posh flats being constructed along the canal and near the heart of the city center. Sheila talks about this area "where Granary Wharf is [and all of the] gentrification":

> That's definitely desirable 'cause they're high priced sort of homes and desirable for going out at night to posh restaurants around there, and there's nice walks down there. [This area is] desirable for a yuppie kind of life, young people I suppose, not families.

When asked "Twenty-somethings?" she answers, "Yeah! People like me when they graduate hopefully." Mitchell, who already has a job in the city center for the following year, also mentions this part of town as desirable:

> I've thought about living in the city center 'cause they've got quite modern flats. And because I'm still quite young, I'd like to be near the hustle and bustle of town and that's where I'll be working; I think there's quite a lot of young people are living in like modern flats in town because they like to be close to work and they like to be close to going out [at night] as well.

Finally, desirable places to live are those that have a sense of community, which Liam defines as the presence of "a social center, the local pub, and the chip shop." It's also important to community that those who run the shop be "very friendly people and tend to know everyone in the area." Liam also notes all the kids that run around, enhancing further a positive neighborhood feeling. Liam also notes that there is a green area to this community, but unfortunately, it's "where the joyriders come and dump their cars."

For Zoe, desirable is what she is accustomed to or familiar terrain: "To be honest though, everything up to here from Woodhouse is desirable because I live there." Anna says something similar: "Because it's familiar, then it's desirable in my mind, anyway. Don't know if that's necessarily right, but if I know [a place], then I feel more comfortable. All the pubs and stuff that are along there are similar to pubs that I have back home." Zoe admits that if she were more established with a "permanent job and I could afford to live where I wanted to, I wouldn't live in Woodhouse because it's a student area . . . a happening place but I wouldn't want to live [laughs] in a street full of students if I'm about forty." She names Alwoodley as a "really posh" place, but she wouldn't want to live there now because there wouldn't be other students surrounding her. Elaine is also quick to point out that she suspects her notions of desirable places will change as she gets older. For now, however, desirable means a vibrant area (Zoe's term) or a hustley-bustley place: Anna likes Kirkstall because of the cinema, "which is always a bit hustley-bustley anyway so you feel quite, you know, happy there as well."

As with the no-go category, places designated as desirable tend to have messy boundaries and a slippery status. For example, Mitchell tries to find desirability somewhere in the betweens: "A nice area to live would be just near the university but away from student houses. I suppose if you see an area as being half desirable but very convenient, in a good location, then it becomes even more desirable." Anna, too, sees the city center as neither/nor: "All around the city center, I wouldn't say it was no-go, but I wouldn't say it was desirable. It is no-go if you're in a certain situation, like it's late at night or you're by yourself." Liam's comments about the city center also illustrate how a place can have more than one status or designation, or that perceptions of it can vary according to time of day or past experiences. While Liam and most of the others definitely mark the city center (downtown) as quite a desirable area they feel comfortable in, Liam also identifies the rail station as "a bit unsavory":

> *L:* Round the station actually—behind the station, yeah I'm going to mark the station, just sort of behind it, 'cause I know it's quite a no-go area—
> *I:* Okay, and do you think that because you've been there?
> *L:* That's being there at night and seeing the people that hang around there at night. There's a lot of . . . undesirable people walking around there when I've been there at night coming back from a club or whatever, and it's just a bit unsavory . . . and again that's specifically around the station area.

These students' desires, in general, influenced their judgments about what areas around Leeds were desirable: how did they see themselves as university graduates, as older members of middle England? There were definitely areas of Leeds where these students felt threatened or uncomfortable, but they also felt extremely empowered in the familiar areas of "student land" as well as in the green, large-garden neighborhoods of their imagined futures.

These mental maps of Leeds illustrate that movement through the spatial world hinges upon contested places, geographies of exclusion, and (sometimes invisible) markers of boundaries. The images we carry around in our heads, even those that come from the reports of others, affect our willingness to explore or our choices of residential areas. Even if people move through certain areas or neighborhoods without fear of physical harm, they may feel uncomfortable or they may have minor confrontations about "who belongs there."

Investigating the "imageability" (Lynch) of cities or areas contributes much to our understanding of the social production of space and people's experiences in space, and these are the forms of mapping that I want to claim as spatial practices of the everyday that can help us to re-imagine acts of writing as material and visual. In *Writing Women and Space,* Alison Blunt and Gillian Rose claim that mapping "is a distinctive form of spatial representation because it can be interpreted as visual and/or textual. . . . the spatial imagery of mapping can expose tensions between the dynamics of the visual and the written" (10). I would add, however, that mental mapping, where the real and the imagined or the physical and the emotional come together, adds yet another layer to mapping and its representations.

Mapping, then, in all of its overlapping forms, contributes to geographic rhetorics by insisting upon the realandimagined production of space and more complex ways of representing places and spaces. Along with walking—forms of *flanerie*—and dwelling—the subject of the final chapter—mapping forms part of the techne for geographic rhetorics, those that focus on moving through the world, encountering the rub of differences, the fissures and gaps in discourse, the borders and fault lines. Maps work metaphorically, but they also do rhetorical work: they provide information that influences action; they persuade users to try a new route or stick with the old one; and they communicate an image of a place that may or may not hold up. Maps, like all texts, function in the betweens of metaphor and materiality: cartography is a useful and profitable "skill" done with tools, but mental mapping is a swirl of memory and experience related to race, class, gender, sexuality, age, or abilities. A geographical rhetoric, then, would not ignore longitude or latitude but would try to capture the layers of meaning and the *feelings* of residents or visitors or trespassers.[12] Contested places like Hyde Park in Leeds are not easily "mapped," but as rhetoricians and educators, it is our responsibility to understand not only where our students come from but also what forms of fear or reluctance keep students locked in place.

Students' highly charged responses to certain places in Leeds and their reluctance to explore neighborhoods beyond "student land" highlights how difficult it is to move learners to have a meaningful encounter with difference. The next chapter turns to the cultural geography method of "streetwork" to show how walking and mapping can help us to understand the complex ways in which space hides consequences from us and the ways in which one's "sense of place" is constructed. Like forms of mental mapping, streetwork exposes the workings of geographies of exclusion: how the landscape, the built environment, the inhabitants, or the force of their own preconceptions and expectations can make people feel excluded or alienated from certain places. This bodes ill, I argue, for composition's growing enthusiasm for service learning and literacy projects if such project designs do not include an awareness of the sociospatial construction of difference.

4

STREETWORK: SEEING DIFFERENCE GEOGRAPHICALLY

Every street tells a story . . .

—Tom's lecture notes

Disney World—one of cultural geographers' prime targets for critique[1]—opens with a fairy tale castle but soon becomes Main Street, U.S.A., where commerce, charm, and concrete come together in a swirling combination of nostalgia, patriotism, and an idyllic capitalist landscape. Places are said to be "Disneyfied" when they seem contrived, false, inauthentic—a place that's trying too hard to seem safe or desirable, like gated communities. The Disneyfication of places, as chapter 1 referred to, has left us with the task of distinguishing authentic from inauthentic places, or with determining the betweens—a task that requires elements of walking, learning to see, mapping, and inhabiting the streets. Of all cultural locations, *the street* is perhaps the most contested, the most up for grabs, and the most provocative.

A rich literature about the street in geography, urban studies, architecture, and cultural theory provides ways of seeing the street as a site of textured, complex everyday practices emblematic of cultural difference. In "The Street in the Making of Popular Geographical Knowledge," David Crouch looks at ordinary or folk knowledges about life "at street level." Defining the street as "a fragmented and uneven broken series of bits," used in numerous and diverse ways, Crouch also claims that the street organizes local knowledge (162) and is full of signs of commodification but also provides a place to be seen. Most importantly, streets become "embodied" with stories, memories, and all sorts of meanings (164); that is, "the body itself is important in the way we make images of the street" (166). To illustrate this embodiment, Crouch refers to children interviewed about their use of a vacant lot, partially concealed from the street, which they transform into a place with meaning, "another world" separate from the run-down flats where they live (167). The children take artifacts from home—a pram, stools, clothes—to remake the space, to transform it. In this way, then, the vacant lot becomes a space ambiguous in ownership, control, and identity (168).

In "The Culture of the Indian Street," Tim Edensor offers examples of "the rich diversity of social activity in Indian streets" in order to make a case for the highly regulated state of the western street (205). Edensor suggests that western tourists are drawn to the exotic, sensual nature of nonwestern streets precisely because their own streets are over regulated.[2] From the figure of the *flaneur* found in Baudelaire and Benjamin, writers have been fascinated by how people navigate or enact agency in the streets. Whether it's a rhetoric of walking in the city (de Certeau) or the battle cry of taking to the streets in protest, the street holds tremendous metaphoric power and captures our imagination. At the same time, however, streets represent sites of fear and vulnerability, especially for women, whose use of public space is limited to "defensive tactics" and leads to the development of a geography of fear (Valentine, "Geography" 386). Geographies of fear may or may not correspond with geographies of crime; statistics about "where" crimes take place are irrelevant because the threat is there, just the same (Hutchings 32).[3]

The intense conflict over streets can be illustrated by the plans of many urban developers and city planners in the building boom after World War II, when in New York City a developer named Robert Moses had a vision of the city completely interconnected by wide, fast, multilane highways and interstates. In the name of urban renewal and with the vision inspired by federal dollars, Moses built sixteen crosstown expressways, a building push that destroyed neighborhoods and the daily lives of tens of thousands of people (*New York City;* Berman, 290–312). Unrestricted automobile traffic was the key to protecting the American economy; those with automobiles needed somewhere to go, like driving home to Levittown. Streets, and the people who inhabited them, were just standing in the way of progress *(New York City).*[4]

Jane Jacobs set out to fight Moses, and she and her followers rose up to stop the destruction of the West Village and Soho by the construction of an expressway through lower Manhattan. An activist for city life, Jacobs was one of the first to resist the relentless modernist crusade against the street, a vision embraced by Le Corbusier and his followers who valued skyscrapers and interstates and thought the streets were dark and dirty. In *The Death and Life of Great American Cities,* Jacobs made popular the saying in geography studies, "eyes upon the street" (35), which she used not as Big Brother surveillance but to express the importance of long-term inhabitance to a neighborhood, particularly in the effectiveness of residential surveillance—one of her three requirements for a successful city neighborhood. Shopkeepers and stoop-sitters and those going about their chores keep an eye on the street, alert to trouble for the children or others. Rather than minding their own business, neighbors check the street routinely for anything out of the ordinary. Jacobs is not without her critics (see Berman 323–26), but her work still draws the attention of geographers and urbanists who study behaviors on the street or who study the history of urban movements. Putting trashcans away or making trips to the corner store are ways of inhabiting a place, and the small, routine acts help us understand larger cultural issues—like eating. Who eats on the street and who doesn't? What does eating in public represent?

Geographer Gill Valentine analyzes the tension between the historical taboo in England against eating on the street and the growing "foodscape" of the streets, where takeaway shops and vending machines and chains of pastry shops, along with rushed lifestyles, are making eating on the street more common. Interested in street culture generally, Valentine explores "the relationship between public acts of consumption and the production of the public space of 'the street'" ("Food" 192). Like many other cultural practices, the taboo against eating on the street developed as a means of regulating the boundary between public and private (193). Eating on the run, in public, is considered by some to be animalistic, uncivilized, or at least unmannerly. According to Valentine, food "has therefore played an important role . . . in producing the street as a particular social environment" and as a "civilised space" (197). As with many other landscapes, a "blurring" is now taking place, a breaking down of once rigidly maintained social codes that makes the street "a more liminal space somewhere betwixt and between home, canteen and restaurant" (202). Eating on the street marks a "private" activity made public, and these types of blurred boundaries are difficult for people. The homeless, for example, trigger such strong reactions, in Berkeley and elsewhere, precisely because they engage in private acts, such as sleeping or urinating, in public places (Mitchell). A bourgeois family picnic in a park may be acceptable but standing on a street corner wolfing down a grinder is more problematic. Sipping from a can of soft drink is one thing; drinking out of a bottle concealed by a brown paper bag is quite another.

What is for some a benign cultural practice—eating a hot dog from a vendor—represents to others a violation of social codes or ill-mannered behavior; the streets, therefore, are a huge borderlands for any number of "others," those marked by class, race, or abilities. In *Eating on the Street:*

Teaching Literacy in a Multicultural Society, David Schaafsma writes of an incident in a Detroit literacy project where educators were in conflict about a particular practice: "Should teachers confront poor black children about eating on the street, a conflict related to broader issues of authority and cultural difference?" (xviii). These leader-educators were divided about how to respond to this practice, which gives Schaafsma a way to illustrate the importance of storytelling about everyday conflicts. For this book about literacy, eating on the street works as a metaphor for larger conflicts and operates, too, as a material practice, involving real streets, real kids, and real food. I am interested in Schaafsma's choice to focus on this particular conflict because eating on the street is, in fact, such a powerful emblem for issues of public/private, for transgressing boundaries, and for codes of cultural difference.

Street practices, formed from a swirling combination of walking and inhabiting, are of increasing interest to composition and literacy studies, as service learning, tutoring, and community writing programs invite students to explore the streets and cultures of local communities. However, this chapter argues that the "academic enthusiasm for difference" (Sibley 23) must be tempered by the sociospatial realities of everyday life. As composition scholars and practitioners advocate leaving behind familiar terrain in order to understand cultural difference and the complex conditions related to research and learning, a growing trend has emerged in higher education to send students out of the classroom, in various ways, in order to position the learner as an outsider, a foreigner, an other—a positioning that, in its discomfort, often stimulates reflection. At the same time, one of the biggest pedagogical and ethical challenges for critical educators involves wrangling with the concept of "difference." Particularly when they're not so inclined, how can people be motivated to engage with lifeworlds other than their own and then use that experience to enact social change? Giving students the experience of a contact zone takes many forms, but one of the most common in recent years has been to send students "out of place," by asking them to go to community centers or other locations outside of the university, and then, in one version, to write about their experiences there. Those advocating service learning and those committed to the study of literacy practices recognize the need to move beyond or outside the academy, to the streets, to offer students "real" rhetorical situations (Heilker) or to understand the material conditions of writers' lives (Aronson; Gere). Sending students off campus serves to magnify cultural differences between the college student and, say, the homeless person, the migrant farmworker, or the community leader they've been assigned to encounter.

How students *interpret* the difference they encounter tells us a great deal about their understanding of the social-ideological workings of culture, and, the theory goes, the experience makes students better writers, or at least better citizens—*if* that is, social and cultural biases are not simply further entrenched (see Herzberg.) Depending on the community service learning design, students may or may not set out equipped with a methodological awareness and a theoretical perspective that will help them in coming to terms with their experience—and, we hope, help them to develop a "social imagination" (a term Herzberg borrows from Kurt Spellmeyer). Advocates of service learning will testify to the transformative nature of these assignments—that students are changed and enlightened and that many of them continue to serve in their assigned and then adopted communities long after the required part ends. Despite the reciprocity and transformation, the starting point is, nevertheless, one of a requirement being imposed by an authority, that is, they "have" to go. Since geographic research tells us of the reluctance of many people to leave their familiar terrain—precisely my point in the preceding chapter—or if it's true that students will not initiate such exploration on their own, then it might be worth thinking about ways to reconcile this reluctance to travel with a growing trend towards service-related or community fieldwork, a trend that extends into many forms of disciplinary fieldwork. If we believe that white, middle-class students, in particular, are too comfortable and too safe and too invested in the status quo, how do we give them educational opportunities that will make them decidedly uncomfortable—a condition where learning might happen—without creating a "punishing pedagogy"(Forbes)?

Streetwork: Where It Can and Cannot Take Us

In geography, fieldwork is king—a fundamental element to the study of geography or to the earning of a degree—just as it is in anthropology and other fields. Geography's visual epistemology, in fact, makes the emphasis on fieldwork understandable, with a strong reliance on "seeing" to obtain or test knowledge (see chapter 2). A geography student can expect a number of field trips, built into nearly every class. In the Leeds degree program, second-year students head to parts of France for three weeks, accompanied by faculty over the Easter break. Students pay the expenses of this required fieldwork, necessary for the degree. Geography departments make this requirement, however, only after giving students a thorough grounding in theory and methodology that prepares them to make the most of their experience. There are as many ways to approach fieldwork as there are disciplines, but the new cultural geography insists on an accounting of the fieldworkers' positionality and challenges the tradition in human geography of studying landscapes.

"Streetwork," the name of a project created by cultural geographers Jacquelin Burgess and Peter Jackson, shifts the venue for geographic research to urban environments, where there are "different kinds of neighbourhoods and a reasonably active street culture" (155). There are bigger differences than venue, however, in the effort to draw upon qualitative methods that refuse the pretense of objectivity and that require the researchers to identify and account for their own positionality, assumptions, and biases—something that traditional fieldwork out of physical geography, for example, would not require. The word *encounter* implies unplanned, unstructured, fleeting, short-lived; distinctly *not* ethnographic, there is no effort to become an insider or an expert. Without trying to gain full access or be accepted—or to give and take in a reciprocal relationship—students investigate and analyze a place they have chosen through a series of heuristics. The methodology includes site visits, description, interviews, and/or historical research, and in their final reports, students must move beyond description into a critical analysis of their encounter.

Evolving over a period of fifteen years at the University College London, the streetwork project relies on qualitative research and forms the core of UCL students' work in cultural geography. In their article "Streetwork—An Encounter with Place," Burgess and Jackson endorse this type of fieldwork for all cultural geography students. Students work in groups and produce "*an interpretive account* of [their] chosen place, conveying [their] experiences as a traveller and explorer" (153, their emphasis). Noting the radical and political connotations of the name, borrowed from a 1973 text titled *Streetwork: The Exploding School* (Ward and Fyson), Burgess and Jackson outline the aims of such a project for second-year students: Streetwork has

> an emphasis on developing the students' powers of observation and sensitivity to both their own and others' environmental experience; the exploration of those environmental, historical, social and cultural characteristics which contribute to a sense of place; and *the appreciation of difference,* one of the hallmarks of contemporary cultural geography. (152–53, my emphasis)

An appreciation of difference, streetwork argues, comes from firsthand experiences in unfamiliar landscapes and the opportunity to reflect on sociospatial logic and the cultural codes that shape experiences in landscapes, neighborhoods, or cities. Because the street has been romanticized, just as the city, the frontier, and other imagined places have been, the purpose of streetwork is not to glorify the streets, nor to pretend that "real" consequences of space can be revealed if only we get the methodology right. But streetwork purposely puts learners in unfamiliar places and asks them to collect data and make sense of it through a theoretical lens informed by cultural studies and postmodern theory. The principle behind cultural geography's streetwork is a familiar one: that we are all immersed in culture constantly, but it takes some distance, a shift in perspective, or a jolt of unfamiliarity to get people to "see" the ways culture operates.

In neighborhoods (as well as discourses), some boundaries are unmarked, the lines rubbed out by repeated crossings, by layers of historical and cultural sediment that map both the habitual pathways of insiders and the transgressive acts of outsiders. Based on the landscape, the built environment, the inhabitants, or the force of their own preconceptions and expectations, people feel excluded or alienated from certain places; feelings of exclusion are culturally "built in" and are often not limited to such familiar notions of difference as age, race, gender, economic class, or abilities. Tracking people's navigational strategies, their tactics of inhabitance, their habits of place, helps us to understand the complex ways in which space hides consequences from us and the ways in which one's "sense of place" is constructed. Streetwork complicates our understandings of the relationship between public and private space, between culture and identity, and between boundaries and their gaps. Rather than simply advocating "more streetwork," however, I also show how streetwork's "encounter with place" is not sufficient, by itself, to move people to welcome experiences with cultural difference. The theories and methodologies of streetwork are necessary to a successful fieldwork project that equips students to analyze their experience in space, but "an appreciation of difference" is not enough—cultivating such appreciation does little to interest students or residents in activism or social change.

When students are sent out to do fieldwork, we may be limiting their understanding of ideological practices if we ask them only or mainly to "observe differences."[5] Such approaches to assignments give students the impression that their view is the norm, or that they are the "center." This "arrogance of believing ourselves at the center," as Adrienne Rich puts it, results from the ignorance at the core of privilege ("Notes" 223, 226). Thus, because their cultural mobility privileges some students, a focus on "difference" may only serve to harden boundaries (Pratt and Hanson) or to solidify their entitlement. As geographer David Sibley warns, "limited engagement, a superficial encounter, might result in the presumption of knowledge which could be more damaging than ignorance if this knowledge were in the province of state bureaucracies or academia" (29). This is tricky territory for composition and community service learning: how are we to avoid superficial encounters that lead to a damaging presumption of knowledge about difference? One part of the solution lies in attention to methodology and an approach that shifts the focus from individual identities to the sociospatial environment.

Figuring out how people construct and reproduce a sense of place is one of the biggest challenges to cultural geographers. It's difficult methodologically and requires qualitative research since "tick-the-box" surveys cannot capture the complex relationship between identity and place. More important, however, is the need to account for and analyze the *implications* of different senses of place—what does it matter or what does it mean? Cultural geography's streetwork is certainly not unique in the fact that students are sent out beyond the campus borders to explore something about the surrounding communities and to have a fieldwork experience that no classroom can provide.[6] However, unlike many community service learning projects, streetwork begins from geographic assumptions that places and senses of place are complicated, difficult to access, and constantly in flux. The focus shifts away from "identity"—sometimes translated as "how these people differ from me"—and towards questions of boundaries; the construction of insider/outsider status; authenticity; surveillance; and sense of place. Planned fieldwork should ask students to collect evidence of the sociospatial environment and to examine sociospatial difference, or the ways difference is reproduced in neighborhoods, on campuses, or on the streets.

A cultural geography streetwork project focuses our attention on issues related to street practices, practices of the everyday that give a place its "character," and how places are inhabited or what contributes to a sense of place. My own fieldwork with Leeds's geography students highlights the entrenched nature of binary oppositions for thinking about spaces and places and the powerful role of imagined geographies in our "real" experiences. The streetwork data offer more evidence for my argument in the previous chapter that border crossing and boundary transgression do not happen without considerable risk or difficulty. Also difficult is developing and sustaining a set of research practices that begin with the importance of positionality or identity, and the acknowledgment that our own locations do much to determine our ability to "see." Dominant assumptions about places may or may not be dislodged by "an encounter"; thus, the *appreciation* of difference (Burgess and Jackson) is simply not an adequate goal for research conducted out of place. Cultural geography's streetwork, never designed to be reciprocal or sustainable, cannot by itself address the problems and challenges of entering unfamiliar communities and understanding their complexities.

The following sections further describe my participant-observation research in a cultural geography class at Leeds University in England and analyze the data in terms of the lecturer's emphasis on such topics as insider/outsider, boundaries, authenticity, and sense of place. In addition to the mapping interviews, a focus of the preceding chapter, this chapter shares field notes, observations, and informal interviews resulting from the ten weeks I spent attending lectures and workshops and "hanging out" with two groups of students as they conducted their streetwork projects.

Streetwork in Leeds: The Methodological Framework

Streetwork was a major focus of the class that welcomed me as a participant-observation researcher in a ten-week module on cultural geography, an elective for third-year students in human geography.[7] Early in the course, the lecturer[8] introduced the streetwork project to students by distributing copies of the Burgess and Jackson article cited above. He shared his own experiences with streetwork as a geography student studying in London, and he conducted a series of "heuristic" exercises to guide students in choosing their place.[9]

Students were asked to form permanent streetwork groups of four to six members and to decide collaboratively on a place to visit for the duration of the six-to-eight-week project. To discourage students from choosing to investigate places within the area that they already knew, Tom guided them in selecting a place by distributing copies of an Ordnance Survey map of the Leeds area, which had all place names marked (though not all streets) (see fig. 3.5). Students were asked to study the map and identify four types of areas, some of them perhaps overlapping: no-go, ethnic, conflict, and normal. Using colored markers, students were to shade in these categories of places and then get together to discuss their shadings.[10]

Once their marks were completed, Tom asked them to look more closely at the blank or unmarked areas of their maps, and to choose a few that they might be interested in knowing more about and ultimately to agree on a location for their collaborative streetwork project. At this point, Tom clarified that they need not restrict themselves to an urban environment. Several students enrolled in this module were also taking an elective in rural geographies, and Tom used this to invite students to choose a rural location for their study. Tom emphasized that "culture" is not limited to urban life and that, with their willingness or ability to travel several miles away from campus, they need not limit themselves to urban or suburban areas.

With weekly workshops designed to help students through the process—covering methodology as well as theories of place—students had six to eight weeks to visit their place three or four times; to observe and take notes; to conduct informal interviews; to collect some historical data in order to explore themes such as those listed below; and to prepare an oral presentation that would report and analyze their findings. Following each one-hour lecture, in the "workshop hour," the streetwork groups met and either fulfilled a structured activity Tom had designed, or used their time together to plan site visits or interviews or to share what they had been reading on their own.[11]

When students were asked to choose their places for the streetwork, one group I joined was immediately attracted to the idea of visiting a rural village. They recited easily and eagerly all of the attractions, particularly the pub as a cozy, warm place to gather and the center of community life. From the assumed stone walls, fields of grazing sheep, and quiet, crime-free life, these students—like most of us—have imagined geographies of rural life. They imagined sitting down with locals at a pub and learning everything they needed to know about a place over a pint. A similar type of fantasy took hold with a group interested in the city center of Leeds. They saw themselves mingling with high-powered corporate types and entering posh office buildings, giving them a sense of what it would be like to work there.

Once a group had agreed on a location (which took an entire workshop hour), each student then listed his or her preconceptions about the place they were about to visit. Tom suggested that one member of the group collect the preconceptions and save them to be consulted later. The next task was for each group to agree on a time and place to go visit their place for an initial visit, a first impression. Most groups prepared for this initial visit by collecting maps of the area, some varied in scale or historical time period; and by searching on the Web. Students in Tom's class were advised to use the buses, buy things, ask directions, take photographs, draw maps, visit the parks or public buildings, read the local newspaper. Observations, snatches of conversation overheard, preconceptions, and first impressions—all were to be considered useful data.

The "themes" that emerge from my fieldnotes and the groups' presentations at the end of the project touch upon the following:

- Sense of place
- Insider and outsider
- Boundaries
- Change and resistance
- Commercialization and authenticity
- Surveillance and control

These themes, however, did not just "emerge naturally" from the data since they were covered in Tom's lectures. He knew that once they had begun to collect data, students would need a framework on which to hang their findings, especially when they would probably experience the overwhelming side to qualitative research methodologies. Consequently, students referred to these themes because they wanted to "get a good mark" and make sure that they were attending to the lecturer's expectations.

In the next section, I present portraits from the research of the two groups I joined as a participant-observer for the duration of this project. I discuss the research processes and interpretive accounts of two streetwork groups, the Eccup group, which studied the rural village of Eccup, and the Leeds group, which chose the financial district of the city center of Leeds. I offer these snapshots to help readers understand how streetwork played out in two groups and to illustrate some of the questions and issues that emerged from our experiences. Later, I'll draw conclusions from these two groups as well as from other streetwork projects in the class.

My aim is, on one hand, to do justice to the processes and findings of these two groups—to try to capture what occurred for them, from their initial decisions to their presentations to the class. On the other hand, my larger aim is to illustrate the challenges of a streetwork project, both methodologically and ideologically. How does one study a sense of place? It's about as difficult as studying composing because, sometimes, no amount of meticulous attention to method can "open up" a place to outsiders, to researchers who, however well intentioned, do not belong. The social production of space, especially geographies of exclusion, worked to keep these students "in their place" and made access and insights particularly difficult to achieve.

Snapshot #1: The Eccup Group

There is no culture here.

—Jake

Since I had joined them briefly the week before, the Eccup group waved me over to join them permanently. The members (all pseudonyms) were Sheila, Zoe, Julian, Kim, Mandy, and Jake.[12] For this second workshop, the group accomplished what it had been assigned to do (the first being devoted to choosing a place): to make a list, individually, of the preconceptions each had about Eccup before making their first visit, and to give these lists to one member of the group who would compile them and save them for later reference. These lists of preconceptions included: fields, green, pastures, trees, hills, a village setting, stone walls and stone cottages, farms,

cows, a pub with locals, and Emmerdale.[13] After compiling individual lists
of preconceptions, which Mandy noted had considerable overlap, the group
made arrangements for their first visit, and I joined them, a couple of days
later, for a drive out to Eccup, four miles north and slightly west of the Leeds
city center. Like good geographers, the group had two maps and intended
to begin developing a sense of place by finding the landmarks clearly visible on the map, such as a reservoir.

While students envisioned a village much like the one on the television
drama "Emmerdale," what they found on their first visit not only disap-
pointed them but set them back considerably in terms of making decisions
about their research. In two different cars, the first challenge was finding
an obvious place to park and then walk around. Fully expecting their parking place to be the pub, students were dismayed to find that it was closed
on a weekday afternoon. Even more distressing, students saw that there was
nothing to walk *to* from the pub car park. Instead of a village center, students found the lone pub on a commuter road, with no surrounding or
nearby businesses; students couldn't quite believe there was no shop or news
agent. The only discernable "center" was a group of houses, which appeared
to be converted farmhouses. Among some other markers of affluence around
these houses, there was not a soul in sight. Students did find two large
working farms, but this initial visit was characterized mostly by bafflement.

Accustomed to very different fieldwork exercises, and after a thorough
look around, Jake commented, "There is no culture here." That comment
became a point of departure for the Eccup group. Initially, students had
preconceptions and a map. Then they depended on the visual evidence of
the first visit—the very green fields and stone walls and farms they had
anticipated. Nevertheless, all they could see upon their arrival was "empty
space," and they were unable to recognize data or to connect what they were
seeing to the content of the course lectures. They couldn't imagine that the
fields or farms had any meaning in terms of culture. Until this point in the
course, about three or four weeks into the term, students may have been
operating from a notion of culture as "high culture"—that is, theaters and
museums, galleries and churches—and they struggled to understand the
concept of culture as it is *constructed*, particularly how it might be constructed in a sleepy rural commuter village. The closed pub (open at 5:00
P.M. on weekdays) and the absence of a shop really threw these students'
expectations about Eccup, and they spent considerable time near the end
of this first visit standing at an intersection of two country roads (again,
not a soul in sight) and debating whether they should, in fact, change their
place. The shift in their understanding, however, began from two research

strategies: talking to locals and discovering the history of the village. The research process of the Eccup group can be characterized by the dominance of issues related to insidership, community spirit, and authenticity.

After seeing the name Dawson (a pseudonym) on the post box in front of a farm along a main road, Zoe called to try to make an appointment to interview the owner. Given the visual clues they had about the size and success of the farm, students speculated that this farmer might be their gatekeeper figure. Sheila reported on her interview with a mechanic at the garage nicknamed "Harold the Bus" who claims that he has worked in Eccup for fifty years. He was extremely suspicious of her and what she wanted, but he did suggest that they speak to an eighty-seven-year-old man who's truly an insider, and there's some mention of a shepherd. Julian and Mandy had visited the pub during open hours, where they'd interviewed the barmaids. There doesn't seem to be a landlord—the pub's ownership seems to be in question or in transition. No one in the pub at the time of their visit was a local; the barmaids said locals are rare. One man comes in each Wednesday and a couple comes in each Thursday, but they aren't from Eccup. The pub's clientele is mostly walkers passing through. This finding does fit with students' map knowledge of Eccup as a central point for public access to paths. However, the information about the pub's clientele blows the rural village myth apart. If the pub does not have regulars, locals who come in routinely, then students end one workshop session by speculating about whether Eccup has any community or identity at all.

Through informal interviews, most of them brief exchanges, students found out that the "newest" people in the area have been there for twelve years (and twelve is apparently not enough to be a true villager). One of the informants, a farmer named John, relates that he never goes into Leeds except to shop at Christmas; he usually shops in Otley and shows his livestock in Harrogate. For the group, this becomes a way of measuring all other residents for their "authenticity." This farmer felt that Eccup was a closer community as recently as five years ago, before the pseudovillage was erected for the filming of "Emmerdale." Before this, if the residents got snowed in, everyone would check on each other. Now, the television production keeps the road open anyway—in part for the tour buses.

Intrigued by the changes the village has gone through, the history of Eccup becomes one of the group's priorities, partly because of Julian, who strongly identifies himself as a historical geographer, but also because the historical "facts," as they add up, relieve students' anxiety that they aren't going to be able to say anything about this "cultureless" village. Kim, who interviewed the vicar, is able to produce a map to illustrate changes in the parish boundaries in the 1970s. Students also traced the "gatekeeper" name—Dawson—and Julian found one living in Eccup in 1872. Eccup school, Julian reports, was built in 1846, attendance forty-three; however, the school was demolished years ago. One informant claims that "the village has disappeared." There is no community center, and people have moved, even if locally. Residents have had very little to share or unite over: there was one anecdote about a search for a body a few years ago—an event that caused big excitement initially—but nothing came of it.

The insider/outsider issue came up repeatedly,[14] for example, when Julian referred to the locals' "hatred of textile people from Bradford." During one meeting, Sheila read a comment a long-term resident made about Rookey Farm (one of the new, neat and tidy farms in the area): "They're just not our sort of people." They are "supermarket people" whereas "authentic" residents shop at the shops in Otley.

Before their initial visit, students in the Eccup group imagined a homey, close-knit village with a pub and shop as the centers of interaction. Their first visit gave a big blow to their romanticized notions, and what they concluded about Eccup couldn't contrast more with their early assumptions. After two more visits and informal interviews with a couple of farmers, waitresses in the pub, and the vicar of a nearby church, students tried to come to some conclusions about Eccup and prepare for their oral presentation. Using such terms as "a place in conflict" and a "vacuum," Mandy observed that Eccup exists below its critical mass while Sheila noted that there are no young people, no school, and that no one seems to be having kids. Julian claimed that despite the signs of gentrification, with houses selling for two or three hundred thousand pounds, there are also abandoned properties, which he sees as "residual depopulation." In the course of this research, sense of place for this group became a sense of loss, a loss of their own romanticized ideals of a rural village as well as a sense of loss in a culture they hoped and expected to find.

Snapshot #2: The Leeds Financial District Group

Out of place, even in smart clothes.

From their planning meetings in class, the Leeds financial district group (FD group) was very clear that they were *not* doing the retail/shopping district. For Anna, Elaine, Nan, Monica, and Vince, therefore, deciding where the retail district "ended" and the financial district "began" were early concerns, and they agreed that a group of imposing bank buildings, all along one street, comprised one of the clearest borders, another being a small supermarket.[15] The first site visit began at the McDonald's in St. John's Centre, a well-known landmark and the location of a busy city center bus stop. Monica had gone to the Geographic Resources Unit and copied an OS map at the scale of 1:2500, or 25.344 inches to the mile (i.e., every building represented). Monica agreed to the importance of delineating boundaries but insisted that boundaries could only be identified "on the street" and not from the maps. Nan announced that her main objective was to see where the boundaries were "transgressed." They planned for the first visit to take in initial impressions of people, the atmosphere, the architecture, and a few "facts" but mostly how it "felt" to be there. They made plans to go on different days of the week and at different times of day and evening, including a Saturday when the area would be dramatically different, abandoned by the Monday-through-Friday employees. For this first walk-through of the area, a dictaphone was passed around as group members commented incessantly about what they were seeing, like all the "To Let" signs which meant, they speculated, that a shift was taking place in the area, perhaps as the financial district moved closer to the waterfront to participate in the gentrification underway for that area. Considerable time was spent in front of a multistory car park that contained a fascinating automatic "stacker." Drivers would pull in and get out, and the car would be moved, with a combination elevator/forklift, to a slot in the car park. Many details were noted, as well: the gold-painted knobs on the tips of the wrought iron railings that separated the buildings from the sidewalks. What particularly grabbed their attention on this first visit were the many signs of CCTV surveillance and the signs in some pubs or restaurants that said "Proper dress required."

The second week of the project, Elaine and Vince reported to the group on the nine interviews they had recorded and transcribed from the day before, mostly people on fag breaks who were willing to talk to them for a few minutes about what it is like to work in the financial district, quick conversations that they had tape-recorded and transcribed. Those workers in the area interviewed by Elaine and Vince did tend to react to the architecture and buildings—comments were made about buildings that didn't seem to "fit," one in particular, and which ones were most aesthetically pleasing. Monica had done some observation in two locations and walked around, but she was convinced that her experience of the area would be patently different if she "looked like everyone else down there." Nan and Anna had visited the art gallery and the benefits office the day before, struck by their juxtaposition on the same block.

The group decided fairly early in the research process to focus their written report on "power and control." The obvious evidence about surveillance contributed to this decision, but so did the students' sensitivity to their own positionality and the issue of insider/outsider. They were painfully aware of their identity as students; there were many comments about not quite feeling comfortable there and some anecdotes about the way they were treated because of their dress. Elaine and Vince, in their usual clothes, were convinced that the reaction they got from some people hinged on their appearance: "Oh I'm very busy—no time for you." Following Monica's idea, Elaine and Vince wondered if they might return in smart clothes, with clipboards, under the guise of doing market research, and how the reactions might differ. Two of the students, Nan and Anna, did try this; they returned to the area dressed in suits and wandered around again, getting brave enough in their smart clothes to speak with, for example, a gallery owner. In addition, three of them went to a pub in the area on a Friday at five o'clock, with visions that it would be full of twenty-somethings just getting off work and ready to welcome the weekend. Contrary to their expectations, the place was occupied by older people and had no young business types at all. Even though they visited the pub in their upscale clothing, the FD group was unconvinced, finally, that clothing was the way in. Clothes, they determined, don't really change the fact that students have no real "purpose" there—or not a purpose that is accepted by the function of the area. They have no office to get to, no clients waiting, no business to be conducted. Students knew they didn't belong there, even in smart clothes, and they began to realize one less-obvious but no less insidious function of all the CCTV cameras that functioned to monitor these city blocks: these students felt watched and out of place.

For obvious reasons, this group concentrated on the built environment and concluded, roughly, that the sense of place of the financial district of Leeds evolved from the buildings and the power and control that they represented. Their attentiveness to architecture and the built environment led them to observe that the lobbies or reception areas of the office buildings were designed to query visitors right away—designed with a "funneling" effect—making it impossible to walk right past. In other words, if outsiders are bold enough to enter the large doors of an imposing building, especially one where they don't have any real business, then they will almost immediately encounter a security guard or information desk whose function is to screen callers and to protect the time and safety of workers within. After some reading on the connection between architecture and control, Anna set forth a thesis that built space affects and determines the activities there. She read passages to the group documenting a long historical precedent for structures of power to be built physically separate and higher (cathedrals or castles).

The group came to dismiss the idea that gender was an issue in this environment; they reasoned that there was no way to find out if the women were really secretaries instead of power brokers. One interview seemed to indicate that women and men were "equal" under the guise of "doing business," that being part of the business world united them somehow. Elaine and Monica agreed that not gender but age seemed a key distinction among people, and there were many comments about how young the suited workers looked. This feature of the crowds made these students even more eager to find connections between themselves and the young business execs.

There was agreement, however, that people of color and the differently abled were not at all visible. In two visits, Monica had seen only one black person, but Anna piped up about how many were at the benefits office. Still, in the presentation, this group was more interested in the built environment and power and control generally rather than issues directly related to race, class, or gender. Nan was hoping to find graffiti as an example of transgression, but the group concluded that the absence of graffiti helped them make their case for the rigid control of the area. Despite the group's interest in exploring how identity is created through place, they did not pursue identities other than those represented by power suits and briefcases.

This group was particularly overwhelmed by bits of data, lists upon lists of observations they weren't sure what to do with: was it significant that there were flower boxes beneath the windows of the solicitors' offices? Because the financial district was so full of "signs" and codes—dozens if not hundreds of buildings; heavy traffic during certain hours; bus stops and many pedestrians—this group, especially in contrast to the Eccup group, faced the challenge of analyzing a tall pile of data, much of it disparate or unconnected observations.

In writing about the control of urban public space at the end of the century, Lees emphasizes that an "overriding concern with 'control,'" mostly as city planners and officials try to practice it, tells us nothing about how space(s) can be appropriated and contested (250). Even though these student-researchers were concerned with issues of control—the area's features led them to this emphasis—they also dismissed evidence that would have focused on challenges to or gaps in that control.

Some Conclusions about Both Groups

Because of the different types of places they chose to explore—one an area marked by pastures and the other by buildings—the experiences of the two groups were quite dramatically different. The day I visited the financial district with the FD group, we noticed a thousand details: different approaches to jaywalking, the way the streets swelled with pedestrians at noon, the absence of litter, and the strict parking regulations. The only dictaphone was passed around constantly, with each member accumulating a long list of details they'd observed. With the Eccup group there was more like stunned silence. We certainly noticed the manure smell right away, and we saw a woman in the door of a farmhouse watching us, but there wasn't nearly the same cascade of details. Because of what they perceived as a "lack of data," the Eccup group was far more confused and at a loss for what to do. In fact, during this first visit, the Eccup group spent considerable time trying to decide if they should change their place! If this same group had been invited to use the methodologies of physical geography to study Eccup, they would have quite comfortably begun surveying and mapping the terrain.

The "nature" of these places led students to concentrate on different modes of interpretation. The Eccup group—studying a rural village—became increasingly interested in history while the financial district group was more interested in architecture and postmodernism. Maps and interviews with locals were far more important to the Eccup group while the FD group concentrated almost exclusively on the built environment. The Eccup group began with what they perceived as empty space; thus, they depended very much on research data to "fill" their presentation. The FD group, on the other hand, was rather overwhelmed by details (observed), and they retreated to theories and a published literature to make sense of it all. They needed ways to *interpret* while the Eccup group searched for ways to *understand.*

As the twelve groups in Tom's cultural geography module chose their places to investigate, the first signs of these students' own cultural positionality became evident. There were only two exceptions to the overwhelming interest in rural villages: the FD group and another that chose a section of Roundhay Road in order to examine the contrasting neighborhoods at two points along the road. (Harehills is the most Muslim-populated area of Leeds, along and off Roundhay Road). Therefore, only one group out of twelve chose to encounter a place characterized by racial, ethnic, or religious difference; none of the groups chose Burmantofts or Seacroft or Lincoln Green, places characterized by tower blocks and a very short distance from the university. From the earliest decisions made in this project, then, students demonstrated a reluctance to enter neighborhoods they perceived as marked by forms of cultural difference. These students as first-years had been warned, after all, to stay out of the no-go area of Chapletown (see chapter 3). Without being told in this instance, they extended that warning to other areas of Leeds occupied by residents of color. Like their tendency to stay in familiar neighborhoods or follow the same routes through town, these white, middle-class students were not eager to take on the (understandable) challenges of going into an area where they were not "the same," where they would be immediately noticed and labeled as outsiders. It's true, too, that most students were already familiar with some of the ethnic areas of Leeds because they were also student neighborhoods—namely, Hyde Park. Because Tom told them to choose a place with which they were unfamiliar, the *student* residential areas, however characterized by diversity, were not an option.

Despite the fact that Tom had lectured on "positionality" and that, in the Leeds FD group, Nan insisted on its importance to their experience, none of the students in the class made the connection between their own whiteness and the choices they made in exploring unfamiliar places. The Leeds FD group accounted fully for their positionality *as students,* defined by age and mode of dress, but the category "race" barely made in onto the map, the only exception being the Leeds FD group's observation that the only people of color they saw were in the benefits office, a point they did not pursue beyond a passing comment in the presentation.

Students' reluctance to encounter glaring racial/cultural difference is one of the themes to which I keep returning; they were ignoring not only South Asians in native dress or Afro-Caribbeans but also the working class "pikeys" that Anna refers to in the preceding chapter. They were attracted to the places most familiar to them or those they wanted to identify with—the rural villages or bustling business district. Their reluctance results, of course, from culture and ideology, structures that design and regulate places to exclude those who don't belong. The imposing buildings of a city's financial district don't need signs on the doors saying "no students in jeans allowed," but there may as well have been such signs. The beauty of surveillance is, in fact, that it reproduces itself. Even without signs saying "proper dress required," students learned very quickly that without both power suits and the positions or authority that they symbolize, even as privileged white students they did not belong in the city's financial district.

Because Tom's lectures had covered "insider/outsider" as one possible mode of analysis for their data, students found it very difficult to talk about place *without* relying on an insider/outsider dichotomy. Students were tempted to simply label their interviewees as one or the other, but then discussions about *who* was *which* began to drag out with no satisfying conclusion. At one meeting with the Eccup group, they seemed relieved when I suggested that they might think of those terms, rather than in a binary relationship, as operating along a continuum—that a certain individual wasn't necessarily one or the other but existed somewhere in between. With traditional container metaphors for space and place, insider and outsider make sense as categories for analysis, but in borderlands or thirdspace, firm conclusions about status or experience or belonging become fuzzier.

Binary logic reappeared in their discussions of authentic and inauthentic places as well as in their efforts to delineate boundaries. It proves very difficult, if not impossible, to define a place without comparing it to other places. The Leeds group could only decide on the boundaries of the financial district by considering the area of the retail district, and the Eccup group could make sense of that village area only by comparing it to the fictional Emmerdale. Even in trying to capture something as nuanced and complex as a sense of place, dichotomies rule. When analyzing geographic difference, inside and outside become all too handy and too easy even for students who understand, theoretically, that boundaries shift and change.

Students did learn, however, about their own role in the construction of knowledge and in the reproduction of cultural norms: "there was no culture" in Eccup until students pieced together the history, interviewed some residents, and toured the Weetwood Farm. When they found out that the manager of the farm couldn't meet with them one day because he was attending a computer class, they began to consider how little they really knew about this village and how much they were relying on assumptions and fictions (like, for example, farmers use tractors but not computers). When they then found, to their great surprise, that the same farm had a Website (<http://www.weetwoodfold.co.uk>) advertising its Highland cattle, students began to realize their own limited notions of culture and how difficult it is, methodologically, to understand difference.

Perhaps most importantly, the students' own class biases or cultural position determined their "findings," and this is, of course, one of the most haunting features of qualitative research (something of which I am well aware). Data is gathered and analyzed in ways that reflect the researchers' own class or level of "empowerment" in the culture. For example, one group, investigating two very different neighborhoods within two miles of each other along Roundhay Road, asked residents of each area to sketch, freehand, their own mental maps of their neighborhoods. The students reported a common resistance to this request by people who claimed not to have any drawing ability, a problem with this research method noted by others (Wiegand and Stiell). But the Roundhay group analyzed its findings in ways that were disturbingly simplistic as well as dependent on class bias. For example, when the maps of those living in the more middle-class area were deemed to be neater, tidier, and more creative than the maps drawn by those in the poorer, working-class area, the students thereby concluded *that the middle-class residents were happier* in their neighborhood and more satisfied with their surroundings.

This is more evidence for Herzberg's concern that hegemonic attitudes are not "overcome" by the experience of fieldwork—that, in fact, students or any researchers find what they expect to find or find what their ideological positioning enables them to see. The Roundhay group's conclusion also illustrates how difficult it is to ask people of privilege to see differences as ideologically inscribed rather than as some sort of personal failing. It also drives home the fact that even well-designed streetwork projects, with some devotion to methodology, are not going to "enlighten" students about entrenched forms of difference. The most striking pattern in my observations replicates the finding of the mental mapping interviews: students stayed out of areas they perceived as undesirable, or perhaps threatening, or those places they just didn't imagine themselves in. They *did* imagine themselves in tranquil rural villages, surrounded by other white, middle-class people who have good jobs and gardens. Thus, students chose places to investigate that fit with their own class identity and their imagined sense of community: two groups, for example, chose villages near Leeds known as tourist sites, probably with populations 98 percent white. One chose Haworth, twenty miles from Leeds and home of the Brontë museum, and one chose Esholt, the (former) television filming site for the popular British soap opera, "Emmerdale Farm." In other words, students chose sites that they were already familiar with through British television and the tourism industry—places already "known" and assumed, therefore, safe.

Despite students' awareness, through the lectures, of what Tom called "operations of nostalgia," most groups, like the Eccup group, did in fact choose to study what they hoped would be an "authentic" village, complete with stone walls and a cozy pub. However, as students discovered firsthand, villages have lost much of their romantic appeal in the change from close-knit farm communities to privatized housing for wealthy commuters, and some villages have sold out to tourism. Those who live in the village are rarely "at home"; they are instead making a living and doing the shopping and being entertained elsewhere. While the authenticity of rural villages did not hold up for these students, they also recognized that many of those who live in these villages now represent economic success. Those who encountered villages came away feeling nostalgic for the old days of England, but, at the same time, they had adopted a much more cynical view of communities and residents living in harmony. Immersed as they were in authenticity, students' notions of community came into question as they debated boundaries and borders. Are boundaries determined by map or by local knowledge?

The Eccup group concluded the latter, and they approached this question by trying to find out where residents did their weekly shopping. Residents were true locals if they shopped in Otley, going into Leeds only for holiday shopping once a year. They were not authentic residents if they shopped at the major supermarkets in Leeds.

In fact, for both groups I observed, one of the major concerns or focuses of the initial visit had to do with boundaries and borders. Not by assignment (i.e., Tom did not ask them to determine the boundaries) but by inclination or training, these geography students wanted to know where these areas began and ended—and how an outsider could tell. The place to start, for them, was to get out and walk, with a map in hand, and to drive down all of the significant roads in the area. At one point, the Eccup group stood at an intersection for quite some time, on the edge of a residential area, referring to the map and trying to decide where their own boundaries should fall for the purposes of their research.

The Eccup group also realized the difficulty of determining sense of place, as this exchange between Zoe and Sheila at one of the meetings illustrates:

Z: There's this argument that says 'Do you get your sense of place from people rather than from the actual location?' Some people say that you do get your sense of place from people; it doesn't matter where you are, it's connection between the same sort of people. But this author was arguing that location does come into it as well because you've got to also have a physical sense of place. But with these farms, I got the idea that the sense of place has got more to do with the people.

S: Definitely. We didn't get a sense of place when we first went there, from the landscape; we only got it from talking to people.

Z: I feel like I'm in the middle of a meadow, I just don't feel like I really belong.

S: I found it sort of sad that the people we spoke to denied the fact that it is a place, denied the fact that it's a community—now, today, in the year 2000, yet they all mentioned the same names even though they deny they've got a community. "No, no, I haven't got anything to do with this; no community here." Like Allen Dawson who said to us about the people who'd moved into Rookey Farm, he had no sense of community with them, yet he knew exactly what their jobs were, exactly what their names were, and exactly what they do on the farm

Z: He knew more about them than I'd probably know about my next door neighbors.

S: Exactly! Didn't the people in the pub say that it's not a community? [Someone says "uh-huh."] But I think it is; I think it really is.

On one hand, the dilemma of the Eccup group illustrates why Burgess and Jackson named their fieldwork project "Streetwork" and sent students to areas of London: it was not necessarily created for the exploration of nonurban areas like Eccup. Cultural geographers like Burgess and Jackson believe that for too long geographers have researched "fields" using the tools of physical geography, measurements, and objective data, approaches that do little to explain how humans interact with place and how culture is constructed via place. Thus, Burgess and Jackson emphasize the importance of the urban environment, where there are "different kinds of neighbourhoods and a reasonably active street culture" (155).

Had Tom, the lecturer, insisted that students explore an urban area of Leeds with which they were unfamiliar, twelve parts of inner Leeds would have been the object of study, and this would have increased the chances that students encountered neighborhoods of distinct difference from their own white, middle-class experience. I think Tom wanted to give students the "rural" option because of the rural geographies elective course some students were taking, but I doubt that he anticipated how many students would choose rural villages over the areas of Leeds that would have been far richer in visual data and much more occupied with potential interviewees. Street practices in a bustling city environment can be observed at almost any hour of any day, but there wasn't much action on the one road in Eccup. Perhaps Tom was uncomfortable with "forcing" students into parts of Leeds that students would have found "alien" if not actually frightening.[16] At the same time, however, if students had remained in urban areas, they might have assumed that culture is only a feature of urbanity or can only be found in busy, bustling places. The village of Eccup also had a "culture," and its workings can be traced even in places that seem quiet, deserted, unpopulated.

Was streetwork a "success" for these students? They did leave the campus of the university and work collaboratively towards an understanding of a place that was unknown to them. They also had the opportunity to practice qualitative research methods, those they had learned in a required second-year course, and to turn their data into a class presentation. However, there is and was no reciprocity or sustainability to streetwork, and like other qualitative research endeavors, streetwork generates questions without necessarily providing answers. Still, its methodology gives advocates of community service or student activism a place to begin with activist fieldwork that can lead to understandings of difference.

Implications for Service Learning

We can say that we want students to encounter difference in order to understand the workings of ideology in our culture, but the very same ideology is working *against* students as they set out on assigned encounters with difference. Therefore, I am unconvinced that any particular method can necessarily open up a community or a street culture to "outsiders" who have no interest in the culture beyond fulfilling an assignment for university credit. While a responsible and ethical methodology is necessary for all research projects, no amount of sophisticated methodology can overcome ideology or allow us to step out of it for a clearer view. Thus, I turn to street-work with a keen sense of its limitations.

Streetwork may expose some geographies of exclusion and how they operate, and it can help us to understand sociospatial logic, workings of power, sites of difference. However, I am not quite prepared to argue that streetwork as conceived and practiced by cultural geographers can address or resolve Herzberg's very legitimate concern that students' experiences in community literacy centers, for example, do little to give them a social imagination. Despite our best efforts, students remain convinced that mis-fortune can be overcome by a bootstraps mentality or that homelessness is the result of individual circumstances. Streetwork as practiced in cultural geography does not offer "the answer" to these dilemmas, especially when it is limited to an appreciation of difference through a superficial encoun-ter with an unfamiliar place.

However, in order to come closer to the goal of educating students about cultural difference, composition practitioners need to inform community service learning projects with the methodological emphasis of streetwork. First, fieldwork assignments or community service projects should devote time and care to *methodology* so that students have a way of analyzing their experiences in some depth and accounting for their own locatedness. Sec-ond, students need not be sent off the campus for them to have plenty of data about geographies of exclusion, the politics of space, or the construc-tion of sociospatial differences. Finally, service learning should be informed by a more radical notion of activist fieldwork, which is less about volun-teerism and more about intervening to effect social change.[17]

As many scholars have admitted, one of service learning's biggest limi-tations results when students fall back on "How can we help these people?" instead of the harder question, "Why are conditions this way?" While ad-vocates of service learning will testify to the transformative nature of these assignments—that students are changed and enlightened and that many of them continue to serve in their assigned and then adopted communities long after the required part ends—the starting point is, nevertheless, one of a requirement being imposed by an authority, that is, they "have" to go in order to get course credit. As Kathryn Forbes and her coauthors point out in "Punishing Pedagogy: The Failings of Forced Volunteerism," community service programs fail, backfire, or are hugely problematic when students, like criminal offenders, are forced into volunteerism. A prevailing attitude in many communities is that those who serve others might be righting a wrong rather than working to change the status quo. Eileen Schell's students, enrolled in a section of "Writing and Learning in the Community," discovered that residents of Syracuse, New York, were not particularly welcoming to those students who were delivering their meals. She writes, "One resident even confronted John, . . . about what 'he had done' to warrant his service. . . . This community resident thought of service as 'forced restitution,' as a sentence the student had received for bad behavior at the university."[18]

A more insidious problem, however, is that the assigned encounter with difference often "devolve[s] into a cultural safari into the jungle of 'otherness'" (Forbes et al. 158). If courses require volunteer work without also requiring a critique of volunteerism, they write, "community service [becomes] at best an exercise in observing otherness and at worst a missionary expedition" (162). Forbes and her coauthors point out that the push towards volunteer work in the curriculum tends to ignore all of the work that has been done in women's studies on grassroots organizing and coalition building. In addition to the sometimes unacknowledged burden that students with service requirements may present to local organizations, as Schell's anecdote illustrates, residents and "the public" think of community service as a type of punishing pedagogy, and one of the challenges, then, is to educate the community, in part, by being able to answer Lorie Goodman's question "*Why* are you doing this?"

Goodman poses this question asked by a woman who was a "guest" at a mission in downtown Los Angeles. Eyeing the students suspiciously, the woman said "Why are you doing this?" Goodman, like all those engaged in service learning, had to do some soul searching about her own pedagogical motivations and ethical grounding for requiring service at a homeless shelter (59–60). On campuses, in particular, populated by a large percentage of white, middle-class, young-adult-aged bodies (like Goodman's students at Pepperdine University), it's tempting to want to give students, often sheltered by their home cultures or by various geographic limits, the experience of seeing some exoticized Other. As Goodman admits, for those who claim to have never seen a homeless person, instructors want to respond by saying, "Let's go, and I'll show you some."

Students and their instructors take with them their preconceived notions, media-driven images, and packaged stereotypes as baggage that is impossible to leave at home and often see themselves as "liberal saviors" (Schutz and Gere 133). To overcome a self-centered arrogance requires an examination of the structural mechanisms that make "difference" different in the first place.

As many service advocates ask themselves, how much understanding can develop from one afternoon's visit to a homeless shelter or a food bank, even if students do write reflectively about it afterwards? Avoiding superficial encounters begins with the recognition, already in place among service learning advocates, that one assignment, one semester, is not going to cut it; this is why it's important to make long-term commitments to communities and to create sustainable projects.

Writing "about" the community keeps more distance between insiders and outsiders, solving the problem that Sibley identifies but creating another one: students or other servers form no attachments and cannot fully understand the "community" in ways that would develop with long-term contact. Writing *about* the community does not require the depth of understanding that writing *for* or *with* the community does (these prepositional distinctions come from Deans). Most difficult but also most preferable is the writing *with,* which supports the idea that public service is not about helping others but is an effort to join others "as relative equals in a common project of social change" (Schutz and Gere 146). Writing with others will help to achieve a common project of social change, but achieving this in one semester is next to impossible.

Unfortunately, when service learning comes to mean "outside," it reinforces the belief in an ivory tower, a golden space for learning and opportunity, where differences are erased by privilege and where everyone is treated "the same." Instead, community service learning might be a site in composition studies where the notion of "community" continues to be interrogated. In the conclusion to his critique of community in the study of writing, Joe Harris urges us to "reserve our uses of *community* to describe the workings of . . . specific and local groups" (20, his emphasis). However, as the experience of the Leeds streetwork groups illustrates, "community" may be an elusive, shifting, fluid notion, even in a local context. Those investigating the financial district of Leeds certainly didn't detect any "community," and neither did those who fully expected to, the group studying the village of Eccup. Community remains a concept firmly attached to the ideologies of authenticity and nostalgia, and in that attachment, it becomes difficult to see the differences among residents or members, or the points of contention.

Since designing, contributing to, and completing "a common project of social change" proves to be difficult logistically, one challenge, then, is to come as close to that goal as possible, but to allow for alternatives or adaptations. As one example, since different communities with different histories and agendas can be found on most college campuses, students don't need to go very far away from the classroom to participate in social change movements or grassroots activism. The college or university environment has plenty to offer in terms of mapping geographies of exclusion, and large-scale, long-term projects are not the only option for introducing students to acts of dissent.

Aaron Schutz and Anne Ruggles Gere conclude their article "Service Learning and English Studies: Rethinking 'Public' Service," with a note about method:

> Despite our best intentions, if we are not careful we may end up reinforcing ideologies and assumptions that we had hoped to critique. *How* we step outside the classroom, how we enter into service learning relationships with communities beyond our own, will be crucial in determining our success. (147, their emphasis)

While these authors give a nod to the importance of method, they do not explore this "how" in their article, at least not in the practical sense.

While they emphasize that public service would require students "to enter relationships with *communities* and not with easily isolated individuals" (145, their emphasis), Schutz and Gere offer little towards a set of practices for such "entering." It's a familiar principle within cultural studies and postmodern theory that our constant immersion in culture makes perspective difficult to achieve: it takes some distance or a jolt of unfamiliarity to get people to "see" the ways culture operates. But this jolt of unfamiliarity must be accompanied by a set of tools to help students *analyze* what they witness, not simply record their impressions. One alternative for reform involves shifting attention to a place-based encounter, to the methodologies suggested by cultural geography and streetwork.

Students can begin to understand the geographies of exclusion just as well on a college campus as they can by being sent "outside," although it is equally important for them to see the university as part of a larger community. Along with sending students to communities that surround and support the university, we also need to encourage their understanding of the politics of space in the immediate university environment.

Research projects of all types, but especially geographical ones, can and should introduce or reinforce the skills of collecting and analyzing data, testing hypotheses or assumptions, and contributing to an ongoing conversation about a topic. Students must be asked to analyze from data they have collected, but they also need the tools to conduct a more structural analysis of culture, one that would encourage them to make connections beyond the site of their encounter. A set of tools can be developed from the social sciences (sociology, psychology, anthropology, geography) whose disciplines put such a high value on fieldwork.

Feminist research methods, in particular, can help students to develop an awareness of the pretense of objectivity and the importance of situating oneself in the research process. Feminist researchers try to involve willing "participants" rather than examine "subjects" and try to remain conscious of the problems with imposing one's own agenda. From a critique of positivism, feminist researchers try to generate questions and conduct analyses from the perspective of women's experiences, or from the location of the other. Ideally, feminist research also has a "consciousness raising component" (Gilbert 90).

Ellen Cushman brings many of these principles to bear in an essay titled "The Public Intellectual, Service Learning, and Activist Research," where she outlines "activist fieldwork" as a cornerstone of a service learning course, a model that combines "postmodern ethnographic techniques with notions of reciprocity and dialogue" (332). Praxis research in service learning can begin with a place-based encounter that insists on accounting fully for "where" the research project originates and develops. However, social science fieldwork doesn't typically ask researchers to "give something back" to the communities they visit. If students benefit from the project by earning college credit, good grades, or the rewards of publishing research findings, then they must, in an ethical research model, find ways to reciprocate or ways to form a long-term relationship with the community.

Cultural geography may give us a window on the construction of difference that other disciplines or approaches do not. Still, I'm not convinced that the Leeds students, through their streetwork projects, encountered forms of difference that truly challenged their own entrenched senses of privilege and entitlement. Streetwork in various forms can certainly *complicate* students' understandings of the relationship between public and private space, between culture and identity, and the scope of boundaries. Understanding more of the forms of alienation and exclusion that students and others face in the everyday can contribute to a richer, deeper awareness of how place constructs or reproduces these forms of alienation; for example, how the built environment of a downtown financial district can exclude all those not dressed in power suits, or how the design of park benches, as Mike Davis shows, keeps the homeless from lying down on them (233–35).

Thus, we need in our college curriculums forms of pedagogy and structured assignments that *do* ask students to analyze the geographies of exclusion, the ways in which certain people are kept out or made to feel out of place. Cultural geography streetwork projects offer one model for guided, interactive fieldwork that asks students to try to understand, and thereby construct, a sense of place. But as these students' choices and processes illustrate, most people tend to resist a direct confrontation with difference as they try to reproduce the types of places in which they feel comfortable. These students tended to stick close to home, both for their class projects and in their lifeworlds generally.

Even for forms of fieldwork that are not geographic in discipline, our focus must shift away from identity—that is, "how these people differ from me"—and towards questions of boundaries and movement, locatedness or surveillance, and sense of place. We must engage more fully with the geographical construction of difference—especially as it influences texts and discourses—and begin to consider teaching and learning, reading and writing, from the standpoint of moving through the world: through forms of walking, mapping, and dwelling. While the assigned encounter with difference can be important in giving students the opportunity and motivation to encounter cultural difference, many students will venture out of their habitual neighborhoods or off their usual pathways only if required to do so. Given these realities, it is important to consider the construction of dwelling, or staying put, and to understand its role in the formation of identities and in acts of writing, particularly when dwelling, too, is impacted by geographies of exclusion. That's the goal of the next chapter.

5

LEARNING TO DWELL:
INHABITING SPACES AND DISCOURSES

All identities are a fluid amalgam of memories of places and origins,
constructed by and through fragments and nuances, journeys and
rests, of movements between.
            —Linda McDowell, *Gender, Identity and Place*

In attempting to study and understand places and spaces—their richness
and variety and mysteries—cultural geographers often use the image of
a *palimpsest,* the imprint of marks on a tablet, overwritten by other marks.
How can writing and composing practices be studied, the Leeds students
might suggest, as "the sum of all the erasures and over-writings" (Crang 22)?
Like a parchment used for writing where earlier symbols remain visible—
a never-quite-clean slate—writing's materiality leaves traces on the text, on
the page or screen, or on the writer. Studying writing/composing as a palimpsest means acknowledging the vague or faint traces left by homeplaces,
changes in the landscape, mental maps, or spatial memory. Places are pal-
impsests, cultural geographers agree, but how to "read the land" is a contentious issue, a tough question. In this disciplinary context of rhetoric and
composition studies, we work with texts, in large part, print and electronic—not landscapes or urban streets. In any case, we're a long way from
the days of parchment, and writing as a palimpsest is, admittedly, just another metaphor standing in for something we don't understand very well
despite years of research or experience. But it is a metaphor that captures
very well writing's complexities and the way in which "inextricably intertwined temporal, social, and spatial relations are being constantly reinscribed, erased, and reinscribed again" (Soja, *Thirdspace* 18). Trying to read
the (material) traces of texts—in their infinite variety—takes time, energy,
method, and imagination.

Geographies of rhetoric and writing begin with the assertion that the way we map the world is a direct but complex result of gender, race, class, and abilities; images and feelings get imprinted in our heads and on our bodies, affecting how we walk through a neighborhood, choose an apartment, find our way across campus, or navigate texts or acts of literacy. In this final chapter, I want to think harder about how to reconcile (or encourage) some of the tensions between metaphor and materiality, especially as those tensions are enacted through practices of inhabitance and embodiment. I argue that learning to dwell, even when those places are imaginary like texts, might encourage a willingness to encounter difference. The concept of dwelling, then, is a third spatial practice I want to claim for geographies of writing: spatial practices related to dwelling have much in common with spatial practices related to textual production; texts, like dwellings, need to be planned, built, and then occupied, filled with meaning, significance, or history. They need to be *arranged,* and those arrangements are often enacted through memory. As earlier chapters have attempted to illustrate, spatial practices are habits adopted in a variety of "first places," whether those be homes or rooms or other settings we often refer to as private space. These habits and patterns go with us as we navigate public space; they "go with us" as part of our bodies and minds.

Organized roughly by different spatial scales (the body, homes, institutions), this chapter argues for attention to *dwellings*—the places we most intimately or frequently occupy—and to *dwelling,* as a way of being in the world that helps us re-imagine acts of writing and theories of composing. In mapping some sites where spatial practices of dwelling and composing come together in both exhilarating and frustrating senses of space, I try to show that dwelling as *metaphor* is helpful in re-imagining acts of writing in *material* ways even though the relationship is a messy one. Constructed as neither public nor private but somewhere in thirdspace, dwelling is a set of practices as well as a sense of place.

My exploration of dwelling raises questions about forms of exclusion and segregation, not in just neighborhoods or communities but also in discourses. Acts of dwelling in a small apartment or a neighborhood park or in on-line environments are contingent upon material conditions and circumstances. When the "place" is crafted through language, how can dwelling happen? And in imaginary dwellings, don't we tend to neglect the consequences of the material, as chapter 1 argued? I'll take up these questions in exploring what practices of dwelling might tell us about spaces for learning, including campuses or software packages, and how dwelling practices for writing invite more attention to the rhetorical canons of memory and arrangement.

Writers dwell in ideas to make them their own; they squat, intellectually, before moving on. This idea of "inhabiting" discursive spaces connects, of course, with concepts from classical rhetoric—*ethos* as haunt, for example—and invites us to revisit the connections between habits and places, between memories and places, between our bodies and the material world. Our earliest dwellings, some believe, become sedimented within structures of feeling that contribute to our responses to all other places.

In the social production of space, Soja's trialectics of spatiality, dwellings are full of classic contradictions and tensions: homes are comforting but reproduce the gendered politics of the culture and often harbor angry, dysfunctional people. Universities are centers for learning but are also organized to keep many outsiders from feeling welcome. The borders of dwellings keep people in or out but as Anzaldúa shows, can create opportunities for different kinds of "crossing" or resistance. All spatial practices, then, contain some of the contradictions embedded in the social production of space. On one hand, placemaking and "nesting" are deeply satisfying human activities, and working to sustain long-term communities is a hugely important social and political goal; on the other hand, the more that people are occupationally and residentially segregated, the more that boundaries harden (Pratt and Hanson).

For composition studies, Richard Marback claims many of these ideas for writing as placemaking, defined as "a material act of building and maintaining spaces that is at the same time an ideological act of fashioning places where we can feel we belong, where we create meaning, and where we organize our relationships to others" ("Learning" 58). How can we "inhabit places verbally as well as physically" (62)? In his attempt to link inhabiting with writing, Marback turns to the curricula and languages of urban planning: "If the city could speak, what would it say to us?"

In inviting students to inhabit discourses (Marback), we must remember that dwelling can also be an act of resistance to the dominant culture (hooks). Writing as dwelling, like writing as travel, cannot stand on its own as a theory of composing or of writing instruction; dwelling makes travel possible just as travel is meaningless without forms of dwelling (Clifford). On one hand, dwelling is necessary as both metaphor and set of material practices to resist the attraction—in theories, discourses, and images of postmodernism—to movement and travel and being on the go. On the other hand, dwelling can also prevent us from encountering difference—a shield from others, from those who do not occupy the same space; dwellings offer a respite from racism, ignorance, crime, fatigue, even weather. Full of contradictions that reflect the social production of space, the concept of dwelling illustrates how geographies of exclusion operate even in intimate, vividly remembered, or metaphorical spaces; dwelling reproduces itself, shaping our practices, as we leave the home and move through the world.

Dwelling on Dwelling

Learning to dwell begins with some thoughtfulness about the meanings of dwelling. I'll touch here on two reflections, Martin Heidegger's "Building Dwelling Thinking" and Gaston Bachelard's *The Poetics of Space.* Heidegger asks "What is it to dwell?" and "How does building belong to dwelling?" Dwelling on the language—for it is fundamentally an essay about language (Do we inhabit language or does language inhabit us?)—Heidegger defines building as dwelling—to build is to dwell; "that is, being on the earth . . . remains for man's everyday experience that which is from the outset 'habitual'" (147). Human beings are dwellers, and "dwelling itself is always a staying with things," a preserving (151). Heidegger claims that "Man's relation to locations, and through locations to spaces, inheres in his dwelling. The relationship between man and space is none other than dwelling, strictly thought and spoken" (157). Building, as he characterizes it, becomes a "letting-dwell," and dwelling is *the basic character* of Being" (160, his emphasis).

In a similarly phenomenological reflection on dwelling, Gaston Bachelard in *The Poetics of Space* writes a "topoanalysis" of the intimate nature of houses as dwellings—the spaces that allow us to daydream—asserting that "the values that belong to daydreaming mark humanity in its depths" (6). Bachelard identifies the common and important phenomenon of dreaming about the house we were born in, a house that becomes "physically inscribed in us" (14). In chapters titled "Drawers, Chests and Wardrobes" and "Nests," Bachelard explores a number of images as intimate spaces tied to memory and as functions of inhabiting the world.

In Bachelard's sense, then, dwellings are hugely important physical spaces that become embodied through acts of living and remembering and daydreaming. However, phenomenological approaches are only one way to treat dwelling. More political concepts of home, like those from bell hooks, remind us how habits in rooms of houses are shaped by patriarchy and capitalism—like kitchens being assigned to women. Dwellings do not need to be particularly inviting to outsiders, nor do they have to be "homes" in the traditional sense. Migratory peoples or nomads—even students who consider themselves transients—learn to *make do* with temporary or makeshift or substandard housing. Learning to dwell doesn't necessarily mean "loving" a place and settling in happily or for years at a time; it means paying attention to place, not just to the borders that surround it, and building thirdspaces. Learning to dwell means tapping into the circulation of practices that don't show up on a map or in a photograph of a village. For many of our concerns in composition and literacy studies, learning to dwell or recognizing the spatial practices of dwelling are important for encountering discourses of otherness, unfamiliar texts or speech practices, or rhetorical moves that surprise us.

Inhabiting writing, learning to dwell, can only begin with an understanding of how geography constructs difference and how differences become inscribed geographically. That is, until we see how *place* affects other social, cultural, and economic differences, the turn to geography becomes just another way to interpret spatial metaphors or just another gesture towards interdisciplinary research. It is important to understand geographies as embodied and how the process of the social construction of space occurs at the level of the body, not just at the level of the city or street or nation. People's responses to place—which are shaped in large part by their bodies, by the physical characteristics they carry with them through the spatial world—determine whether they will "enter" at all, or rush through, or linger—and those decisions contribute to how a space is "used" or reproduced. Bodies and places impact upon each other; a body becomes marked with the residue of a place, but places are also changed by the presences of bodies. Those changes can't happen, however, if people won't cross borders, won't engage with a new place, or can't overcome their fear or aversion to a particular location.

Bodies in Space/Places as Embodied

Bodies matter to place and space. As Linda McDowell puts it, "bodies in space raise all sorts of questions about the space and place they occupy" (*Gender* 40). She suggests that our awareness of our own body in space is never sharper than when we are sitting in an airline seat in economy class. How bodies juggle for more personal space in such cramped quarters—like occupying a crowded elevator or lecture hall—brings home the relationship between our bodies and space. One's sense of personal boundaries ("I need my space"), however, is culturally constructed, and the more economic privilege one has, the more privacy—witness the growth of gated communities in America. Clearly, families and communities in most of the world do not have the same requirements for privacy that the wealthy have.

When Adrienne Rich names the body "the geography closest in," she does so with a deep awareness of the ways in which experiences in the social world are structured by one's race, class, gender, body type—and how, in turn, the body then carries with it signs of those experiences, signs of struggle.

Marked on her own body are her Jewishness and lesbianism and motherhood; she carries Baltimore with her and her father's voice inside her, and cultivating this awareness of one's own body helps her to resist speaking *for* the bodies or experiences or histories of others:

> To say "my body" reduces the temptation to grandiose assertions. . . . To locate myself in my body means more than understanding what it has meant to me to have a vulva and clitoris and uterus and breasts. It means recognizing this white skin, the places it has taken me, the places it has not let me go. ("Notes" 215–16)

Rich reflects for the rest of the essay on that whiteness as a location for questioning the authority of white-centered theory, and for asking, "'Who is *we?*'" (231). For feminist theorists, beginning with the body as the geography closest in is a way of resisting patriarchal epistemologies that insist on objectivity or subscribe to a Cartesian mind-body split.

For women, the body is a site for reproduction, and in this way, women may be more keenly aware of body or bodily politics. The fact that women's bodies can be occupied by another being—that women's bodies sustain life—has given rise to the prominent yet problematic woman-as-nature and landscape-as-woman metaphor. In addition, women's rights to control their own bodies or the cultural pressures on women to have aesthetically pleasing bodies make issues of physicality and identity particularly keen for women: "The primary physical site of personal identity, the scale of the body is socially constructed. The place of the body marks the boundary between self and other in a social as much as a physical sense, and involves the construction of a 'personal space' in addition to a literally defined physiological space" (McDowell, *Gender* 40). Because bodies occupy a space between self and other, they "catch" and hold the imprints or layers that create one's *habitus.*

Clothing also marks a space between bodies and the "outside world," a space where identities and rhetorical codes meet, inscribed upon people's bodies. Wendy Dasler Johnson, in "Cultural Rhetorics of Women's Corsets," uses sentimental rhetoric as a heuristic to read what corsets might tell us about bodies and women's writing; admitting that "bodies may still seem to be an odd site for understanding persuasion and poetry," her work illustrates how "discourse is embedded in material culture" (205). Verbal and nonverbal discourses, a range of rhetorical codes, "still shape human subjectivity . . . because our bodies too are shaped by cultural practices, practices that convince us of a particular sense of self" (223).

Only bodies can make places meaningful, and the bodies that occupy a place give it meaning. Bodies that are beautiful, bodies that are big, bodies that are slow, bodies that are pregnant, bodies that are tattooed (or corseted): all of these bodies make their way through social space, being imprinted by place as they also leave their trace upon places. Places only become meaningful when bodies occupy them, when people move through them or stay a while or something in between. If the bodies in a place are pretty much all the same, bodies marked as different will sense borders and boundaries, even if they haven't been erected intentionally.

Understanding how geographies are embodied—how bodies imprint a place with identifiable or palpable characteristics—can then lead to an inquiry into why some bodies feel excluded from certain places or how the social production of space operates via keeping some bodies in and some bodies out. David Sibley in *Geographies of Exclusion* draws from psychoanalytic theory, particularly object relations theory, to trace strong emotional responses to place. Sibley finds Melanie Klein's contribution to this body of work especially important, the idea that the emerging self develops a sense of "border," of separateness and self. Some people, this theory suggests, will have "a greater boundary consciousness than others" (Sibley 7). The factors that contribute to this border mentality, which emerges in infancy, include dirt, feces, soil, ugliness, and imperfection, in other words, "puritanical, western obsessions" (7):

> Thus, the boundary between the inner (pure) self and the outer (defiled) self, which is initially manifest in a distaste for bodily residues but then assumes a much wider cultural significance, derives from parents and adults who are, by definition, socialized and acculturated. (7)

In its crudest sense, humans want to distance themselves from shit.

Sibley also refers to Julia Kristeva's essay on abjection to set up his thesis about how otherness and social boundaries are constructed and maintained. Dangers to identity come from without: from disease, decay, infection. Kristeva insists, however, that the abject is always there, and that "this hovering presence of the abject" creates anxiety and drives humans to make separations between "us and them" (Sibley 8). Kristeva writes about food loathing, in particular, and the visceral responses some people have to certain foods or certain smells. Many responses to smells are class-related, and Sibley goes on to argue that such responses are reinforced by the culture of consumption. People living outside the culture of consumption, like gypsies, become the target of intense vilification (102–8).

Aversion to places does not always develop from firsthand encounters or from visual evidence. Drawing upon hearsay, family stories, "common knowledge," or media images, notions about a place build up and over time, become difficult to undo. Many of us are warned about staying out of dark or dangerous places, and then we pass that information along to others as though it is true. The interviews with students in Leeds demonstrate the power of these warnings, heard in their social geography lectures, in the attitudes towards Chapletown, where only one student had actually been yet which all of them mentioned it as a no-go area. Sibley's book is helpful in accounting for the strong responses students had to certain areas—the aversion, if you will. For example, despite the fact that all of Zoe's friends live in Hyde Park, she seems particularly repulsed by the place:

> *I:* Why'd you decide that you did not want to live in Hyde Park?
> *Z:* Well, to be honest, Hyde Park to me looks like a ghetto—really. I think my parents would have been scared [laughs] if they'd seen where I was living cause it is really bad. Compared to other student areas in other cities, Hyde Park is terrible. The houses don't have gardens; there's hardly any trees; every house has got grating on it—you know bars and alarms everywhere; the streets have got rubbish on them, it just looks horrible.

Liam identifies an area he would bypass for some of the same reasons:

> *L:* See, I'd actually go around Burley rather than walking through the center; you know there's quite a lot of terraced housing at the bottom of the hill . . . and there's a lot of housing around there that I wouldn't walk through at all.
> *I:* Can you tell me why or describe the housing?
> *L:* Um, housing is terraced, vandalized, bins everywhere, litter actually everywhere, kids running around screaming and . . . well there's no specific fear actually; I'm not officially scared of being mugged.
> *I:* Or attacked?
> *L:* Yeah, I mean if I walked through Burley, I wouldn't think someone's gonna come at me. I just don't like the feel of the place; I just don't like it.

Both passages also show, of course, the class-based nature of responses to place. Liam's strong reactions to Burley were accompanied by a similarly strong attraction to green spaces; during our interview, he walked me to a window to show me how near the fields were. Zoe's reactions were probably influenced by her family's experience with urban crime: during a visit from her parents to Leeds, their car was "nicked" and burned on Prince Phillip's playing fields. Perhaps unsurprisingly, these middle-class white students had strong aversions to places marked by terraced housing or security bars, aversions that just might "get in the way" of learning.

In addition, Liam's insistence that he just doesn't like the *feel* of the place illustrates how intangible and difficult to name sense of place can be—how elusive and embodied. Places also contain embedded histories that aren't necessarily "seen" but rather "felt." How do students or any other "trespassers" recognize boundaries and borders? How do they know when they don't belong? Sensing where boundaries lie and who can cross them constitutes a type of knowledge or understanding that's extremely difficult to name or to research. Julian claims "intuition," as the following exchange shows:

> *I:* Well, there aren't any parts of Leeds that you recognize as being scary, dangerous?
>
> *J:* They're the areas that I don't go, this is the funny thing I know, I just *know* not to go there.
>
> *I:* Right, how do you know? You've heard or—
>
> *J:* Well, I've started walking up towards it, and as soon as I get near it, sort of alarm bells start ringing.

The alarm bells are not innate, of course, but develop from Julian's experiences in space, from the ways in which space has been constructed through English culture and education. Despite the fact that Julian claims "he just knows," what's more noticeable in these interviews is the consistency with which students described the no-go or undesirable places; clearly visual evidence contributes significantly to their judgments about places:

> *J:* You notice that everything's boarded up and there's nobody about the estates. There's lots of broken, damaged—just the whole place is terribly rundown; it's like walking into a war zone . . . it's like suddenly turning up in Bosnia [laughs].
>
> *I:* So it's physical or actual?
>
> *J:* Yeah, you see burned out cars, you see broken windows, you see high security fences everywhere and rubbish strewn everywhere and a few kids perhaps running around the place looking wild.

And here's Sheila describing the characteristics of urban deprivation: "like more graffiti, more litter, vandalism, and then things like the houses stop being private and go into more like public housing—flats, in particular . . . and the shops tend to have things like physical barriers, like grilling on the windows." With striking consistency, students describe the undesirable places in physical terms, and never mention the people, the inhabitants (other than, interestingly, screaming kids).

It's as if these no-go places are disembodied, uninhabited, deserted, and they do often appear that way because the residents feel so alienated from the tower block architecture, from the masses of concrete with no green space or public gathering place. The postwar "urban renewal" that destroyed old Victorian neighborhoods and replaced them with modern high-rises literally drove people off the streets by eliminating streets altogether.[1] The idea is to keep residents inside, on the eleventh floor, not outside on the stoop or in the back garden where they might talk with neighbors and work to create an active, vibrant neighborhood. There are very good reasons why people find housing estates to be no-go: because there are no corner shops, no corners at all, and no stoops or sidewalks or small plots of garden. The high-rises emerge from huge tracts of land, much of it concrete and characterless.

The presence or absence of bodies is one feature that gives a place a particular reputation, or gives it a certain "feel." Even in the village of Eccup, though all of the other signs of urban deprivation were missing, students noticed right away that there were no *bodies;* conversely, then, the absence of people can mean either deprivation or privilege. References to rubbish, trash, and other types of "dirt" also serve to support Sibley's thesis that people can be repulsed by places, but these responses are learned behavior, ideologically constructed and not a feature of the places themselves. As the attitudes and hearsay and assumptions about a place build up and accumulate, then, over time, the boundaries around them can harden, making it more difficult for others to move in and out.

Hardened Boundaries

Cities get their character from the material conditions that, according to Sibley, are sources of revulsion: there is more dirt in the city, more trash, litter, graffiti, more food and body odors, more traffic noise—all of which contribute to strong responses to place, even if it is to respond positively to the hustle bustle and stimulation of the senses. While cities have been glorified and vilified and everything in between, geographers know that modern cities, by design, work to keep people apart. The geography of cities—the placement of boulevards or interstate highways; the location and design of housing projects; even bus routes and subway stops—contribute to residential segregation. Since Victorian times, when the bourgeoisie felt threatened by the masses, social divisions between rich and poor have been reinforced and controlled by increasing spatial segregation (Jackson 83–89). The desire of merchants and employers to distance themselves from their workers meant also that they moved away from their shops or small factories, living elsewhere while "vast tracts of working-class housing" went up to house the poor, with the result that nonresidents dared not enter except for the police sent to enforce order (Jackson 89).[2]

Geographers help us to identify and analyze the social and political pressures to keep people divided, which result in a number of different types of segregation. Studying residential and occupational segregation for women in cities, for example, can help to explain how geography constructs difference. In "Geography and the Construction of Difference," a case study of working women in Worcester, Massachusetts, Pratt and Hanson conclude that women in Worcester are "very much rooted in place and this is a vehicle for the construction of differences among women" (5). Arguing, ultimately, that "geographies of placement must be held in tension with an ideal of displacement," these geographers show how the spatiality of social life contributes to identities becoming rigid—frozen in place—therefore making change or community-building very difficult. In situating their study, the authors depend on Minnie Bruce Pratt's 1984 essay for its insights into reading the social in spatial terms, "the ways that places can veil or heighten awareness of differences and varying axes of difference" (Pratt and Hanson 8). Pratt, they claim, "describes what every social geographer knows":

> that the spatial arrangement of social groups in cities and towns often separates one from the other, screening differences and inequality, and thereby diffusing conflict. . . . Residential segregation is part of the "othering" of "the other"; it is part of the construction of difference while simultaneously shielding that difference. (8)

Like Janet Wolff, Pratt and Hanson are concerned with exile and nomadism and marginality as locations because these notions may actually serve to "harden boundaries" between feminists and between feminist theorists and other women: "An overvaluation of fluidity as a subject position may lead away from a careful consideration of the processes through which identities are created and fixed *in place*" (9, my emphasis).

From their position that geography fixes identities and hardens boundaries, Pratt and Hanson conduct an empirical study of four communities in metropolitan Worcester, interviewing both employers and employees in each area. Their findings lead them to conclude that "most people are fixed in and by space" (12); for example,

> one firm . . . hires exclusively Latino women for the first shift and primarily Vietnamese and Cambodian women for the second . . . . This is because the majority of the Latino employees at this firm do not have access to an automobile and only the first shift is served by public transportation. (15)

Women's working lives, this study shows, are dependent upon where they live, their access to transportation, and their childcare responsibilities; at the same time, work keeps them within the boundaries of their local communities.

Concluding that there is a *stickiness* to identity "grounded in the fact that many women's lives are lived locally," Pratt and Hanson object to suggestions that people travel or move through the city with the kind of casualness, freedom, or frequency that some theorists posit (25). Dwelling, in this sense, is not the practice of freedom of choice; people do not live just where they want. As the Leeds geography students had learned, people who are "the same"—by religion, race, or home country—tend to congregate in the same neighborhoods. When new immigrants arrive, they want to live with others like them. Students, too, want to live with other students, not with middle-class families or in working-class or tower-block neighborhoods. This stickiness and fixedness explains, in part, residential segregation, and residential segregation explains how geographies of fear develop. Like bell hooks as a girl making her way across town to her grandmother's house, some walkers, especially women, speed up, change course, or proceed with a pounding heart.

Gill Valentine, in "The Geography of Women's Fear," suggests that women think most about their own risk when they perceive "unregulated space," where the behavior of men cannot be observed by the public or other women:

> Unlike men women find that when in public space their personal space is frequently invaded by whistles, comments, or actual physical assault from strange men. This inability of women to choose with whom they interact and communicate profoundly affects their sense of security in public. (386)

Hardened boundaries may actually serve the purpose, then, of giving women a feeling of security; if they stay on home turf, they will feel safer or more able to deal with the trouble that might arise.

Women's fearfulness in public space might also explain why females are said to have a lesser or impaired spatial sense compared to males. According to geography educators Wiegand and Stiell,

> Many studies . . . have drawn attention to the superior performance of males compared with females over a broad range of spatial tasks. Boys have been shown to draw maps of their home area, for example, that are more accurate and detailed than those of girls and these differences appear to persist into early adulthood. (195)

The researchers attribute these differences to "boys' greater environmental experience and their action in space" (195). These differences might be attributed, instead, to how men occupy space and how this affects women walking, as this interview passage with Anna illustrates: "There's a garage down in Hyde Park, which is just the dodgiest garage you've ever seen in your life. These Asian men sort of sit outside and just watch you as you walk past, and it's really intimidating, especially if you're a girl and you're by yourself." From their position sitting outside, often in plastic chairs lined up and leaning against the building, these men stay connected to their territory but also take up some of the sidewalk, and their gaze extends their occupation of space even further into the street.

Whether or not Anna's map of Hyde Park would be "accurate" from a cartographer's standpoint, her map, to be meaningful, must include the dodgy garage and reflect her responses to being watched. The taxi drivers *dwell* in front of that dodgy garage in ways that Anna cannot possibly imitate. She treats Hyde Park only as a territory to be passed through; her main objective is to keep herself to herself. Dwelling, then, can only happen with a sense of comfort, familiarity, or empowerment. For that block around the dodgy garage, the men *owned* that street, and over time, as women like Anna turn or cross or hurry past, the space of that street changes, is changed by these spatial acts, precipitated by social and cultural and racial difference.

For Anna and others, their experiences from Hyde Park to the university illustrate how boundaries harden through a repetition of routes or through habitual pathways. In addition, being a girl, by yourself, in public space, has enormous consequences, especially when factoring other embodied differences, like being a Muslim female in traditional dress. As Claire Dwyer asks, how are embodied differences negotiated in the construction and contestation of identity? Dwyer studies the dress of Muslim women to pursue these questions; through a methodology of discussion groups (in two girls' schools), Dwyer shows how dress is "a contested signifier" for young British Muslim women (7). Other contested signifiers would include tattoos or other forms of body art, jewelry, clothing, accessories, hair styles— even a style of walking, the shape of pregnancy, or the look of illness. These signifiers, whether contested or dominant, contribute to the ways in which identity is constructed and negotiated on the street.

Identity is constructed on the street by dress, mannerisms, time of day, or people's previous experiences in space. Brent Staples, for example, chronicles the different ways his "body" is received or interpreted, whether he is dressed in sweat pants or business clothes. An avid night walker in cities, Staples learned as a young black man that his nightly constitutionals made people who encountered him cross the street or go the other way. Out of self-protection and a reluctance to frighten others, he learned to "take precautions" to make himself "less threatening" (39). His movements on the street are designed to ease people's fears and keep himself from being shot: "I give a wide berth to nervous people on subway platforms during the wee hours . . . . If I happen to be entering a building behind some people who appear skittish, I may walk by, letting them clear the lobby . . . so as not to seem to be following them" (40). Most creatively, Staples whistles melodies from classical music. Whistling a "sunny" selection from Vivaldi does wonders, he says, for reducing nervous tension on the street. "It is my equivalent," he writes, "of the cowbell that hikers wear when they know they are in bear country" (41).[3]

The reaction to being scared on the street might send many people home to a "safe" environment, but the literature of feminist geography has contributed much to a more complicated concept of homes. The home is, of course, one context for the exercise of power (Sibley 91). We learn about power, in fact, by being raised in homes; it is in the home that we learn how to navigate space and how "control" operates; our house "is our first universe" (Bachelard 4). Despite the role of a house as a respite for the imagination, a place to daydream and build intimate relationships, the arrangements of home life make borders and boundaries clear to us and keep them enforced; as a repository of memory, homes are also hugely politicized places.

Home Dwellings

Dwelling safely and securely means learning to read the "keep out" signs that aren't really there. Knowing when to stay out of an area is a critical skill of street smarts, of cultural literacy, one that we learn in some of our earliest "home" experiences. Despite most Americans' belief in the sanctity of the home, feminist geographers have demonstrated how homes are not immune from the politics of space in the everyday. Like all spaces, homes reproduce the politics of gender as they construct our sense of boundaries and borders, of what is acceptable and forbidden. Women's experiences and emotions in domestic spaces are so geographically rooted, they can vary with the floor plan—women can get angry in the kitchen, for example, but not in the bedroom (Blunt and Rose 2). Movements between the kitchen and the bedroom—and the risks or pleasures that might reside in each room—constitute those ordinary journeys of the everyday that are accounted for more thoroughly in the spatial theories of women.

In bell hooks's spatial writings, she emphasizes that uses of space in the everyday functions of home life offer opportunities for resistance to the dominant culture and that homeplaces are essential to women of color as a safe harbor from white patriarchal culture. The dedication to home is consciously exercised in practices of the everyday, and as hooks shows, homes maintain their sanctity because their dwellers must, at some point, leave them and venture out into the streets, shops, or schools—to cross the tracks into more frightening territories.

Too often, in binary thinking, homeplace can represent shelter and goodness only when set against its binary opposite, "cold, cruel world," or gains its power only when set in opposition to the street. This view, however, enforces the idea that there is no "movement" within a homeplace or that they are always stable, quiet places. Like all spaces, homes have a contradictory, provisional nature; they are representative of thirdspace, too, or have a complex set of "betweens." We want to believe that for those who get out and move through the world, either by necessity or desire, homeplaces offer shelter and respite. To those engaged in movement, however ordinary it may be, home is a place to end up and to unburden oneself, as hooks describes it. Without trying to undo those powerful emotional responses to homeplace, we also need to consider homeplace or dwelling as always in flux, as forms of paradoxical or contested space.

Bachelard believes that "the house we were born in is an inhabited house . . . physically inscribed in us. . . . a group of organic habits" (14). We adopt certain gestures from the house itself or become attuned to its features and qualities: "We are the diagram of functions of inhabiting that particular house. . . . The word habit is too worn a word to express this passionate liaison of our bodies, which do not forget" (15). The house I was born in is inscribed in me: I knew the house I grew up in so well that I could walk through it in the dark; as a teenager in past her curfew, I learned to step completely over stair number fifteen, the creaky one very near the door of my parents' bedroom. Movements, gestures, and habits develop from first places, and we learn much from our homes about the arrangement and uses of space.

My parents bought a big house in which to raise their growing family when I was about nine months old, my mother pregnant again with their fourth child. Two more would arrive—six kids in eight years—and 917 South Highland would be home for twenty-eight years. Memories of those rooms are vivid; I sometimes dream about particular passageways, like the stairwell to the basement, lined with shelves holding canning jars and tools, cleaning rags and vegetable bins; and I can still picture the wallpaper patterns or the contents of closets. My memories are not just visual images, however, because I can still hear the *noises* of 917: pounding feet on uncarpeted stairs; the slam of screen doors; conversations rising through duct work; the shouting to be heard and being yelled at, simultaneously, to pipe down. The noise and confusion often sent me in search of a private place among so much shared space.

An avid reader who craved quiet, I searched for places to hide from nosy younger siblings and be alone, places that rotated because of temperature or season. In her "Writing on the Bias," Linda Brodkey situates her own literacy and her love of reading within the space of her four-room work-

ing-class house: "In such small quarters, interior space is social by definition, since to be in a room is to be in either the company or proximity of
others" (39). This social arrangement of space, particularly in the kitchen,
fosters her reading habit: in a middle-class household, children might be
perceived as "hostile" for reading during meal preparation; she was in fact
praised for her ability to read while surrounded by others.

If the number of rooms (seven) and the rule "no reading at the table"
are any indication, my own household was more middle-class. I still can't
read while surrounded by others; I still crave quiet and privacy for certain
parts of the day; and I do think my own lessons about social arrangements
of space and functions of space can be traced to this homeplace. Did my
reading habit lead to my desire for private space when it was either forbidden or difficult for me to do in the presence of others, as Brodkey could?
Or did my desire for peace and quiet send me to books? I think I learned
early on that dwelling in the pages of books was more pleasant than listening to siblings fight or to my father's commands.

Certain rooms in 917 dictated certain behaviors or had prescribed—if also
diverse—uses; in this way, the arrangement and uses of rooms teach children
or other dwellers how to behave or what is considered acceptable. Homes
embody issues of class, in the ways they are arranged or decorated or by the
smells coming from the kitchen. Homes hold, in fact, many answers to questions about what can happen *where*. Our living room, the front room, was
designated only for company—drop-in visitors like the Avon lady—or for
family and friends on holidays. Kept mostly unheated in the winter and
never cooled in the summer, the front room was not for kids to play in,
although reading or quiet games were acceptable activities. Site of the
Christmas tree, the front room was a lived-in place only a few days a year.
The dining room had far more uses, well beyond the traditional holiday
dinners or birthday parties. In the everyday, the dining room table served
as homework central and, for a stressful few days in April, my dad took it
over to do taxes. The dining room also held the ironing board, a busy place
in an era when even the sheets were ironed and when both parents wore
starched and ironed uniforms for some years. The dining room held the window air conditioner, and on the hottest days or nights of summer, somebody
could be found sleeping on the floor of the dining room, safely out of the
path to and from the kitchen. In a house of little kids, one corner of the dining room held a record player and some toys and games. Later, my sisters
and I each had a dining room chair to store our handbags and schoolbooks.

For the eight members of our household, there were three toilets but only
one bathtub, so especially as five girls hit puberty, the bathroom on the

second floor became a very contested place. By then, we were allowed to lock the door again after years of a "no lock" policy—instituted after my sister, submerged under water and singing to herself, didn't hear my father calling her through the locked door. My dad, assuming the worst because of the gas stove, broke the doorframe to get in. Under the guise of safety, I learned at a young age, then, even the bathroom isn't private space, a fact to which mothers with young children will attest, as they are routinely followed into their own bathrooms.

In the third-floor converted attic I shared with two sisters, the large open floor plan offered no privacy, so my parents bought us each a "divider," a six-foot hinged room divider made of plywood and cardboard. We set them up like barriers to keep sisters out and to mark our own spaces for bed and desk. As we got older and had a phone installed, we pulled the receiver around the corner into the closet where we could talk privately, huddled underneath the hanging clothes and on top of the shoes.

My brother, the only boy, had his own room. The smallest bedroom, but it was all his, and even my mother didn't have her own room. The small room off my parents' bedroom that once served as a nursery became my dad's office, with her sewing machine in one corner. Like the ironing board in the dining room, the sewing machine in the corner of dad's office served as a reminder of the multiple functions of rooms and the ways that even the smallest of rooms needed to be shared space.[4] Both also illustrate how the furniture and items of domestic life (ironing boards or sewing machines) take up space in our homes and contribute to the gender politics of domestic space. Learning to share and negotiate space, and to recognize their multiple uses, is a lesson carried with us from childhoods in homes. Mental maps of homes, like this one of the home I was raised in, do not depend on the sizes of the rooms but on how the space is used, produced and reproduced in other, later homes or in other spaces. Bachelard claims that "all really inhabited space bears the essence of the notion of home" (5). The notion of home follows us, in a sense, into other places and spaces; a study of dwelling leads us to the importance of memory.

Memory and Place

In her novel *White Teeth,* Zadie Smith captures the intimate connection between memory and place—vividly remembered, the places come complete with smells and sounds.

> Irie stepped out into streets she'd known her whole life, along a route she'd walked a million times over. If someone asked her just then what memory was, what the *purest definition* of memory was, she would say this: the street

you were on when you first jumped in a pile of dead leaves. She was walking it right now. With every fresh crunch came the memory of previous
crunches. (378–79)

Our spatial practices of the everyday and our ways of being in the world
are formed through the memories that make them at first familiar, perhaps
comforting, and then habitual. The power of memory to shape our experiences in space is one of the messages of the *Phaedrus,* clearest in the opening scene and the late passage about writing, a message that reappears in a
twenty-first-century novel, where the character reflects on memory as a
moment in time and space, including smells and sounds, like the crunch-
ing of leaves on a deeply familiar street. A wave of memory brings back
memories of other moments, other times and spaces, and they fuse together
in a palimpsest. Geographer David Crouch acknowledges the importance
of memory in the culture of the street:

> Memories are part of culture and depend, in various ways, upon the physi-
> cal setting. . . . Memories are of course contingent, unstable, and constantly
> reworked in further practices. They inform us today in a different way from
> the way they may inform a practice tomorrow. These practices are rituals
> which are inscribed on the knowledge of the street, as the bits of the street
> where they happen . . . are inscribed in the rituals themselves. (166)

Memory's role in walking, mapping, and dwelling cannot be underesti-
mated; our spatial practices of the everyday or our way of being in the world
are formed through the memories that make them at first familiar, perhaps
comforting, and then habitual.

Despite Plato's alarm that the development of writing would "ruin"
memory, memory is alive and well in the everyday practices of a culture
immersed in digital imagery, electronic environments, and print; memory
is not in any danger of diminishing, despite popular predictions about its
demise, because we cannot navigate space without it. Remembering the
parts of a discourse, as the ancients knew, was an art of "placing" the bits
to be memorized, situating them in the mind like rooms in a house; in this
way, then, memory and arrangement are inextricably linked. Not quite as
organic as the "body" metaphor for an essay's structure (head, trunk, legs
and feet), the house metaphor works because rooms become intimately
familiar places and because so many (western) houses have the same rooms:
kitchen, sitting room, bedroom, bath. Those who have to memorize have
often created mnemonic devices based on place or location; for example, a
waitress repeats her customers' orders to the kitchen by memorizing where
they are sitting at the table's settings.[5]

In the classical art of memory, knowledge was stored in "places"—the topoi represented specialized or common places for storing ideas or references. In *The Art of Memory,* Frances A. Yates traces the technique of impressing places and images on memory from the classical tradition, through the middle ages, and into the scientific era of the seventeenth century. One of the most common mnemonic devices was the architectural type—Quintilian's technique of memorizing a speech by assigning each part to the room of a house. Memorable places in Yates's history include, for example, the memory theater of Guilio Camillo, complete with pull-out illustration, and other memory treatises. Yates makes the usual comparison between our world and the ancient world, where "devoid of printing, without paper for note-taking or on which to type lectures, the trained memory was of vital importance" (4). An important distinction between natural and artificial memory is first found in *Ad Herennium,* which also conveyed an "astonishingly visual precision" to the memory *loci:* as Yates puts it, "Who is that man moving slowly in the lonely building, stopping at intervals with an intent face? He is a rhetoric student, forming a set of memory *loci*" (8). Notice in this quotation the implicit connection, once again, between memory and place; the rhetoric student is in a building doing his intellectual work. Socrates and Phaedrus were also rhetoric students, choosing very intentionally a spot along the stream, near the plane tree, that would help them to enhance their memory of Lysias's speech. Students sent on a streetwork project or a service learning assignment, too, are rhetoric students, searching for places to make their learning matter.

As should be clear by now, *places* are hugely important to learning processes and to acts of writing because the kinds of spaces we occupy determine, to some extent, the kinds of work we can do or the types of artifacts we can create. Roxanne Mountford quotes a seminarian who says, "The architecture of a church affects what kinds of sermons I can preach" (58). Women ministers often feel silenced by a traditional raised pulpit and choose instead to wander around the sanctuary while speaking; coded as male, the pulpit "embodies power and authority" (Mountford 59).[6] As we have seen, this is a powerful spatial logic that holds true in many institutions and forms of the social world, certainly in college classrooms.

One of the problems with university teaching is that classrooms are not easily inhabited; they tend to look all alike, cool and sterile, the only stuff on the walls advertisements for study abroad or schemes for earning money. Dwelling in a traditional college classroom resembles more an act of encampment than placemaking. In a composition classroom, the inhabitants are temporary—only for three hours a week, in and out—and often required to be there to fulfill the university/universal requirement to pass first-year composition. Inhabiting a classroom does not seem possible in Bachelard's sense, if we think about dwelling only in terms of a "where." However, since dwelling is not only about where but also about *how*—a set of embodied spatial practices—then learning to dwell can carry over into imagined geographies: into discourses, acts of writing, and/or in written texts. For re-imagining the work of writing through both the places and practices of dwelling, it's necessary to begin with mapping some of our most familiar spaces.

Dwelling in University Spaces: Mapping URI

One way to make connections to places from which we feel alienated is to plunge in, spend time there, and figure out what creates and upholds the hardened boundaries or the geographies of exclusion. First-year students, especially those who are first-generation college students, often feel a sense of alienation or displacement on a college campus, at least before they have dwelt within its spaces long enough to begin to feel at home. Starting from this point as well as from the belief that we need not go outside the campus boundaries to explore or understand the construction of difference, I designed a project, drawn from streetwork, called "Mapping URI," where students began with maps of the campus and, working in groups, marked the areas of campus with which they were completely unfamiliar, places where they'd never been. They decided together on an area to visit and on the boundaries for that area, and we reviewed fieldwork methodologies in class. The goal was for them to collect data and analyze it and then write an essay that both presented their findings and reflected on the experience, particularly in terms of *how it felt* to visit that unfamiliar place and what they sensed about being an insider or outsider. They walked to their chosen area, walked the boundaries they had located on the map, and then began to write their own maps, which, in turn, reflected their identities as students.[7]

Our discussions in class ranged across some of these questions: Where do students feel comfortable and welcome on campus, and where do they feel like outsiders? How do they know where the boundaries are, or what signs can they read about their being welcomed or not? What are the limitations of a two-dimensional map of the campus in representing their experiences as they move through different buildings, quadrangles, or parking lots? For example, while students are welcome in classrooms, lecture halls, libraries, or the cafeterias, how are they treated when they enter hallways of faculty offices, or when they wander into a research lab? How are they spoken to when their teaching assistant, responsible for 299 other students, doesn't recognize them? Where are they allowed to park as residents or as commuters, and how are these two groups of students treated differently by the administration or by the layout of the campus? Are there houses of worship for all of the major religions, and any minor ones? What are the states of repair or disrepair of some of the buildings on campus, and what does this indicate about the value of the work that goes on within in them? And finally, within the student-centered cafeterias, will anyone notice the glaring segregations, as all the African American and other students of color sit together on one side, while all white students stay on another?

One of the motivations behind designing the Mapping URI assignment came from teaching the introduction-to-college course and realizing how little first-year students know about universities as social, cultural, and academic institutions. Like many universities now, URI requires a one-credit course for first-year students designed to build learning communities and improve retention rates. Proven costly to take for granted that students come prepared for the mysteries and challenges of college, this type of course is typically called something like University 101. More than a crash course in survival skills, it can also function as the only "small" class students have and offers opportunities for friendships that large lectures don't have.[8]

Realizing that most first-year courses do not encourage an understanding of the university, which students need in order to understand the cultures that produce and value universities, I have emphasized academics and intellectual work in my own version of University 101 and have tried to introduce students to the university as a research institution. I shouldn't be surprised, but it's somewhat rare for first-year students to know that a university's *raison d'etre* is not, in fact, teaching undergraduates. Students are surprised to learn that most full-time faculty are hired not for their teaching experience but for their promise as scholars or their potential to attract grant monies, and students are often dismayed to learn that college faculty do not need a license to practice. The undergraduates at my comprehensive state university do not realize that many faculty members are expected to publish and be professionally active, that their teaching assistants are engaged in "original research," or that some of their instructors have their own offices while others must share a cubicle. In most of the ways the university functions for first-year students, there is no connection between the million-dollar grants for cancer research and the Biology 100 lab, or between the forensic science partnership on campus and the unit on crime in their sociology lecture, or between the textbooks they read in class and the actual humans who write them.

"Introduction to the University" courses were designed to make students feel more at home. On the contrary, my experiences teaching University 101 and the Mapping URI project with my first-year writing students tell me that undergraduates are excluded from many areas of university life, particularly academics and research—and the greater the distance from these areas (for instance, for first-generation college students), the greater the alienation. If my claim is viable—that the social production of space at a university works to exclude students while it also claims to be the doorway to students' knowledge and success—then efforts to define this university sociospatial logic are worth more attention.

The most striking finding in the set of papers I received: Students who dared to enter distinctly "non-student" areas were treated with deep suspicion, even rudeness, and they reported feeling very much out of place and unwelcome. For at least two of these sites, the workings of exclusion were fairly understandable: a construction site for a new building (where safety was an issue) and a child development center (where unknown adult visitors are all treated with distrust). Other sites included a building of faculty offices (no classrooms); a faculty club (called "The U Club"); the fine arts building (whose architecture some call an eyesore); and greenhouses (the research lab for botany students). In the greenhouses, students were quite welcomed by, interestingly, a graduate research assistant, but for the other sites, students had negative reactions. One student's thesis statement, which she shared with the whole class one day, was taken up by others: "Appearances can be deceiving; thus places that seemed really welcoming on the outside (the University Club) were not, and the places that look cold and intimidating (the fine arts center) were really quite warm and welcoming." As with the Leeds students, there were only two categories: warm and welcoming, or cold and intimidating. The tropes of nice place/bad place, like insider/outsider, are too dominant to avoid, and avoiding these binaries is a formidable challenge to those engaged in studying sense of place.

In their Mapping URI project, two students wrote about the exclusions and politics of space regarding religion: one examined the absence of a Hindu temple or Muslim mosque on campus, while another focused on the striking contrast between the nice Catholic center and the rundown Hillel center; a third explored the seemingly intractable problem of parking for commuters. Some students turned this essay into an argument about the poor treatment of students by several offices or personnel on campus. Apparently, there are legendary tales about the woman in the registrar's office who disdains students, and many were willing to share their testimony, which my students eagerly collected. (When I was a student, it was the mean woman in the health center.) Of course, there are an equal number of stories about how horrible students are to staff and faculty, but my point is that we needn't send students off campus in order to get them to understand geographies of exclusion, maintained border lines, or sedimented histories that characterize many spaces for learning and living.

Like Sheila, who was turned away from the golf club near Eccup for wearing jeans, my own students were treated with suspicion (a secretary said "What are you doing here? What do you want?")—all because they looked like, acted like, and were *students*. More than one staff member asked my students "Who is your professor?" and word got back to me that other faculty and staff on campus did not appreciate my assignment. The attitude seemed to be that "we are trying to get work done here or conduct business here and we can't be bothered with talking to your students!" In other places, students quickly concluded that they were not welcome because of the codes and signs they saw in these places. For example, as they examined brochures at the entrance to the University Club, brochures that mentioned "memberships" as well as various social functions, they got the hint right away, despite the nice, homelike exterior, that they weren't invited to join. Students reported that as they looked into the dining room and the meeting rooms, they felt extremely uncomfortable and didn't stay long enough to interview anyone.

In hearing these accounts from my students and others, I suppose I could call into question students' behavior (Were they rude? Did they act inappropriately? Were they just not determined enough?). One could also critique the nature of hearsay in order to dismiss these stories, which may certainly have been exaggerated in the telling. However, I am more inclined to ask why, even in an age when students are identified as "consumers," they are treated as interlopers, as bothersome, as bodies out of place. Students, in fact, "don't belong" on a university campus, at least when they dare to enter spaces designated for researchers, experts, faculty, or staff.

In addition, despite its wisdom, URI's no-alcohol policy, enforced even for homecoming, has created a culture where living on campus is decidedly uncool, and the place it's really happening is "down the line," the bus line, that is, south from campus to the beach rental housing that so many students occupy from Labor Day weekend to the end of May. Owners then return for the summer, possibly to face complaints about loud parties and parking, but are quick to rent again to students for the price of a mortgage payment plus. The fall and spring neighborhoods of students that develop cause headaches for the local residents, those who are not just summer residents. In places like Bonnet Shores and Eastward Look, transient students and year-round residents clash over noise, trash, and parking, just like they did in the Headingley or Meanwood sections of Leeds. These town-and-gown conflicts, competing senses of place and neighborhood, are important for students to examine and understand because attitudes towards places carry over into a variety of learning situations. Learning to dwell in a classroom or neighborhood requires knowing where the boundaries lie and what risks are involved in crossing them.

The same geographies that construct our notions of gender, race, class, age, or abilities also construct spaces of learning, which in turn become particularly complicated or fraught with meaning. When students walk into classrooms, they come with years of experience walking into classrooms; each person's mental map of past classrooms will be different. How do those students' different experiences in the sociospatial world walk in with them, and how can exploring this difference become the intellectual work of a writing class?

Students, as transient members of academic or university communities, need strategies for movement and dwelling, ways to negotiate between their habitual spatial practices and the task of writing. Students might be invited to map places meaningful to them, new and unknown places, or create new places—realandimagined rooms, towns, cities, or planets. Students learn resourcefulness, or to walk and map with some efficiency and purpose: "Where am I, and how can I find out?" Students can be asked to use their memories—to retrace their way through a Website (why did you go there next?) or find their way through an unfamiliar part of campus. How do they remember landmarks? What stayed with them about their journey? How many cell phone numbers, e-mail addresses, or song titles do students remember? What do such lists tell us about the culture in which many people can recall hundreds of song lyrics or the arrangement of rooms but not many poems, essays, or arguments? Writers working on issues of place and space can keep a place journal,[9] create maps, visualize arguments, or explore campuses and surrounding neighborhoods. Whatever the assignment, a geographical emphasis encourages the use of memory and particular attention to the arrangement and uses of space and may open up a set of town-and-gown issues that are well worth analyzing. The Mapping URI project got me to thinking about other geographies of exclusion in familiar or assumedly "democratic" or public spaces, especially those constructed by language.

Inhabiting Dwellings or Discourses

Inhabiting a dwelling means enacting a number of familiar and everyday spatial practices. Being an inhabitant means having memories of a place, being able to picture it in your mind and call up rooms, passageways, and details like doorknobs or odd windows. Inhabiting a place means knowing where the scissors are without even thinking or knowing how the furniture used to be arranged, or knowing how to jiggle the fireplace flue handle just so. Occupying a dwelling means that your clothes, books, photographs, and other personal artifacts surround you and that you can tell a story about many of the items. You can walk to the kitchen in the dark or to the baby's room with your eyes closed.

What does any of this have in common with inhabiting discourses? Discourses don't have roofs or walls or provide shelter, but as many of us recognize from favorite books or stories, discourses can hold memories or represent a meaningful time and place; if familiar, they invite us to dwell within them. If unfamiliar or strange, it takes much longer, and dwelling doesn't happen when people feel excluded or that they don't belong; they have to stay long enough, in the text or the neighborhood, to know where the bullies hang out and where the best curry is. Parallels between texts and dwellings illustrate how writing can be inhabited, involving both the metaphorical and the material. While dwelling might seem an apt, rich metaphor, it is not merely metaphor because dwelling within discourses is an act performed in the material world, in the place where our phones, lists, coats, spoons, or dogs reside, but one that also demands our full metaphorical imagination.

For readers, how does inhabiting a text happen? You approach and take inventory, looking around and getting a sense of the terrain. You notice if there are signs that are familiar or if there are any features that are recognizable—and if the unfamiliar or foreign elements add up quickly, then there has to be a good reason for entering the area at all. Inhabiting a text begins first with entry or with going in and then proceeds with acts that gauge the text's hospitality, if you will. After the equivalent of checking for bars on the windows, for litter on the ground, or the people moving through the area, visitors to a text will decide if they can safely stay a while, perhaps browsing or lingering. Inhabitance develops only through habit and familiarity, or when the "visitor" has spent enough time in that space and others like it to move through it with confidence and knowledge. De Certeau claims the act of reading as a form of dwelling:

> The thin film of writing becomes a movement of strata, a play of spaces. A different world (the reader's) slips into the author's place. This mutation makes the text habitable, like a rented apartment. It transforms another person's property into a space borrowed for a moment by a transient. Renters make comparable changes in an apartment they furnish with their acts and memo-

ries; as do speakers . . . through their own "turns of phrase" . . . ; as do pedestrians, in the streets they fill with the forest of their desires and goals. (xxi)

Like sense of place, encounters with texts are about *feeling*—structures of feeling or felt senses that are deeply emotional, visceral, embodied. Just as some walkers experience fear of certain neighborhoods, some readers are going to experience aversion to certain prose styles, citations, or "big" vocabulary words. Disinclined to go where their instincts tell them to stay out, students look to us to understand why they feel excluded from texts or just can't find a good reason to engage. Therefore, it's too easy to just insist that students get over it and reread the hard passages. Where exactly do they feel like an outsider, and where do they feel that they could straddle a threshold? Those who can't find ways to *dwell* develop other moves—they just move on.

Within the discourses of composition studies, which are often written in response to or from intersections of various postmodern or critical theories, readers from different neighborhoods, if you will, disagree about whether dense theoretical writings have the equivalent of bars on the windows or signs saying "Proper dress required." The debate about "accessibility," style, and density, recently brewing its way to a boil, can demonstrate how power is constructed spatially and geographically—and how some textual dwellings can be as intimidating as a mansion or skyscraper.

Wendy Bishop quotes a sentence written by Gary Olson and claims that it has "no clothes, and no heart (no organs at all, no human substance)," leaving her with no place to stand (26). Despite her claims to genuine inquiry, many readers have interpreted Bishop's line of argument as an attack on those who write about theory or from the standpoint of theory, which becomes conflated with those who write "dense prose." Most recently, Sharon Crowley joins this conversation by defending Judith Butler against critics who are outraged or at least put off by her writing. The density of Butler's prose generally alarms some critics; Crowley, however, thinks that Butler's political agenda is well served by her "powerfully ethical rhetorical theory" (164). In fact, Crowley believes that form follows content and that Butler simply cannot make her arguments in writing characterized by coherence or (the myth of) a common language.

Besides defending Butler and her project, however, Crowley also wants to reprimand the Wendy Bishops and others, whose "rage for clarity marks a class war in composition and rhetoric," one where the "boss compositionists"—those with the money and power—have built their empires, so to speak, on the backs of clarity, brevity, and sincerity (166). There's no room in the regime for critical accounts of language, then, or language that takes risks—for language that threatens the ruling party. "The rage for accessibility," according to Crowley, "is yet one more manifestation of the old colonizing desire to identify and control" (166).

Some would argue, with Crowley, that certain styles of writing (postmodern, political, theory-laden, or fragmented) are appropriately rhetorical and provide important resistance to the hegemony of clarity, coherence, and unity. Those siding with Bishop might say that modernist values of clarity open texts up to a broader and more diverse audience, which also seems an admirable goal. Because of my own experiences in teaching both graduate and undergraduate classes where this issue of "accessibility" is a running theme, I am grateful to both Bishop and Crowley for taking this issue on and taking it public. The responsibility of writers to make texts "accessible" (but to whom?) *is* a conversation worth having. We need to talk more often and more bluntly about the geographical walls that divide readers from writers, or those that divide neighborhoods where different readers and writers reside. Taking on this topic, however, shouldn't mean having to name names and quote sentences, since we've all written, and have had published, sentences that leave some readers with little to get a handle on. But neither should it mean taking a position of defending one of the accused; being "right" in the style wars seems unimportant if we also neglect the very real ways in which some readers—even well-educated, eager, or sincere readers—feel excluded from certain texts, discourses, or conversations.

In the betweens of this exchange in the pages of rhetoric and composition discourses, one thin layer of the palimpsest, lies a history of other exchanges that only certain readers will find; in their allusions and asides and citations, texts have always excluded some readers. In analyzing textual geographies of exclusion, then, it may help to be reminded of the tenacity of some forms of residential segregation.

Residential segregation is so powerful that even city planners fall prey to the rumors and assumptions that circulate about certain areas. Jane Jacobs tells of wandering around the North End of Boston, impressed by housing improvements and a bustling street life, only to be told repeatedly by city planners and bankers that it was "a slum." Statistics about the North End showed otherwise (10), but the experts insisted that their theories were truer than real, daily life in the North End (and bankers weren't likely to spend a day there, wandering around and speaking to residents). Like neighborhoods, texts can have hardened boundaries, making it difficult for outsiders to see the place as it "really is" unless they are willing to spend time wandering around and seeing for oneself. Residential segregation is also the tendency for people to gather with their own kind, if they can, surrounded by those with similar values or incomes or ethnic heritage. Rarely are neighborhoods so pure, however, that no diversity exists; for example, white students live in the student neighborhoods of Leeds, sharing the streets and sidewalks with South Asians.

The Bishop and Crowley exchange over the density of prose offers an opportunity to deepen our understanding of textual geographies of exclusion. We know from geographic research that many people turn around and walk away from territories that look threatening and that many more can't find good reasons to leave home at all. In fact, those threatening neighborhoods are often characterized by *density*—dwellings crowded together, extending up several stories or divided only by sidewalks, narrow streets, or alleyways. Density in prose is less easily defined, but it nevertheless results in many readers turning away. Granted, there can be many routes through a text—readers don't have to follow an essay in the order in which it appears on the page. Skipping around, like acts of *flanerie,* send us in search of something new to see—a new enticement—and is a form of resistance to containerized ways of reading.

How are texts inhabited differently if one is a writer or a reader, positioned differently in a space of literacy? Readers (as visitors or transients) and writers (as dwellers or owners) are never going to experience a text in the same way. However, as De Certeau implies, a finished text, one that the writer will not change again or has published, is one where the writer has moved out and left his text for readers to inhabit. It becomes a different dwelling, then, and the writer's familiarity grows dimmer and more distant. Readers may become inhabitants, then, just as close friends or extended family members may become dwellers in our homes, if they come often enough and learn what cupboard the coffee cups are kept in. Readers inhabit a text when they cease to be outsiders and move through it with some familiarity, confidence, or fully engaged memories of what goes where or where a certain "turn" leads.

How do *writers* inhabit texts or make texts habitable? It's easy to talk about writing a text like making a bed or setting a table—the metaphor of inhabitance is so *inviting,* but making a text habitable is a material act, tactile and physical, made up of movements, motions. We can follow a pedestrian through a street to see the moves she makes, the turns she takes, but we can't follow a writer into a text—or it's proven very difficult to "study" how writers write. What we do know about writing's materiality is that acts of writing require tools: ink and parchment, or pencils and Big Chief tablets, or computers and software programs.

The architecture and the tools are, of course, hugely significant to any act of building or dwelling—and not just in a suggestive, metaphorical way. Think, for example, about Lynn's notebooks in Emig, or my niece's computer game, or the desktop interface examined by Selfe and Selfe. These items or tools or icons—see Trimbur on typography—are the stuff of material and geographical rhetorics. Harder to do is to detect the materiality of writing beyond the use of tools, in ways that shed insight on how writers use, for example, habitual spatial practices or how their memories of other texts influence, for example, the style, shape, and arrangement of new ones. Writers inhabit their texts by spending hours of time within them; they know where everything is or have memories of building it. A writer grows familiar with her text in ways that a reader, even who visits several times and feels quite at home in its pages, cannot replicate. Turning pages, or hitting the page up and page down keys, using the "find" or "go to" commands to get to specific (remembered) parts, or using a post-it note or penciled checkmark—these are a writer's acts of dwelling. Writers inhabit a text when they can still remember "where they were," physically, emotionally, and intellectually, while writing it.

Writing's materiality begins with *where* the work of writing gets done, the tools and conditions and surroundings—not to determine a cause and effect relationship between the writing's quality or success and the site of its production, but to trace the threads or remnants of literacy practices. Along with knowing more about where writers write, though, geography contributes to a richer understanding of the habits and memories and "moves" that characterize our own acts of writing, particularly those moves that become habitual but are not "taught." Like Johnson-Eilola's daughter says, "you just play." To watch someone click around on his or her own computer is to witness a compelling form of self-taught expertise; everyone manages his or her desktop differently, with different "moves" that others might not rely upon or even recognize. Trying to explain the process of copying a document, for example, to another folder, results in the most tedious possible sentences ("First, click on the folder to see the contents; then doubleclick on the document to open it; then click File, Edit, Select All, Copy; then File New, Paste, Save As"), which is why software manuals are rarely opened and why most people learn to navigate a computer interface through trial and error, through time spent in front of the screen, trying different buttons or repeating the same moves. Learning one's way around a computer interface, like learning one's way around a neighborhood or campus, takes time spent walking and mapping (or clicking and dragging) that eventually becomes dwelling. Dwelling practices for writing—movements shaped and made possible by pen, keyboard, mouse, page, screen, dexterity, familiarity, or habit —are limited by or made possible by material conditions. In any case, readers can't dwell in a text if they can't find a way in, and writers can't dwell in ideas or questions of arrangement or style unless they have the time and space necessary for such intellectual work. I want to suggest, then, that dwelling as *metaphor* is helpful in re-imagining acts of writing in *material* ways, even though I agree with one reader that I haven't done much in these pages to unlock those physical movements that we call writing, uses of a mouse or keyboard, pencil or stylus, screen or page.

What I've learned from this project is that it's a geographical instinct to try to orient yourself when in an unfamiliar place, behavior learned from homes and other dwellings, streets, and cities; it's a habitual response to being faced with newness or unfamiliarity. Therefore, when conversations about a text or discourse or image begin with its size, length, or shape, it seems a fairly natural place to start. From the standpoint of geographic rhetorics, mapping the text would be the place to begin: arrows to mark a point of entry and other signs that indicate turning, yielding, or slowing. If students remark that they can't find a way in, that's an opportunity to examine the geographical dimensions of texts and the ways in which container metaphors, for example, limit our ability to imagine writing as spatial practices and make very difficult the task of describing writing as a material act: the layers and traces and shadows are difficult to track, precisely why container metaphors have prevailed.

One part of my participant-observation study with the Leeds geography students suggests how the places and the tools do affect composing—that material conditions and the regulation of textual space not only impact upon decisions made but also contribute to the construction of a writer's *habitus*. As the Eccup and financial district student groups fulfilled their assignments of composing a group presentation on their streetwork, I saw how time and space issues become hugely significant for collaborative group projects, particularly when students did not own their own computers and when they were dedicated to composing together.

Crowded Computer Labs

The cultural geography lecturer, Tom, reviewed the oral presentation assignment during the second week of lecture as part of his introduction to the streetwork project. He did not assign a specific format for the oral presentation, but later, he did stress a limit of ten minutes. Later, when it became clear that the groups needed more time for the qualitative research, Tom granted the class an additional week to prepare the presentations. For the two groups in which I was a participant-observer, the single biggest challenge by far was finding a time when all group members could meet and a suitable place for a collaborative meeting, where all could be heard and decisions made.

More fortunate than students on many campuses, geography students did have a room in the building designated for their use; called the Foyer and furnished as a lounge, students used this space to meet, read, rest, or have a snack. A roomy space with large windows and a teakettle, the Foyer was conducive to socializing but not to studying or to planning the parts and content of a presentation. One group that tried to meet in the Foyer was soon chased out, unable to concentrate because of the constant stream of students coming in and out and the generally noisy atmosphere. They moved to a small conference room on the third floor but were continually interrupted by staff coming in to use the copy machine located there. Interruptions don't necessarily mean the work stops completely or can't go on—most of us learn to concentrate despite them—but neither of the two groups was able to talk and plan without them. The other group tried having its first meeting in an empty laboratory adjacent to the Foyer, but after a short time, a faculty member came in to say the room was needed for a class. The same problems arose when it was time for the group to begin composing the presentation using computers. Where could lab space be found for groups of five to seven students to gather around one screen and consult with each other?

Here's an entry from my field notes that captures one student's concerns about getting her work done:

> Zoe mentioned today that she does not have her own computer and that the queues lately in all of the computer clusters have been very long, especially when most of them close at five. Those in the library are open until 9:30 but are packed. Two or three, she thought, stay open twenty-four hours. She is worried because the campus will close on Holy Thursday and not re-open until the day dissertations [like senior theses] are due. I am reminded of the difficulty students have when they do not own their own computer. Some projects in geography, furthermore, require the use of software or Websites that can only be accessed via certain terminals.

One of the libraries did have a group-work area, a large room with work-tables arranged in pods, with two terminals at each pod and two monitors per terminal. The financial district group was disciplined and lucky enough to arrive early one morning and claim a pod, which was an excellent space for what these groups needed to do, but by 11:00, the line to use this room extended out the door and down the hall. With no posted time limits, students often moved in for the day, and the line stayed long and moved slowly in the hours that I spent there on two different dates. During the same week, the Eccup group also managed to find a pod for about five hours one day, but on the day they were due to present, members of the group had to enter class less prepared than they wanted to be after difficulties struck. Mandy and Sheila reported to the group that they had worked for two hours that morning trying to make the final changes but weren't able to save the presentation on the mainframe. The entire group made its way to a different lab, where a technician confirmed that the mainframe had been acting up all morning. When they tried to log in to edit the presentation, they could not save or log out—and no one could figure out the problem. Then adding insult to injury, when they tried to rehearse in the hour before class, no lecture theater could be found that was free.

Collaborative assignments put students in situations where the material conditions for composing undoubtedly affect the process and the outcome. While those teaching at community colleges or urban universities are probably sensitive to the demands they can or cannot fairly make on their students, it had not occurred to me that even these very privileged students (at least by the standards of the English university system) have a number of difficulties fulfilling collaborative assignments. For example, since most Leeds geography students do not have their own computers, they are given a certain amount of disk space on the mainframe or the server. That's all they get, and on some terminals, they are not allowed to save to disk. So for a Web page or a large PowerPoint presentation, they have to delete all possible unnecessary files and hope for the best. When students are expected to produce results together, and one student of the group has the data on her account, that creates problems for how others are to access it. If Julian, Sheila, and Kim want to spend some time working on the presentation, but they can't find Mandy, they're out of luck unless Mandy has given them her password and permission to access her account. The "hassles" of collaborative work faced by these students made me pause to think again about how much we take for granted regarding material conditions for getting done the work of learning. Furthermore, when they turned to PowerPoint as a tool for creating their oral presentations, students entered a pre-formed space, a set of containers that bypasses invention and randomizes arrangement. Rather than worry that images are taking over writing, perhaps we should be concerned that in the world of software development, writing has become a task, rather like filing.

PowerPoint and Arrangement

We need the slide that binds.

—Sheila

PowerPoint risks squeezing out the provider of process—that is to
say, the rhetorician, the storyteller, poet, the person whose thoughts
cannot be arranged in the shape of an AutoContent slide.

—Ian Parker
"Absolute PowerPoint"

Nearly every group in the cultural geographies class, eight out of ten, concentrated its efforts on creating a PowerPoint presentation, despite the fact
that Tom, the lecturer, had not at all assigned PowerPoint specifically.[10] However, because the lecture halls in the Roger Stevens Lecture Theaters had
podiums with computer terminals, Internet access, and projection screens,
the Eccup and FD groups never even questioned whether PowerPoint was
appropriate or necessary or the best choice; it was a given from the moment
they started. As I watched these two groups of students putting their streetwork presentations together for the class, I realized how hugely influential
this software can be in influencing the composing processes. Ideally, most
writers agree, form follows content, or should. However, this dictum clashes
with the fact that spatial practices of dwelling, learned from firstplaces, don't
change much in virtual or electronic environments. People adapt to the space
they're allotted, whether that means expanding or shrinking to fit the space.
Dwellers get rid of stuff to fit into a small efficiency apartment or buy more
to fit a bigger one. In this sense, then, writers in electronic environments
also adapt to the borders or boxes of some software programs, illustrating
that new technologies don't make the container metaphor obsolete. In fact,
as an analysis of PowerPoint easily demonstrates, form rules over content,
and the container metaphor reigns supreme.

Many commentators on PowerPoint have made this or similar observations. In fact, critics have reviled PowerPoint, lamenting its rise not only
to the top of Microsoft sales charts but also into our collective consciousness as "the" way of organizing information to present to a group (Gates;
Parker; Nunberg). One thread of this debate echoes the ambivalence about
visual culture and media communications, for example, that this software's
success is "part of a general decline in public speaking" (Nunberg 331). Like
the book and other technologies, PowerPoint is influencing "the structure
of thought itself" (Nunberg 331). Ian Parker names PowerPoint more than
a tool, rather a social instrument "with an oddly pedantic, prescriptive
opinion about how we should think" (76).

While one critic believes that PP "can give visual shape to an argument
. . . [and] makes the logical structure of an argument more transparent"
(Parker 86), others are convinced that PP is taking the speaker out of the
equation—signaling a decline in public speaking skills, a concern reminiscent of the ambivalence in many fields about visual culture. While such
ambivalence should be addressed head-on, my own experience observing
the two streetwork groups confirms that too often "the *tool* takes over the
process" and presenters "fixate on fonts without actually thinking" (Gates
46, her emphasis). Too many writers (users of PowerPoint) are using effects
rather than ideas. If PowerPoint presentations lack verbs, as Nunberg claims,
that also means that they lack assertions or arguments.

Collaborative group projects of all sorts may suffer from "too many
cooks" syndrome, but the use of PowerPoint, given all the choices possible,
did seem to exacerbate this problem. For example, the financial district
group spent a good five minutes clicking through different color choices
for the bullets, and the conversation went something like this: "'I don't like
those open bullets; let's change them.' 'No, no no, yes! That one.' 'No, that's
tacky . . . .'" With one keyboard and three onlookers, every change in format or appearance garnered much discussion, leading Sheila, at one point,
to announce that she was taking control. Even more time consuming was
the effort to scan in photographs, taken with a nondigital camera. Students
in both groups had volunteered to take photographs of their streetwork sites
and to develop the photos, which all enjoyed seeing. On one hand, their
use of photographs, maps, or other images was fully expected in the context of a geography class. Not simply "added on" to enhance the presentation, the photos or maps contributed to the effort of each group to capture
"a sense of place" or to document their encounter with place as accurately as
possible. On the other hand, both groups spent more time and energy scan-
ning in photos than they did in discussing the argument their presentation
was making.

Had this been a writing or a rhetoric class, the pros and cons of Power-
Point would have been more a part of the discussion, and the lecturer might
have warned students about spending too much time on the bells and
whistles. Significantly, though, these geography students used PowerPoint
to compose; their writing process began with the arrangements allowed by
the software design, not with ideas they hoped to communicate. Rather than
relying on the software to present information to an audience after it had
been developed and arranged, they turned to it first as they contorted their
data, smishing and squashing it to fit within the (literal) boxes designed
by the presentation software. As the boxes began to fill up and the number

of slides increased, Kim noted to her peers that the boxes near the end of the slide show were crammed with text, far more than an audience could absorb. This resulted, perhaps, from trying to make the presentation "look good" in the earlier slides; then realizing that they had actually "said" very little, students filled some boxes with content—once again demonstrating the container function of PowerPoint.

Those skeptical of electronic technologies can legitimately ask: "Is assigning a PowerPoint presentation assigning *writing?*" PowerPoint was not invented for composing, yet its use is ubiquitous in business culture and in college classrooms, making its flaws or features harder to see. PowerPoint is clearly a medium of delivery, but the users I observed depended on the software not only to deliver but also to invent, draft, and arrange. PowerPoint's design, however, promotes a containerized version of communication, with fairly inflexible "shapes" for the work of composing. It's not a gross exaggeration to suggest that habitual PP users, those whose ideas are embodied in the shape of slides, may really begin to believe that developing ideas is only about filling in empty boxes, with headings and bullets. This is a familiar problem in writing instruction: rather than seeing what shape an essay or argument might take, among many options available, writers often simply adhere to a known form: the five-paragraph theme, the comparison/contrast essay, the research paper, the thesis paragraph.

Taking risks with arrangement, like entering an unfamiliar place, requires writers to move beyond questions of similarity or difference to decide where things go. Writers often answer questions about arrangement by relying on their memories of other spaces, other texts. In a containerized notion of space, like goes with like, or familiar patterns rule: the coffee table goes in front of the sofa, or the strongest point goes last. Arrangement was prescriptive in classical rhetoric, yet it needs to be fluid in a postmodern or material rhetoric.

PowerPoint does not have this fluidity; however, if it *can* be rehabilitated for rhetorical instruction—for helping composers map their way through an argument, for example—PowerPoint's only virtue may be that it does draw attention to arrangement—but that's only if the user chooses to bypass AutoContent. In fact, the *order* of the slides was a significant bone of contention in the Eccup group and led to the most significant discussions of the group. As different group members sat down in front of the screen to run through what they had so far, they would each switch the order of the slide presentation, offering often quite compelling reasons for moving a slide before or after another one. This went on for quite some time, where every run through the slide show resulted in a reordering. Finally, Julian suggested that they stop *"because it all depends on what we say in between the slides."* He realized what I had been thinking for some minutes: it depends on how the slides get narrated or tied together. The work of rhetoric comes *between* the slides. Once they began to focus on the "transitions" rather than on the slides themselves, the presentation began to come together, despite the very strong pull to reorder the slides again and again. Focusing on arrangement, therefore, becomes a way of focusing on the *betweens,* the places where language moves "outside the box" to welcome readers or outsiders.

To try to resist containerized writing instruction and promote the rhetoricality of writing, composition scholars have argued persuasively for the importance of invention. From this context—decades of effort to rehabilitate invention—writing instructors may not see the necessity of focusing on arrangement or memory, especially when what students seem to lack most is *ideas* for writing. "Why then," Susan Jarratt asks, "in the face of these persuasive and historically informed arguments for invention [i.e., Crowley], would one want to resuscitate disposition?" (69). Jarratt points to the "spatiality of invention," both classical *topoi* and the insistence that writers are located in time and space (70). Disposition extends to ask not only "where does this go?" but also "why can't it go there?" Disposition, Jarratt argues,

> marks the connection between rhetorical practices and the postures or orientations connected with social positions. . . . disposition extends the inquiry beyond the immediate rhetorical situation to social relations more generally. It is a way to account for the presence or absence of difference within historical and geographical spaces. (71)

Disposition or arrangement is important to geographic rhetorics, then, because it asks us to examine how difference is produced in rhetorical situations that take place in the trialectics of space. How are spaces arranged to organize the control of difference, or to silence those "too different" for the space?

Geographies of Writing

Whether the geography of difference is constructed in a journal article, a book, a classroom, a town, a housing estate, or a city neighborhood, we can cultivate spatial practices that advocate dwelling as well as walking and mapping. Dwellings, those places we inhabit most fully and most meaningfully, should be places we can retreat to, places that make us feel safe and allow us rest. Maybe this means, for rhetoric and writing classes, something so simple as giving students opportunities for rereading and rewriting whenever possible—letting them revisit several times—fewer texts but more travels through them. But encouraging dwelling can only mean simultaneously encouraging movement. Student writers should be encouraged to dwell in some landscapes and just keep moving through others. I'm not trying to be coy: our dilemma is caught up in the swirl of spatialities that affect all acts of walking, dwelling, or composing. Should we keep going? Doubleback? Take a sharp right? There are no prescribed responses possible since each act of writing *takes place* differently—in a distinct environment (Dobrin).

As they exist in our memories, in our daily lives, in our rooms or our imaginations, places and spaces are a swirling combination of metaphor and materiality. We carry this swirl of spatialities—some perceived, some conceived, some lived—around with us in every encounter with a place, whether that place is Granby Road in Leeds or a document saved on a hard drive. While something that *swirls* doesn't seem a very helpful or practical response to the challenges of writing instruction, composition instructors committed to working for social change need to understand something about students' sense of place because their notions of difference are deeply geographical, indeed ecological and environmental, and because their habitual spatial practices serve to "lock in" their identities, masking the politics of space and clouding the importance that place has in literacy, learning, or communication. Many educational goals can be achieved in street culture, the built environment, or the natural world. Those committed to or interested in critical pedagogy, activist learning, literacy projects, sustainable communities, or community service learning might be particularly interested in geographies of writing—the spatial practices that emerge from our memories of firstplaces and combine with our encounters with intimidating neighborhoods or difficult texts. As teachers of writing in the twenty-first century, we need to know more about the spatial practices that students bring with them and how to tap into their embodied practices—in screen culture as well as street culture—for their acts of composing, their habitats and places meaningful to them. We need to understand more about how spatialities become imprinted on a body and form a *habitus,* a set of embodied practices that learners and writers carry around with them—like skin, hair, clothing.

People experience space as confining, comforting, hospitable, frightening, confusing, exhilarating, or boring. But if we can get people to overcome their prejudices about places, then maybe they can be "moved"—*persuaded*—to encounter difference, to walk beyond the city walls. Still, even if a combination of methodology and circumstance opens up a certain neighborhood, moving through it *changes the space.* Places, streetscapes, homes, classrooms, Website, or texts are all altered by embodiments, different bodies who move through, settle, move on. Through walking, mapping, and dwelling, geographic rhetorics analyze how people feel in spaces both familiar and unfamiliar, how they manage to inhabit unwelcoming places, or how they respond to unsettling encounters with difference. Through memory and arrangement and forms of *flanerie,* geographies of writing invite engagements with difference at street level, complete with visuals, smells, sounds, and the tools that make both movement and dwelling possible. A better understanding of those tools seems an important next stage since many composition theorists are coming to the same conclusion that we don't know enough about writing's materiality.[11] As Trimbur puts it, we don't know enough about "the composer's work in producing the resources of representation in order to signify at all, to make the special signs we call writing" ("Delivering" 189). Dobrin has called this elusive knowledge "the thingness of writing" (at CCCC, 2002), but it cannot be studied in isolation from the imaginative, metaphorical, and affective elements of composing. Geographies of writing suggest that college students in writing classes, as agents who move through the world, know a great deal more about "writing" than they think they do—not that they are holding out on us, but that we haven't yet tapped their spatial imaginations or studied their moves.

This study of writing as spatial practices, informed by postmodern and cultural geography and parallel to so much work in ecocomposition, continues a tradition in composition studies of foraging in other disciplines for theories and approaches that help us to understand writing. New maps of writing, maps I've only begun to explore in these pages, will devote a layer to the *where* of writing—not just the places where writing occurs, but the sense of place and space that readers and writers bring with them to intellectual work of writing, to navigating, arranging, remembering, and composing. Writing can be studied or understood only in a cultural context— and only through the thin, smudged layers of a palimpsest, without the sharp focus of a digital camera.

Rather than worry about a loss of memory and the onslaught of visual images in postmodern culture, we should investigate encounters with place and space and reconsider the kinds of movement (and stillness) that characterize acts of writing and places for learning. Writers, as they construct identities through discourse, are enacting their own lived experiences in the sociospatial world. Words on the page, the visual image, the map, the built object—all reflect a series of moves made for habitual, intentional, or accidental reasons. Keeping track of some of these moves might give glimpses into the social production of space, embodied in the moves a writer makes and the products of a writer's work.

I have tried to argue that geographic rhetorics might give us new understandings of learning to see, at street level, where borders lie. I leave it to my readers to map their own ways through the sociospatial world of learning and writing with the reminder that spatial metaphors—from how writers find a way "in" to where the boundaries are for different discourses— are not meant to be overcome, only recognized for the power they wield over our imaginations and for their frequent neglect of material conditions. Entering borderlands means learning to inhabit *los intersticios,* "the spaces between the different worlds" that women of color, in particular, inhabit (Anzaldúa 42). But layers of geographic research show just how difficult these crossings can be. The fixedness of relationships between identity and place and the hardening of boundaries around neighborhoods makes it hard to inhabit, even momentarily, the spaces that others inhabit everyday, and there are good reasons why a group of white privileged students and their teachers or researchers wouldn't be welcome in many neighborhoods or by many villagers or street dwellers. A person's sense of place can feel invaded or violated, and it's important to respect certain boundaries, to transgress others, and to know the difference. Border crossing is promising, exciting, and exhilarating, both theoretically and in the everyday. Border crossing is also risky or difficult or uncertain. Understanding diversity issues and literacy practices demands that we hold simultaneously these conflicted notions about space and place.

NOTES
WORKS CITED
INDEX

NOTES

Introduction

1. Plato's concerns about memory and writing have now resurfaced in a classic history-repeats-itself way. A recent newspaper headline reads: "Electronic gadgets may make human memory obsolete," and the story cites one hundred million mobile phones (all with speed dialing) and eight million personal organizers as evidence for the decline in people's ability to retrieve once-accessible information, like telephone numbers or birth dates—the type of factual information that electronic devices store.

2. My reading of *Phaedrus* has been most influenced by Jasper Neel, *Plato.*

3. Chapter 1 discusses thirdspace in some depth, but I borrow the term from postmodern geographer Edward Soja's 1996 book titled *Thirdspace.* His analysis of this concept begins with Henri LeFebvre, but also draws from Gloria Anzaldúa, Gayatri Spivak, Edward Said, Homi Bhaba, and Michel Foucault.

4. This distinction between strategies and tactics comes from de Certeau (xix–xx). See also Probyn 86–87.

1. Between Metaphor and Materiality

1. *Space* and *place* are two distinct terms here; of the two, *space* is probably the less understood or the more-taken-for-granted. As logic or common sense would indicate, space is "bigger" than place, but the two are intricately related. Places emerge from space with the passage of time: "Spaces become places as they become 'time-thickened.' They have a past and a future that binds people together round them" (Crang 103). Space is the more conceptual notion—a realm of practices—while place is defined by people and events. In one sense, places are fixed positions on a map, or you can follow directions to get there. Space, if you will, structures our habitats but cannot be inhabited. Places touch people's lives and evoke memories and emotions.

2. See Philip Eubanks's argument regarding conduit metaphors, referred to again below, which he says elicit "nearly unanimous condemnation" (93). While he does cite several articles or theorists in rhetoric and composition, Bowden isn't included in his analysis; I assume he would disagree with her about the limitations they enforce in theorizing or teaching writing.

3. But see Merrifield's account of how LeFebvre's work was initially ignored, at least by Althusserian Marxists ("Henri LeFebvre" 167–70).

4. For examples of embodied rhetorics see Selzer and Crowley's volume *Rhetorical Bodies.*

5. As Lester Faigley points out in *Fragments,* it's perhaps easiest to contrast modernism and postmodernism through architecture (4–5).

6. This perceived loss contributes, in part, to the desire for substitute—i.e., electronic—spaces, in on-line environments and through satellite communications.

2. Reading Landscapes and Walking the Streets: Geography and the Visual

1. On the discourse of crisis, precipitated by such outcries as Newsweek's 1975 piece "Why Johnny Can't Write" (Sheils), see Faigley's chapter 2 in *Fragments of Rationality* and Trimbur's "Literacy and the Discourse of Crisis."

2. So what happens for those who cannot see? I'm intrigued by the tension in geography studies between 1) an expanding literature on geographies of disabilities; and 2) the continued persistence of the visual epistemology of geography. I cannot adequately address here the contributions that visually impaired people can make to geography and cultural studies, but "learning to see" is not entirely dependent on 20/20 vision; it draws on all the senses, on a type of embodiment or inhabitance. For example, Tom, the cultural geography lecturer mentioned "smellscapes" when introducing the streetwork project to students (see chapter 4).

3. Cultural geography is also being mined for its connections to literary studies. Writing in *American Literary History,* Sara Blair surveys "the common ground between Americanist literary studies and the new geography" (550) and speculates about what literary critics and historians might contribute "to new understandings of spatial practices, of the production of spatial and social differences, and of space, time, and nature as material frames for everyday life" (549). She finds, as I do, that "each field of inquiry . . . encompasses habits, histories, a mode of attention, from which the other can richly profit" (545). The new models and vocabularies of cultural geography can lead to a remapping of not just American studies but also other fields interested in the social. "In a very real sense, the new geography constitutes a powerful expressive form, giving voice to the effects of dislocation, disembodiment, and localization that constitute contemporary social orders" (Blair 545).

4. What would an abstract notion of culture be? The idea that culture is generally "good for people" or makes them civilized, or a dictionary definition not grounded in place.

5. By paying good money for the images, geographers can download onto their GIS systems images of a particular forest or town, for example, and can track changes in the environment or population. This data is very expensive, but if professors can get a cloud-free image of the New Forest, they'll "buy it" because so many of their students work in/on the New Forest, and "somebody's grant" can pay for it. But who's selling it?

6. Neil Postman's *Amusing Ourselves to Death* provides one example of this type of criticism: "embedded in the surrealistic frame of a television news show is a theory of anticommunication, featuring a type of discourse that abandons logic, reason, sequence and rules of contradiction" (105).

7. "What Is a Visual Argument, and What Is It Doing in a Writing Class?" CCCC, Chicago, 2002. As an example of a powerful visual argument, she also shared the "upside down map," reproduced here in chapter 3. See George for a published version of this presentation.

8. Featherstone says, though this is just one of many points, that flanerie is a method for reading texts, for reading the traces of the city. It is also a method of writing, of producing and constructing texts.

9. The use of the masculine pronoun is tough for me, or I'm very much aware of the "he," thus my use of forms of *flanerie*. Although I have no objection to *flaneuse* (Wilson's term), it's also important to recognize the sex and sexuality of the *flaneur*, who's often read as a dandy and coded as gay. Theoretical work on the *flaneur* tends to front this issue and tries to maintain levels of ambiguity or encourages foraging (see Munt on the lesbian *flaneur*).

10. Because they cannot give in to unstructured time or undirected rambling, Americans, White says, are "particularly ill-suited to be flaneurs" and would rather follow guidebooks, intent on self-improvement (40).

11. I'm using "composing" in the sense that Peter Smagorinsky outlines—where composing doesn't stand in for an act of writing but represents "constructing meaning across the curriculum" (164). He argues against letting any single medium dominate learning or teaching and challenges the assumption that writing is the best tool for every student learner in every situation. This definition of composing—bigger than just writing—encompasses visual arguments, oral presentations, and streetwork.

3. Maps of the Everyday: Habitual Pathways and Contested Places

1. This episode was broadcast 28 February 2001 on NBC, titled "Big Block of Cheese Day."

2. As Susan Miller wrote to me in an e-mail, at the very beginning of this project, "you have to know which way is *up* to read a map." And she's right: as attractive as mapping is for all kinds of projects, reading or following maps requires a specialized form of literacy.

3. Readers of postmodern theory will recognize the term *cognitive mapping* as Fredric Jameson's. In an essay of the same name, he borrows Kevin Lynch's model from *The Image of the City* and tries to synthesize it with Althusser's formulation of ideology, which

> has the great merit of stressing the gap between the local positioning of the individual subject and the totality of class structures in which he or she is situated . . . this ideology, as such, attempts to span or coordinate, to map, by means of conscious and unconscious representations. (353)

In attempting to extrapolate Lynch's spatial analysis to class relations and social structure, Jameson also claims that "the incapacity to map socially is as crippling to political experience as the analogous incapacity to map spatially is for urban experience" (353).

4. Leeds is a growing city of over 700,000 residents, and Leeds-Bradford makes up the largest metropolitan area of West Yorkshire. The University of Leeds, just half a mile from the thriving city center, has a student enrollment of 21,000. Because of a serious shortage of on-campus housing, most of these students live off-campus, in the areas of Headingley (where I also lived), Hyde Park, Woodhouse, and Meanwood.

5. For research and context regarding mental maps, I relied upon Gould and White and Wiegand and Stiell. To ensure that my interviews were methodologically sound, I reviewed the work of qualitative researchers in my own field (Gesa Kirsch, Ruth Ray, Jennie Nelson) and took the opportunity to learn from some new ones (Robert Burgess, Sara Delamont, Gill Valentine). I can't really say, however, that I have side-stepped the criticisms Soja levels at mental mapping, but since he doesn't really define thirdspace epistemologies (choosing to "leave the discussion . . . radically open" [*Thirdspace* 82]), researchers have to depend on secondspace methods for understanding how people interact with the sociospatial world.

6. I have edited these passages considerably, with readers in mind, to sharpen the speaker's point or to eliminate what I considered to be distracting wordiness. Single periods mean a full stop. Ellipses mean I have eliminated words, but if ellipses appear in brackets [. . .] that means I have cut out whole lines. I added marks of punctuation, in particular, and eliminated most of the "ums" or other fillers because my purpose here is not discourse analysis as a sociolinguist might perform. Instead, my purpose is to illustrate, through students' own words, contested relationships to place and space.

7. Students recognized, however, that the term *no-go* is quite specific in social geography as places where the police refuse to go (a term that evolved from Northern Ireland—see Keith).

8. Although I'm a bit uncomfortable using the blanket term "Asians," it is the term that students used. More specifically, however, this area is populated by Pakistanis, and Hyde Park does have one of the largest concentrations of ethnic minorities in Leeds—much smaller, however, than areas of Bradford. Widely recognized to have the largest ethnic minority population in the north, and just a few miles from Leeds, Bradford has a 15.60 percent population from minority groups, according to the 1991 census.

9. It's well known among students that Headingley is just a bit more posh than Hyde Park. Zoe notes: "I wouldn't be able to afford to live in Headingley though, because it's sort of popular to live there—the housing is just too expensive. The cheapest you can get is probably about £45 a week which is too much for me."

10. Anna also identifies Chestnut Avenue as particularly Asian, a street that also holds the title, according to Anna, of being the most burgled street in England.

11. Bodington Hall is a large expanse of "green" land, sports pitches and the like, and a huge residential hall—the home of many first-year students. Located four miles from the campus, built in this location because there was simply no room nearer to the city and university, students rely on the bus to get back and forth between the campus and Bodington Hall.

12. I can imagine some readers wondering why I didn't work also with Asians in the neighborhoods of Headingley or Hyde Park. A seven-month stay, in university housing and possible only through university connections, made me feel uncomfortable about asking Asian residents to participate in this study when I'm not sure I could have argued or articulated what's in it for them. If I could have stayed longer, maybe, but I would have had to think very carefully about how to get access as well as make the interaction somehow reciprocal.

4. Streetwork: Seeing Difference Geographically

1. See, for example, Zukin.

2. But Edensor also romanticizes the Indian street in problematic ways, ignoring, for example the politics of gender.

3. But certainly women's experiences in the street differ by class, race, or abilities.

4. Ric Burns's documentary *New York City* and the film "Wonderland" make a good pairing for classes studying urban "renewal" or urban geographies, sense of place, or the politics of space in city planning.

5. I don't mean to imply that I think all SL or CSL projects ask students only to observe differences; I know that some are quite demanding and methodologically sophisticated, tightly linked to critical pedagogy, and that the number and range of projects vary considerably.

6. As I need to emphasize, this project out of cultural geography is not and doesn't claim to be "reciprocal" in the way that community service learning projects do strive to be. I suspect that cultural geographers advocating streetwork might soon need to confront or acknowledge this lack of reciprocity, and they would certainly find arguments in composition to help them think through these issues (see, for example, Cushman).

7. Students in the cultural geography seminar in which I was a participant observer were third-year students. Required in the second year was a course I also observed on research methods. Both qualitative and quantitative methods were covered, and students had to complete group projects practicing each type. The instructor for the third-year course in cultural geography, therefore, did not "re-teach" research methods, e.g., interviewing, but built on students' second-year experiences with the research methods course and offered quick reviews or referred to students to sources.

8. At the beginning of the term, I had gained access and met with the instructor, whom I call Tom. At the beginning of the second lecture, he gave me two minutes to introduce myself to the class of forty-six students and to prepare them for my presence, particularly my observation, chronic note taking, and occasional

questions. I said that I might well be asking some of them to be interviewed or to share with me some of their thoughts about the class.

9. During these exercises, after students had self-selected into groups, I floated among three different groups, those nearest my desk in the bolted-chair lecture hall and some students I had spoken with before. By the end of the second week of forming groups and choosing a place, I asked two groups if I could join them for the duration of the project, and both were very welcoming. The Eccup group chose a village north of Leeds, and the Financial District Group chose an area of "power" in the city center. I joined them for their initial visits and two subsequent ones.

10. This class activity, conducted early in the term in the "workshop" hour that followed a "lecture" hour, triggered the part of this research project that involved interviews and mental mapping, the subject of the preceding chapter; they grew out of but were separate from the streetwork project.

11. In an interesting difference between the U.S. and the U.K. university systems, the students I observed at Leeds weren't required to buy books and were rarely given assigned readings that everyone was expected to complete. Instead, lecturers distributed bibliographies or reading lists that students were responsible for on the end-of-term exam, which determined a large portion of their grade or degree granted. The libraries had several, sometimes many, copies of certain books (at least for geography) that were recommended reading, which soon explained why the libraries were so busy and crowded. In any case, students would report to their group members the reading they had been doing.

12. Readers of chapter 3 will recognize Sheila, Zoe, and Julian (and Anna and Elaine) as interview subjects for the mapping interviews. When I asked for volunteers, these students were willing, I think because they were already acquainted with me, as the streetwork groups were already underway as I began my interviews.

13. "Emmerdale"—a.k.a. "Emmerdale Farm"—is the name of a long-running television soap opera in the U.K., whose characters occupy a rural village in the north of England and which had recently begun filming on a "fake" set just north of Eccup, after filming for many years in a "real" village, Esholt.

14. I'm referring in most of these paragraphs to a group meeting on 22 March 2000, which I taped and partially transcribed.

15. This supermarket is a good example of a shifting or ambiguous boundary, however. It did signal the beginning of the retail shopping area, but many workers in the financial district went there to buy food for lunch or to purchase items before going home.

16. Tom's own identity as white and middle-class served, perhaps, to encourage him to "protect" these already sheltered students from the shock of too much difference. I think many teachers might do the same, consciously or not.

17. I am indebted to Donna Bickford for helping me think through many of the ideas in this section.

18. Schell reports that her students were initially shocked to learn the negative attitudes held towards them by members of the Syracuse community, and they did

begin to see themselves through the residents' eyes. "In turn, the students were forced to alter their view that the university was the center and the city neighborhoods the margins."

5. Learning to Dwell: Inhabiting Spaces and Discourses

1. This was Le Corbusier's vision, implemented to some extent by the developer Robert Moses in New York in the late 1940s and early 1960s: high towers, open spaces, and no more corridor streets (*New York City: A Documentary History*). Instead streets were to become "machines for traffic," free of pedestrians and store fronts (Fyfe 2–3). Ric Burns's documentary portrays Moses with a relentlessly modernist view of cities—where the new is always better than the old—and undisguised disdain for do-gooders who tried to save the old neighborhoods.

2. And by the time of race riots of the late twentieth century, even the police wouldn't enter places like Notting Hill, Brixton, or Hackney (see Keith).

3. I just want to mention my own ambivalence about this Staples essay. I've had success with it in class discussions (first-year composition), but the author's rather sunny acceptance of people's reactions to him bothers me; and I think students like it because Staples does not really politicize the topic of black men on the streets. Still, his strategies for responding—his efforts to put others at ease—are striking.

4. See Aronson about the student, mother of two in a small apartment, who used her tiny bedroom as a study, the occupants next door audible through thin walls (289).

5. Thanks to Lori Gemma for her extended example of this practice; she wrote an essay in a graduate seminar on rhetoric and geography about the art of waiting tables through enacting memory.

6. As Nan Johnson argues, however, even when nineteenth-century women orators did take the stage to speak, the podium had to be reconfigured, ideologically, as domestic space.

7. This design, like the streetwork it imitates, makes no claims to reciprocity; this manageable assignment, as a slice of streetwork, concentrated on the early and difficult steps of gaining access because the first important step is to get people to enter an unfamiliar area.

8. Enrollment for the URI course is capped at twenty-five to give some students their only small class of the year (except, in many cases, for first-year writing). In addition, as the course was under development, a local philanthropist gave $1 million to institute a service learning component. Therefore, in the way that service learning comes packaged with other agendas, most sections of this introductory course require service learning, though that can take many, many forms, some of which qualify as free labor to local economies.

9. The outlines of my own place journal assignment I borrowed from Buell, who presented at URI in the spring of 1999 and shared his own place journal assignment.

10. What Tom did emphasize in making this assignment was data analysis, particularly the question, "how much have your results been affected by your methods and decisions?"

11. One of my readers shared a concern, rightly, that the earlier version of this chapter did not sufficiently address writing's materiality or the "tactile" nature of writing. I hope that my revisions have done more to address this gap, but I also know that more studies are needed that depend upon empirical research to trace writers' *moves* in composing.

WORKS CITED

Anzaldúa, Gloria. *Borderlands/La Frontera: The New Mestiza.* San Francisco: Aunt-Lute Books, 1987.

Aronson, Anne. "Composing in a Material World: Women Writing in Space and Time." *Rhetoric Review* 17.2 (1999): 282–99.

Bachelard, Gaston. *The Poetics of Space.* Trans. Maria Jolas. Boston: Beacon, 1994.

Barnes, Trevor J., and James S. Duncan, eds. *Writing Worlds: Discourse, Text and Metaphor in the Representation of Landscape.* New York: Routledge, 1992.

Berman, Marshall. *All That Is Solid Melts into Air: The Experience of Modernity.* New York: Simon and Schuster, 1982.

Bickford, Donna M., and Nedra Reynolds. "Activism and Service Learning: Reframing Volunteerism as Acts of Dissent." *Pedagogy: Critical Approaches to Teaching Literature, Language, Composition, and Culture* 2.2 (2002): 229–52.

Bishop, Wendy. "Places to Stand: The Reflective Writer-Teacher-Writer in Composition." *CCC* 51.1 (1999): 9–31.

Bizzell, Patricia. "Cognition, Convention, and Certainty: What We Need to Know about Writing." *PrelText* 3.3 (1982): 213–39.

Blair, Sara. "Cultural Geography and the Place of the Literary." *American Literary History* 10.3 (1998): 545–67.

Blunt, Alison, and Gillian Rose, eds. *Writing Women and Space: Colonial and Postcolonial Geographies.* New York: Guilford, 1994.

Bourdieu, Pierre. *Distinction: A Social Critique of the Judgement of Taste.* Trans. Richard Nice. Cambridge: Harvard UP, 1984.

Bowden, Darsie. "The Limits of Containment: Text-as-Container in Composition Studies." *CCC* 44 (1993): 364–79.

Brandt, Deborah. "Accumulating Literacy: Writing and Learning to Write in the Twentieth Century." *College English* 57.6 (1995): 649–68.

Brodkey, Linda. "Modernism and the Scene(s) of Writing." *Writing Permitted in Designated Areas Only.* Minneapolis: U of Minnesota P, 1996. 59–81.

———. "Writing on the Bias." *Writing Permitted in Designated Areas Only.* Minneapolis: U of Minnesota P, 1996. 30–51.

Bruffee, Kenneth. "Collaborative Learning and the 'Conversation of Mankind.'"

Cross-Talk in Comp Theory: A Reader. Ed. Victor Villanueva Jr. Urbana, IL: NCTE, 1997. 393–414.

Buck-Morss, Susan. *The Dialectics of Seeing: Walter Benjamin and the Arcades Project.* Cambridge: MIT P, 1989.

Buder, Leonard. "Open-Admissions Policy Taxes City U. Resources." *New York Times* 12 Oct. 1970: A1+.

Buell, Lawrence. *The Environmental Imagination.* Cambridge, MA: Belknap, 1995.

Burgess, Jacquelin, and Peter Jackson, "Streetwork—An Encounter with Place." *Journal of Geography in Higher Education* 16.2 (1992): 151–57.

Burgess, Robert G. "The Ethnographic Interview in Educational Research." *Studies in Qualitative Methodology.* Vol. 1. Ed. Robert G. Burgess. Greenwich, CT: JAI, 1988. 137–55.

Carvajal, Doreen. "Honey, I'm Almost Home: The Unbearable Blather of Being." *New York Times* 20 May 2001: WK7.

Cintron, Ralph. *Angels' Town:* Chero *Ways, Gang Life, and Rhetorics of the Everyday.* Boston: Beacon, 1997.

———. "Just Places? And the Rhetoric of Aesthetics." Conference on College Composition and Communication. Palmer House Hilton, Chicago. 21 Mar. 2002.

Clark, Gregory. "Writing as Travel, or Rhetoric on the Road." *CCC* 49.1 (1998): 9–23.

Clifford, James. *Routes: Travel and Translation in the Late Twentieth Century.* Cambridge: Harvard UP, 1997.

Cloke, Paul, Chris Philo, and David Sadler. *Approaching Human Geography: An Introduction to Contemporary Theoretical Debates.* New York: Guilford, 1991.

Connors, Robert J. *Composition-Rhetoric: Backgrounds, Theory, and Pedagogy.* Pittsburgh: U of Pittsburgh P, 1997.

Cosgrove, Denis. "New Directions in Cultural Geography." *Area* 19.2 (1987): 95–101.

Crang, Mike. *Cultural Geography.* New York: Routledge, 1998.

Crouch, David. "The Street in the Making of Popular Geographical Knowledge." *Images of the Street: Planning, Identity, and Control in Public Space.* Ed. Nicholas R. Fyfe. New York: Routledge, 1998. 160–75.

Crowley, Sharon. "Judith Butler, Professor of Rhetoric." *JAC* 21.1 (2001): 163–67.

Cushman, Ellen. "The Public Intellectual, Service Learning, and Activist Research." *College English* 61 (1999): 328–36.

Davis, Mike. *City of Quartz: Excavating the Future in Los Angeles.* New York: Vintage, 1992.

Deans, Thomas. *Writing Partnerships: Service-Learning in Composition.* Urbana, IL: NCTE, 2000.

de Certeau, Michel. *The Practice of Everyday Life.* Trans. Steven Rendall. Berkeley: U of California P, 1984.

Delamont, Sara. *Fieldwork in Educational Settings: Methods, Pitfalls, and Perspectives.* Washington, D.C.: Falmer, 1992.

Demetz, Peter. Introduction. *Reflections: Essays, Aphorisms, Autobiographical Writings.* By Walter Benjamin. Ed. Demetz. New York: Harcourt, 1978. vii–xliii.

Dobrin, Sidney I. "From Writing Processes to Cultural (Re)Production: Compositions Theoretical Shift." Paper presented at the Conference on College Composition and Communication, Palmer House Hilton, Chicago, 22 Mar. 2002.

———. "Writing Takes Place." *Ecocomposition: Theoretical and Pedagogical Approaches.* Ed. Christian R. Weisser and Sidney I. Dobrin. Albany: State U of New York P, 2001. 11–25.

Doheny-Farina, Stephen. *The Wired Neighborhood.* New Haven: Yale UP, 1996.

Drew, Julie. "The Politics of Place: Student Travelers and Pedagogical Maps." *Ecompositon: Theoretical and Pedagogical Approaches.* Ed. Christian R. Weisser and Sidney I. Dobrin. Albany: State U of New York P, 2001. 57–68.

Dwyer, Claire. "Veiled Meanings: Young British Muslim Women and the Negotiation of Differences." *Gender, Place and Culture* 6.1 (1999): 5–26.

Edensor, Tim. "The Culture of the Indian Street." *Images of the Street: Planning, Identity, and Control in Public Space.* Ed. Nicholas R. Fyfe. New York: Routledge, 1998. 205–21.

Emig, Janet. "Mina Pendo Shaughnessy." *CCC* 30 (1979): 37–38.

Eubanks, Philip. "Understanding Metaphors for Writing: In Defense of the Conduit Metaphor." *CCC* 53.1 (2001): 92–118.

Faigley, Lester. *Fragments of Rationality: Postmodernity and the Subject of Composition.* Pittsburgh: U of Pittsburgh P, 1992.

———. "Material Literacy and Visual Design." *Rhetorical Bodies.* Ed. Jack Selzer and Sharon Crowley. Madison: U of Wisconsin P, 1999. 171–201.

Featherstone, Mike. "The *Flaneur,* the City and Virtual Public Life." *Urban Studies* 35.5–6 (1998): 909–25.

Forbes, Kathryn, et al. "Punishing Pedagogy: The Failings of Forced Volunteerism." *Women's Studies Quarterly* 27.3–4 (1999): 158–68.

Friedman, Susan Stanford. *Mappings: Feminism and the Cultural Geographies of Encounter.* Princeton: Princeton UP, 1998.

Garner, Dwight. "Stand-Up Poet." Rev. of *Sailing Alone Around the Room* by Billy Collins. *New York Times Book Review* 23 Sept. 2001: 10.

Gates, Phyllis. "Where's the Power? What's the Point?" *Across the Board* May–June 2002: 45–47.

George, Diana. "From Analysis to Design: Visual Communication in the Teaching of Writing." *CCC* 54.1 (2002): 11–39.

George, Diana, and John Trimbur. "The 'Communication Battle,' or Whatever Happened to the Fourth C?" *CCC* 50.4 (1999): 682–98.

Gere, Anne Ruggles. "Kitchen Tables and Rented Rooms: The Extracurriculum of Composition." *CCC* 45.1 (1994): 75–92.

Gilbert, Melissa R. "The Politics of Location: Doing Feminist Research at 'Home.'" *Professional Geographer* 46.1 (1994): 90–96.

Glenn, Cheryl. "Remapping Rhetorical Territory." *Rhetoric Review* 13.2 (1995): 287–303.

Goodman, Lorie J. "Just Serving/Just Writing." *Composition Studies* 26.1 (1998): 59–71.

Gould, Peter, and Rodney White. *Mental Maps*. 2nd ed. Boston: Allen and Unwin, 1986.

Gregory, Derek, Don Martin, and Graham Smith, eds. *Human Geography: Society, Space and Social Science*. London: Macmillan, 1994.

Haas, Christina. *Writing Technology: Studies on the Materiality of Literacy*. Mahwah, NJ: Erlbaum, 1996.

Hamilton, Walter, trans. *Phaedrus and Letters VII and VIII*. By Plato. New York: Penguin, 1986.

Harley, J. B. "Deconstructing the Map." Barnes and Duncan 231–47.

———. *The New Nature of Maps: Essays in the History of Cartography*. Ed. Paul Laxton. Baltimore: Johns Hopkins UP, 2001.

Harris, Joseph. *A Teaching Subject: Composition since 1966*. Upper Saddle River, NJ: Prentice-Hall, 1997.

Harvey, David. *The Condition of Postmodernity: An Enquiry into the Origins of Cultural Change*. Cambridge, MA: Blackwell, 1990.

Heidegger, Martin. "Building Dwelling Thinking." *Poetry, Language, Thought*. Trans. and intro. by Albert Hofstadter. New York: Harper, 1971. 145–61.

Heilker, Paul. "Rhetoric Made Real: Civic Discourse and Writing Beyond the Curriculum." *Writing the Community: Concepts and Models for Service-Learning in Composition*. Ed. Linda Adler-Kassner. Washington, DC: American Association for Higher Education, 1997. 71–77.

Herzberg, Bruce. "Community Service and Critical Teaching." *CCC* 45.3 (1994): 307–19.

Hill, Carolyn Ericksen. *Writing from the Margins: Power and Pedagogy for Teachers of Composition*. New York: Oxford UP, 1990.

Hitt, Jack. "Atlas Shrugged: The New Face of Maps." *Lingua Franca* 5.5 (1995): 24–33.

Hoggart, Richard. *The Uses of Literacy*. New York: Penguin, 1992.

hooks, bell. "Homeplace: A Site of Resistance." *Yearning*. Boston: South End, 1990. 41–49.

Horner, Bruce. *Terms of Work for Composition: A Materialist Critique*. Albany: State U of New York P, 2000.

Horwitz, Sari. "No Longer a World Apart: Grant Brings Geography Home to District Students." *Washington Post* 19 Mar. 1994: A1, A8.

Hutchings, Claire. "Creating Fear by Design." *Geographical Magazine* 66.8 (1994): 32–34.

Jackson, Peter. *Maps of Meaning: An Introduction to Cultural Geography*. New York: Routledge, 1989.

Jacobs, Jane. *The Death and Life of Great American Cities*. New York: Vintage, 1961.

Jameson, Fredric. "Cognitive Mapping." *Marxism and the Interpretation of Culture*. Ed. Cary Nelson and Lawrence Grossberg. Urbana: U of Illinois P, 1988. 347–60.

Jarratt, Susan C. "New Dispositions for Historical Studies in Rhetoric." *Rhetoric and Composition as Intellectual Work.* Ed. Gary A. Olson. Carbondale: Southern Illinois UP, 2002. 65–78.

Jessup, Emily. "Feminism and Computers in Composition Instruction." *Evolving Perspectives on Computers and Composition Studies: Questions for the 1990s.* Ed. Gail E. Hawisher and Cynthia L. Selfe. Urbana, IL: NCTE, 1991. 336–55.

Johnson, Nan. *Gender and Rhetorical Space in American Life, 1866–1910.* Carbondale: Southern Illinois UP, 2002.

Johnson, Wendy Dasler. "Cultural Rhetorics of Women's Corsets." *Rhetoric Review* 20.1–2 (2001): 203–33.

Johnson-Eilola, Johndan. "Living on the Surface: Learning in the Age of Global Communication Networks." *Page to Screen: Taking Literacy into the Electronic Era.* Ed. Ilana Snyder. New York: Routledge, 1998. 185–210.

Kaplan, Edward K., trans. *The Parisian Prowler* (Le Spleen de Paris, Petits Poemes en prose). By Charles Baudelaire. Athens: U of Georgia P, 1989.

Keith, Michael. "Racial Conflict and the 'No-Go Areas' of London." *Qualitative Methods in Human Geography.* Ed. John Eyles and David M. Smith. Cambridge: Polity, 1988. 39–48.

Keith, Michael, and Steve Pile, eds. *Place and the Politics of Identity.* New York: Routledge, 1993.

Kirsch, Gesa. *Women Writing the Academy: Audience, Authority, and Transformation.* Carbondale: Southern Illinois UP, 1993.

Kress, Gunther. "'English' at the Crossroads: Rethinking Curricula of Communication in the Context of the Turn to the Visual." *Passions, Pedagogies, and Twenty-First Century Technologies.* Ed. Gail E. Hawisher and Cynthia L. Selfe. Logan: Utah State UP, 1999. 66–88.

Kunstler, James Howard. *The Geography of Nowhere: The Rise and Decline of America's Man-Made Landscape.* New York: Touchstone, 1994.

Lauer, Janice. "Composition Studies: Dappled Discipline." *Rhetoric Review* 3 (1984): 20–29.

Least Heat-Moon, William. *PrairyErth (A Deep Map).* Boston: Houghton, 1991.

Lee, Alison. *Gender, Literacy, Curriculum: Re-writing School Geography.* Bristol, PA: Taylor and Francis, 1996.

Leeds City Council Site Map. 27 Aug. 2001. <http://www.leeds.gov.uk/sitemap/sitemap.html>.

Lees, Loretta. "Urban Renaissance and the Street: Spaces of Control and Contestation." *Images of the Street: Planning, Identity, and Control in Public Space.* Ed. Nicholas R. Fyfe. New York: Routledge, 1998. 236–53.

LeFebvre, Henri. *The Production of Space.* Trans. Donald Nicholson-Smith. Malden, MA: Blackwell, 1991.

LeGuin, Ursula. "The Fisherwoman's Daughter." *Dancing at the Edge of the World: Thoughts on Words, Women, Places.* New York: Grove, 1989. 212–37.

Leighly, John, ed. *Land and Life: A Selection from the Writings of Carl Ortwin Sauer.* Berkeley: U of California P, 1963.

Lemann, Nicholas. "Atlas Shrugs." *New Yorker* 9 Apr. 2001: 131–34.

Lynch, Kevin. *The Image of the City.* Cambridge: MIT P, 1960.

Lyons, Robert. "Mina Shaughnessy." *Traditions of Inquiry.* Ed. John Brereton. New York: Oxford UP, 1985. 171–89.

Mahala, Daniel, and Jody Swilky. "Geographical Designs: Rethinking Reform in the Humanities." *JAC* 21.1 (2001): 97–127.

Maher, Jane. *Mina P. Shaughnessy: Her Life and Work.* Urbana, IL: NCTE, 1997.

Marback, Richard. "Detroit and the Closed Fist: Toward a Theory of Material Rhetoric." *Rhetoric Review* 17.1 (1998): 74–90.

———. "Learning to Inhabit Writing." *Composition Studies* 29.1 (2001): 51–62.

Martin, David. "Geographical Information Systems and Spatial Analysis." *Methods in Human Geography: A Guide for Students Doing Research Projects.* Ed. Robin Flowerdew and David Martin. Harlow, Essex: Longman, 1997. 213–29.

Massey, Doreen. *Space, Place, and Gender.* Minneapolis: U of Minnesota P, 1994.

McComiskey, Bruce. Rev. of *Rhetorical Bodies,* ed. Jack Selzer and Sharon Crowley. *JAC* 20.3 (2000): 699–703.

McDowell, Linda. *Gender, Identity and Place: Understanding Feminist Geographies.* Cambridge, England: Polity, 1999.

———. "The Transformation of Cultural Geography." *Human Geography: Society, Space and Social Science.* Ed. Derek Gregory, Don Martin, and Graham Smith. Minneapolis: U of Minnesota P, 1994. 146–73.

Mental Mapping, 9–12 Lesson. National Geographic Society. 27 Aug. 2001. <http://www.nationalgeographic.com/resources/ngo/education/ideas912/912mental>.

Mental Mapping Project. Department of Geography, University of Oklahoma. 24 Sept. 2002. <http://geography.ou.edu/courses/1103bg/mentalmapping.html>.

Merrifield, Andy. "Between Process and Individuation: Translating Metaphors and Narratives of Urban Space." *Antipode* 29.4 (1997): 417–36.

———. "Henri LeFebvre: A Socialist in Space." *Thinking Space.* Ed. Mike Crang and Nigel Thrift. New York: Routledge, 2000. 167–82.

Miller, Susan. *Textual Carnivals: The Politics of Composition.* Southern Illinois UP, 1991.

Mitchell, Don. "The End of Public Space? People's Park, Definitions of the Public, and Democracy." *Annals of the Association of American Geographers* 85.1 (1995): 108–34.

Monastersky, Richard. "The Warped World of Mental Maps: Students Worldwide Share a Skewed Vision of the Continents." *Science News* 142 (3 Oct. 1992): 222–23.

Monk, Janice. "Place Matters: Comparative International Perspectives on Feminist Geography." *Professional Geographer* 46.3 (1994): 277–88.

Morrish, William, and Catherine Brown. *Planning to Stay: Learning to See the Physical Features of Your Neighborhood.* Minneapolis: Milkweed, 2000.

Mountford, Roxanne. "On Gender and Rhetorical Space." *Rhetoric Society Quarterly* 31.1 (2001): 41–71.

Muchiri, Mary N., Nshindi G. Mulamba, Greg Myers, and Deoscorous B. Ndoloi. "Importing Composition: Teaching and Researching Academic Writing Beyond North America." *CCC* 46 (1995): 175–98.

Munt, Sally. "The Lesbian *Flaneur*." *Mapping Desire*. Ed. David Bell and Gill Valentine. New York: Routledge, 1995. 114–25.

Nash, Catherine. "Remapping the Body/Land: New Cartographies of Identity, Gender, and Landscape in Ireland." *Writing Women and Space: Colonial and Postcolonial Geographies*. Ed. Alison Blunt and Gillian Rose. New York: Guilford, 1994. 227–50.

Neel, Jasper. "The Degradation of Rhetoric; Or, Dressing like a Gentleman, Speaking like a Scholar." *Rhetoric, Sophistry, Pragmatism*. Ed. Steven Mailloux. New York: Cambridge UP, 1995. 61–81.

———. *Plato, Derrida, and Writing*. Southern Illinois UP, 1988.

Nelson, Jennie. "Reading Classrooms as Texts: Exploring Student Writers' Interpretive Practices." *CCC* 46 (1995): 411–29.

New York City: A Documentary History. PBS. Produced by Ric Burns, 2001.

Nietzsche, Friedrich. "On Truth and Lies in a Nonmoral Sense." *The Rhetorical Tradition*. 2nd ed. Ed. Patricia Bizzell and Bruce Herzberg. Boston: Bedford, 2001. 1171–79.

Nintendo.com. *Banjo Kazooie*. 9 July 2002. <http://www.nintendo.com/games/gamepage/description.jsp?gameId=52#about>.

Nunberg, Geoffrey. "The Trouble with PowerPoint." *Fortune* 20 Dec. 1999: 330–31.

Parker, Ian. "Absolute PowerPoint." *New Yorker* 28 May 2001: 76–87.

Peck, Wayne Campbell, Linda Flower, and Lorraine Higgins. "Community Literacy." *CCC* 46 (1995): 199–222.

Peters Projection Map. 19 Sept. 2002. <http://www.webcom.com/~bright/petermap.html>.

Phelps, Louise Wetherbee. "The Domain of Composition." *Rhetoric Review* 4 (1986): 182–95.

Poster, Mark. "The Net as a Public Sphere?" *Wired* Nov. 1995: 135–36.

Postman, Neil. *Amusing Ourselves to Death: Public Discourse in the Age of Show Business*. New York: Penguin, 1985.

Pratt, Geraldine. "Spatial Metaphors and Speaking Positions." *Environment and Planning D: Society and Space* 10 (1992): 241–44.

Pratt, Geraldine, and Susan Hanson. "Geography and the Construction of Difference." *Gender, Place and Culture* 1.1 (1994): 5–29.

Pratt, Mary Louise. "Arts of the Contact Zone." *Profession* 91 (1991): 33–40.

Pratt, Minnie Bruce. "Identity: Skin Blood Heart." *Yours in Struggle: Three Feminist Perspectives on Anti-Semitism and Racism*. Ed. Elly Bulkin, Barbara Smith, and Minnie Bruce Pratt. Ithaca: Firebrand, 1988. 10–63.

Probyn, Elspeth. *Sexing the Self: Gendered Positions in Cultural Studies*. New York: Routledge, 1993.

Ray, Ruth. *The Practice of Theory: Teacher Research in Composition*. Urbana, IL: NCTE, 1993.

"Redoubling the Efforts at Teaching Geography." *New York Times* 19 Nov. 1993: C11.

Rendell, Jane. "Displaying Sexuality: Gendered Identities and the Early Nineteenth-Century Street. *Images of the Street: Planning, Identity, and Control in Public Space.* Ed. Nicholas R. Fyfe. New York: Routledge, 1998. 75–91.

Rheingold, Howard. *The Virtual Community: Homesteading on the Electric Frontier.* New York: HarperPerennial, 1994.

Rich, Adrienne. "Notes Toward a Politics of Location." *Blood, Bread, and Poetry: Selected Prose 1979–85.* New York: Norton, 1986. 210–31.

———. "Teaching Language in Open Admissions." *On Lies, Secrets, and Silence: Selected Prose 1966–1978.* New York: Norton, 1979. 51–68.

Roberts, Susan M., and Richard H. Schein. "Earth Shattering: Global Imagery and GIS." *Ground Truth: The Social Implications of Geographic Information Systems.* Ed. John Pickles. New York: Guilford, 1995. 171–95.

Rose, Gillian. *Feminism and Geography: The Limits of Geographical Knowledge.* Minneapolis: U of Minnesota P, 1993.

Rose, Mike. *Lives on the Boundary.* New York: Free, 1989.

Sauer, Carl O. "The Education of a Geographer." *Land and Life: A Selection from the Writings of Carl Ortwin Sauer.* Ed. John Leighly. Berkeley: U of California P, 1963. 389–404.

———. "The Morphology of Landscape." *Land and Life: A Selection from the Writings of Carl Ortwin Sauer.* Ed. John Leighly. Berkeley: U of California P, 1963. 315–50.

Savage, Mike. "Walter Benjamin's Urban Thought: A Critical Analysis." *Thinking Space.* Ed. Mike Crang and Nigel Thrift. New York: Routledge, 2000. 33–53.

Schaafsma, David. *Eating on the Street: Teaching Literacy in a Multicultural Society.* Pittsburgh: U of Pittsburgh P, 1993.

Schell, Eileen E. "Literacy and Service Learning in the Twenty-First Century: Connecting Our Writing Classrooms with Communities Outside the University." Paper presented at the Spillman Symposium, Virginia Military Institute, 13 Nov. 1999.

School of Geography, University of Leeds. Home page. 23 Sept. 2002. <www.geog.leeds.ac.uk>.

Schulten, Susan. *The Geographical Imagination in America, 1880–1950.* Chicago: U of Chicago P, 2001.

Schutz, Aaron, and Anne Ruggles Gere. "Service Learning and English Studies: Rethinking 'Public' Service." *College English* 60.2 (1998): 129–49.

Schwartz, John. "Loose Lips Sink More Than Ships." *New York Times* 6 July 2001: WK4.

Selfe, Cynthia, and Richard J. Selfe Jr. "The Politics of the Interface: Power and Its Exercise in Electronic Contact Zones." *CCC* 45 (1994): 480–504.

Selzer, Jack, and Sharon Crowley, eds. *Rhetorical Bodies.* Madison: U of Wisconsin P, 1999.

Sennett, Richard. *The Fall of Public Man: On the Social Psychology of Capitalism*. New York: Vintage, 1974.

Shabad, Theodore. "Geography, A Lost Art." *New York Times* 15 Jan. 1985: C1–2.

Shaughnessy, Mina. *Errors and Expectations*. New York: Oxford UP, 1977.

Sheils, Merrill. "Why Johnny Can't Write. *Newsweek* 18 Dec. 1975: 58–65

Sibley, David. *Geographies of Exclusion: Society and Difference in the West*. New York: Routledge, 1995.

Silber, Ilana Friedrich. "Space, Fields, Boundaries: The Rise of Spatial Metaphors in Contemporary Sociological Theory." *Social Research* 62.2 (1995): 323–55.

Slagle, Diane Buckles, and Shirley K. Rose. "Domesticating English Studies." *Journal of Teaching Writing* 13 (1994): 147–68.

Smagorinsky, Peter. "Constructing Meaning in the Disciplines: Reconceptualizing Writing Across the Curriculum as Composing Across the Curriculum." *American Journal of Education* 103 (1995): 160–84.

Smith, Jonathan M. "Geographical Rhetoric: Modes and Tropes of Appeal." *Annals of the Association of American Geographers* 86.1 (1996): 1–20.

Smith, Neil, and Cindi Katz. "Grounding Metaphor: Towards a Spatialized Politics." *Place and the Politics of Identity*. Ed. Michael Keith and Steve Pile. New York: Routledge, 1993. 67–83.

Smith, Zadie. *White Teeth*. New York: Random, 2000.

Soja, Edward W. *Postmodern Geographies: The Reassertion of Space in Critical Social Theory*. New York: Verso, 1989.

———. *Thirdspace: Journeys to Los Angeles and Other Real-and-Imagined Places*. Malden, MA: Blackwell, 1996.

Sorkin, Michael. Introduction. *Variations on a Theme Park: The New American City and the End of Public Space*. Ed. Sorkin. New York: Noonday, 1992. xi–xv.

Staples, Brent. "Just Walk on By: A Black Man Ponders His Power to Alter Public Space." *Literary Cavalcade* 51.1 (1998): 38–41.

Student Handbook, 1999/2000. School of Geography, University of Leeds, 1999.

Sullivan, Patricia, and James E. Porter. *Opening Spaces: Writing Technologies and Critical Research Practices*. Greenwich, CT: Ablex, 1997.

"Teachers Lament Geography Scores." *New York Times* 12 Mar. 1985: C11.

Tompkins, Jane. *West of Everything: The Inner Life of Westerns*. New York: Oxford UP 1992.

Trimbur, John. "Consensus and Difference in Collaborative Learning." *College English* 51 (1989): 602–16.

———. "Delivering the Message: Typography and the Materiality of Writing." *Rhetoric and Composition as Intellectual Work*. Ed. Gary A. Olson. Carbondale: Southern Illinois UP, 2002. 188–202.

———. "Literacy and a Discourse of Crisis." *The Politics of Writing Instruction: Postsecondary*. Ed. Richard Bullock and John Trimbur. Portsmouth, NH: Boynton-Cook, 1991. 277–95.

Tuan, Yi-Fu. *Space and Place: The Perspective of Experience*. Minneapolis: U of Minnesota P, 1977.

Turner, Frederick Jackson. "The Significance of the Frontier in American History (1893)." *History, Frontier, and Section.* Albuquerque: U of New Mexico P, 1993. 59–91.

Valentine, Gill. "Food and the Production of the Civilised Street." *Images of the Street: Planning, Identity, and Control in Public Space.* Ed. Nicholas R. Fyfe. New York: Routledge, 1998. 192–204.

———. "The Geography of Women's Fear." *Area* 21.4 (1989): 385–90.

———. "Tell Me About . . . : Using Interviews as a Research Methodology." *Methods in Human Geography: A Guide for Students Doing Research Projects.* Ed. Robin Flowerdew and David Martin. Harlow, Essex: Longman, 1997. 110–26.

Villanueva, Victor. "On the Rhetoric and Precedents of Racism." *CCC* 50.4 (1999): 645–61.

Vitanza, Victor, ed. *CyberReader.* Boston: Allyn, 1996.

Wainwright, Martin. "Appeal for Calm after Muslim Riots." *Guardian* 20 June 1997: 14a.

Ward, Colin, and Anthony Fyson. *Streetwork: The Exploding School.* London: Routledge, 1973.

White, Edmund. *The Flaneur: A Stroll Through the Paradoxes of Paris.* New York: Bloomsbury, 2001.

Wiegand, Patrick. "How Teachers Can Stop Continental Drift." *Topic* 21 (1999): 1–6.

Wiegand, Patrick, and Bernadette Stiell. "Mapping the Place Knowledge of Teachers in Training." *Journal of Geography in Higher Education* 21.2 (1997): 187–98.

Wiener, Harvey. Rev. of *Errors and Expectations,* by Mina P. Shaughnessy. *College English* 38 (1977): 715–17.

Williams, Raymond. *Marxism and Literature.* Oxford: Oxford UP, 1977.

Wilkinson, Paul. "Police Attacked with Stones." *Times* 12 July 1995: 3f.

Wilson, Elizabeth. "The Invisible Flaneur." *New Left Review* 191 (1992): 90–110.

Wolff, Janet. "On the Road Again: Metaphors of Travel in Cultural Criticism." *Undoing Place? A Geographical Reader.* Ed. Linda McDowell. New York: John Wiley, 1997. 180–93.

Wonderland. Dir. John O'Hagan. Rhinestone Productions, 1997.

Wood, Denis. *The Power of Maps.* With John Fels. New York: Guilford, 1992.

Yates, Frances A. *The Art of Memory.* U of Chicago P, 1966.

Zukin, Sharon. *Landscapes of Power: from Detroit to Disney World.* Berkeley: U California P, 1991.

INDEX

Nedra Reynolds is a professor of writing and rhetoric at the University of Rhode Island, where she teaches in and directs the College Writing Program. She has published in *CCC, Rhetoric Review, JAC,* and *Pedagogy,* as well as in several collections. She is the author of *Portfolio Keeping: A Guide for Students* and *Portfolio Teaching: A Guide for Instructors.* She coedited the sixth edition of the *Bedford Bibliography for Teachers of Writing.*